Faith, Politics, and Power

Faith, Politics, and Power

The Politics of Faith-Based Initiatives

REBECCA SAGER

OXFORD
UNIVERSITY PRESS

2010

OXFORD
UNIVERSITY PRESS

Oxford University Press, Inc., publishes works that further
Oxford University's objective of excellence
in research, scholarship, and education.

Oxford   New York
Auckland   Cape Town   Dar es Salaam   Hong Kong   Karachi
Kuala Lumpur   Madrid   Melbourne   Mexico City   Nairobi
New Delhi   Shanghai   Taipei   Toronto

With offices in
Argentina   Austria   Brazil   Chile   Czech Republic   France   Greece
Guatemala   Hungary   Italy   Japan   Poland   Portugal   Singapore
South Korea   Switzerland   Thailand   Turkey   Ukraine   Vietnam

Published by Oxford University Press, Inc.
198 Madison Avenue, New York, New York 10016

www.oup.com

Oxford is a registered trademark of Oxford University Press.

Library of Congress Cataloging-in-Publication Data
Sager, Rebecca.
Faith, politics, and power : the politics of faith-based initiatives/
Rebecca Sager.
    p.   cm.
ISBN 978-0-19-539176-3
1. Faith-based human services—Political aspects—United States.
2. Public-private sector cooperation—Political aspects—
United States. 3. Interorganizational relations—United States.
I. Title.
HV530.S27 2009
361.7'50973—dc22   2009014138

9 8 7 6 5 4 3 2 1

Printed in the United States of America
on acid-free paper

To my family and husband—without their faith in me and my work, this project could not have been.

Preface

Since 1996, federal and state governments have been increasing their implementation of a variety of faith-based practices. From creating new Offices of Faith-Based and Community Initiatives to passing new statutes ensuring more access for faith-based organizations,[1] state and federal actors have by and large jumped on the faith-based bandwagon. In his final State of the Union address, President Bush once again addressed what he saw as the importance of faith-based initiatives. He argued that the federal government had not done enough to implement faith-based initiatives:

> When I came into office, the nation's traditions of religious freedom and equal opportunity were facing unnecessary obstacles. Throughout America, religious and community groups were providing effective assistance to people in need, but there was a great reluctance on the part of the federal government to help them. There was the notion that somehow that [sic] there needed to be a clear separation of church and state, and therefore, we shouldn't be using taxpayers' money to help programs that were helping to meet important national goals. (Bush 2008)

While the president and many supporters of faith-based initiatives may have been disappointed with the lack of federal policy progress, what they may not have realized was how far many states had already gone in creating faith-based policies and practices.

State faith-based policy implementation is in fact more advanced in many ways than implementation at the federal level. States have passed significant faith-based legislation, something the federal government has never been able to do, and state implementation of these initiatives has begun to shape governmental and faith-based organizational culture. The consistent efforts of state liaisons, faith-based conferences, and new faith-based policies have created greater opportunities for partnership between faith and government sectors, but have very rarely come up with the resources to make these new efforts work for extended periods of time.

In this book, I outline how and why states have begun to adopt these types of practices. My focus is on the disparity between practical and symbolic action; while there has been a great deal of activity, little of it is in the realm of raising money or increasing spending, but rather in the realm of symbolic politics. State faith-based practices have become the cultural goods that are the product of twin efforts of the conservative movement: changes in the role of religion in the public square and changes in the role of government in providing social services. While some see the implementation of these initiatives as an ephemeral phenomenon, there is reason to believe that the initiatives can affect policy in the future by reshaping our cultural understandings of how church and state could or should work together.

What might be surprising to many who have followed the initiative is that neither the greatest hopes of the faith-based initiatives' supporters nor the greatest fears of their opponents have been realized. The "armies of compassion" have yet to take over the roles of government agencies and the poor and needy to whom they were supposed to offer help are still seeking services and aid. On the other hand, the greatest fears of opponents—rampant proselytizing and religious mandates—have not materialized either. The changes that are occurring are more subtle, but they are no less important. Rather than ushering in major new funding for state-run social services, I found that the faith-based initiatives have been implemented through an array of symbolic policies geared toward creating political allies and changing the role of religion within government. In the aftermath of the faith-based initiatives, religion's role in state government has become something utterly new; religious groups have been granted a new place at the political table, and an atmosphere of church-state collaboration rather than separation has been created.

Acknowledgments

I would like to acknowledge the following for their generous funding of this project: the Louisville Institute, the Society for the Scientific Study of Religion, the Association for the Sociology of Religion, the Horowitz Foundation, the Religious Research Association, and the National Science Foundation. I am also indebted to the tireless assistance of Mark Chaves, Sarah Soule, Joe Galaskiewicz, and Brint Milward. Without their continuous time and support this book would not have been possible. I also want to thank Keith Bentele and Liz Rank for providing much needed advice and help. Finally, I also want to send my undying gratitude to my mother, Judith Sager, whose hours of love and help have made this project possible.

Some of the information in chapters 4 and 6 appeared in articles in the *Journal of Church and State* and *Sociology of Religion*. However, the chapters are substantively different from the articles.

Contents

Abbreviations

CBO	community-based organization
CCF	Compassion Capital Fund
FBL	faith-based liaison
FBO	faith-based organization
OFBCI	Office of Faith-Based and Community Initiatives
PWORA	Personal Work and Responsibility Act
RFP	request for proposals
TANF	Temporary Assistance for Needy Families

Faith, Politics, and Power

I

An Introduction to the Faith-Based Initiatives

I believe it is in the national interest that government stand side by side with people of faith. . . . I understand in the past, some in government have said government cannot stand side by side with people of faith. I viewed this as not only bad social policy—I viewed it as discrimination.

—George Bush, speech, June 2004

Mass publics respond to currently conspicuous political symbols: not to facts . . . [but] to the gestures and the speeches that make up the drama of the state.

—Murray Edelman, *Politics as Symbolic Action*

In the summer of 2004, I attended my first conference on the faith-based initiatives in Washington, D.C. The room was filled to capacity, and there was a palpable air of excitement and anticipation about the promises held out by the initiatives. The conference began with a prayer by Rick Warren, pastor of Saddleback Church and author of *The Purpose-Driven Life*, a very popular account of how to turn conservative Christian identity into social service activism. He told the audience that it was time to start a revolution in the name of faith. At this, the audience came to its feet in applause.

Several hours—and several speeches about the power of faith to heal—later, President George W. Bush arrived. As he often had when he was governor of Texas, the president started his speech with a story. In this case, the story was about addiction and the ability of faith to save one from addiction; he spoke of how his own belief in the Bible and

Jesus saved him from alcoholism. But this was not the only story he told. He also related stories about welfare mothers saved by their neighborhood churches, about prisoners "brought to the light" by Chuck Colson's Prison Ministries, and about children helped out of drug addiction by Teen Challenge. He told the audience that he could not think of a better place for a prisoner to go than to church. He said that change really happened only when loving people told those in need that they loved them and that God loved them; he emphatically argued that it was only through experiences such as his and those that they had heard about earlier, all stressing the importance of spiritual change, that real cultural and spiritual rejuvenation could happen. Along with these stories about the importance of faith in helping the addicted, the poor, and the needy, he made promises: the faith-based initiatives would offer help to the helpless and hope to the hopeless, bringing in new money and new organizations to provide new and better social services. He was speaking the language of the evangelical faith, and almost everyone in the room was moved by the idea that if faith-based groups were just given money, the social ills we had suffered in the past would be remedied.

This was the first federal conference sponsored by the White House Office of Faith-Based and Community Initiatives.[1] Although excitement at that gathering was high, little of the new money that was promised to supporters to fight poverty and addiction has materialized. The main exception has been the Compassion Capital Fund (CCF), established in 2001 through the Department of Health and Human Services. While a substantial amount—almost $200 million dollars—has been distributed to various faith- and community-based organizations (Office of Community Services 2008), this is a far cry from the $8 billion that Bush promised (Cooperman and VandeHei 2005). Instead, the faith-based initiative has become primarily a series of policies, practices, and promises that seem to be more about changing culture and politics by altering the relationship between religion and government than about bringing substantial sums of money to religious and community groups to deliver social services. Through these policy changes, faith-based initiatives at the state level assure religious groups that their religion is protected and encourage state actors to partner and incorporate these groups in new ways. However, in the place of bringing the promised new funds to support new faith-based efforts to provide social services, the initiatives have become a series of actions that are bringing religion into the public sphere in a new— and fundamentally different—way (Kuo and Dilulio 2008; Wineburg 2007).

A Series of Initiatives

Instead of one initiative that has gained traction at the state level, many states are part of what Jay Hein, former director of the White House Office of Faith-Based and Community Initiatives, has called the "quiet revolution" (Farris

2008). In this quiet revolution state and federal institutions have been creating myriad faith-based practices, policies, and promises with very little notice or oversight. These state faith-based initiatives vary in depth and breadth, creating a complex and dynamic environment that is constantly changing over time and space. Some states have created no faith-based policies or practices, whereas others have actively sought out religious organizations and enacted laws and adopted policies that have attempted to change the cultural dynamics between religious groups and the state.

There is no one way to create state faith-based initiatives; however, there has been one common outcome: rather than money or material change, the "goods" of faith-based initiatives can be seen as the cultural changes they have created. Instead of the once-prominent norm of church-state separation, some states are part of a larger social process that is generating a new perspective on the way church and state should interact, one that relies on accommodation, cooperation, and collaboration (Flowers 2005). Regardless of how one measures state faith-based activity over time—by money spent, legislation passed, or other bureaucratic implementation—it is clear that many states are marching toward creating an ever greater and more complex faith-based landscape.

Faith-Based Initiatives as Symbolic Policy

In this book, I examine the stories of those most intimately involved with these faith-based initiatives—their own personal stories of faith and stories of hope about the promise of the initiative. By examining both the stories of those involved and the policies that states have created through administrative and legislative efforts, we can begin to see a full picture of faith-based implementation. As a society, we tell stories about the world—or how we think the world should be—through our government policies. Policies are not just pieces of paper but ideas about larger meanings, recounted to the public with the stamp of authority upon them. Faith-based initiatives are no exception to this. By examining these faith-based initiatives as they become policy and by looking at the stories about faith-based polices and their creation, we can begin to see how these initiatives came about and how their implementation tells a larger story about the role religion should or should not be playing in the public square.

State implementation of the faith-based initiatives has created a largely unnoticed system in which church-state boundaries have been blurred in some states in hopes of creating a political system that relies more heavily on religious organizations and partnerships with them (Singer and Friel 2007). Of course, these processes of implementation and adoption vary over time and space (Winston, Person, and Clary 2008), but the overarching cultural effect of the initiatives has been to create a new process of interaction between secular and faith-based groups. These changes and the alterations of the cultural landscape on which religion and public life rest should cause us to ask larger normative questions about the relationship between the secular and the religious, and what it should or should not look like in the future.

In his examination of the role of social policy in politics and social life, Murray Edelman (1964:6) argued that it is not so much the material consequences of policies that are important, but rather what the policies represent: "Every symbol stands for something other than itself" and evokes responses that are not based only or primarily on facts and evidence, but on beliefs that are central to a person's idea of the world. He argued that many public policies amount to a series of symbols that appeal to certain groups, representing ideas and values that they hold deeply, and thus reassuring group members. These symbols may also appeal to a wider array of groups and thus change the culture in which they are embedded by becoming part of the larger social structure.

Expanding on this work, Roger Cobb and Charles Elder (1972:1) argue that symbolic politics are important because "decision-makers actively engage in the manipulation of symbols and rationalize their action through them." Specifically concerned with symbols in the political world, Cobb and Elder attempt to provide a synthesized understanding of symbolic politics:

> Political symbols are simultaneously elements of a political culture
> and stimulus objects for the individuals of a system, they provide a
> linkage between the macro and micro levels of behavior.... Their
> potency as instruments of arousal and reassurance arises then not so
> much from any commonality of meaning attributed to them, as from
> the scope and intensity of sentiment attached to them and the
> common perception that they are in some way important to the
> system. (1972:4)

In other words, a policy need not mean the same thing to everyone. Rather, it needs to appeal to a variety of deeply held beliefs or meaning systems in either an affective or instrumental way. Cobb and Elder argue that the linkage of levels of behavior through the use of symbols is done by appealing both to people's emotions and to their instrumental needs. Symbols are a reflection of culture and, at the same time, a creation of new cultural dynamics.

Deborah Stone (1988), following the work of Edelman and Cobb and Elder, argued that symbols create a way for politicians to argue that they have done something, since taking action of some sort, even if it is merely symbolic action, is sometimes more important than the details of the policies. Thus, by creating amorphous political symbols, politicians can create a perceived sense of accomplishment and bring more constituents to their side. This duality and malleability of political symbols is readily evident in the multiple constituencies working to realize the faith-based initiatives—and in the tension that is created among various supporters of a policy once the practices are in place. Faith-based initiatives potentially appeal to various constituencies, creating a system of support around the initiatives that is based on a variety of very different reasons. This system of support is both the result of change and the stimulus for greater change to come.

Symbolic Policy and Cultural Change

According to Cobb and Elder, instrumental and affective concerns can appeal to multiple constituencies because the policies and practices of symbolic politics stand for something much greater than themselves. When examined through the lens of symbolic policy, state faith-based policies can be seen as a result of a cultural change that was begun by evangelical movement actors and furthered by groups that also viewed the faith-based initiatives as important, but often for different reasons.

Using data collected from those most closely involved with the initiative and statistical analyses of relevant state factors, I have found that there are two main reasons faith-based practices and policies have been supported at the state level. First, because of the devolution of the welfare system created by the Personal Responsibility and Work Opportunity Act in 1996—the law in which the first of the faith-based initiatives were embedded—some states had to seek alternatives to avert the fiscal crisis this act threatened to precipitate. One of those options was the original formulation of the faith-based initiative, with its promise of having religious groups help deliver social services. Second, in addition to those instrumental political concerns, some political activists and government officials found the language of the initiatives appealing, with its emphasis on reintegrating religion into the public square and then relying on faith-based groups for much-needed social services.

For those who find the faith-based initiatives appealing in an instrumental way, the initiatives are symbolic of how help can be given to others even though the government is moving out of the social services business. Thus, implementing these policies seems a promising way to fill a void in social insurance. For others, the appeal of the policy is less instrumental and more affective. The appeal of faith-based initiatives then comes from their role in creating deeper connections between the faith-based world and the secular world of government. The belief in making these bonds stronger is often coupled with the feeling that by making these bonds stronger, more FBOs would become part of the social services sector and would offer something different and better to those in need. These policies then come to symbolize something much larger than their actual words; the rhetoric within which they are embedded becomes part of a meaning system that taps into powerful feelings, yielding an overall impact on culture and politics that is greater than the individual policies (Lindsay 2008).

According to scholars of political symbolism, symbols represent the parts of culture that are often intangible and create meaning for people in a world that is turbulent and uncertain. Faith-based policies are like other symbolic politics in this way: their primary importance is not that they add a new member to a board or create a new office, but that they attempt to evoke responses based on deeply held notions of right and wrong. For the affective supporter, they represent something much greater than their actual form—they represent a hope that social ills can be remedied by the church. The stories, anecdotes, and words of social movement actors are transformed into real polices that legitimize the goals of the social movement. As theorists in political science argue, the importance of symbolic politics is the change it effects in narratives and norms (Brysk 1995). Although many who support the initiatives truly believe in helping others and fighting to give religious groups the money to do so, in most instances the reality does not match the rhetoric of the initiatives' political supporters. Whatever may be the *intent* of individuals working with the faith-based initiatives, the *effect* of the initiatives seems to be symbolic to a great degree—beliefs, not money.

Symbolic Politics: Creating a New Norm of Church-State Relations

The initiatives, as they stand, increase the importance of religion in the public sphere through policies and practices that appeal to cultural norms that would enhance the presence of religion in the public square, rather than meeting the original promises made to the faith community about new money for social services. These new policies also may assure these groups of something crucially important to them: that the government will not interfere in their activities. Political proponents of the faith-based initiatives have reframed the debate about church-state separation to suggest that such separation creates discrimination against religious groups; they then propose that to remedy this, government must actively reach out to religion in a spirit of cooperation and integration, rather than separation. Thus these measures, which show accommodation rather than separation, work to alleviate these fears.

Two Goals

My research has shown that state faith-based practices are for the most part a series of symbolic policies and practices that work to reshape the relationship between church and state in the United States while simultaneously offering states a way of partially offsetting the loss of federal assistance in social services administration. The symbolic policies discussed here illustrate this in two ways. First, state faith-based policies are part of larger legal and cultural processes that are reframing the Jeffersonian notion of a wall separating church and state. While some may disagree with the interpretation that there is a wall of separation, it had been the legal norm for much of the twentieth century, and the faith-based initiative is one way in which this is being redefined.[2] Second, because these policies and practices reframe the question of the ideal church-state relationship, an idea attractive to many, they appeal to several important political constituencies that have not traditionally worked together, thereby creating the potential to forge new alliances (Lindsay 2008).

A Brief History of Faith-Based Initiatives

Although religious groups have received government money to provide social services for much of American history, faith-based initiatives largely represent a new effort by both state and federal governments to encourage even greater participation. This drive to get FBOs to take on more responsibility in the social services sector has created a growing debate, not only about the role that religion should play in social services delivery, but also about deeper normative questions regarding the relationship between church and state.

Why the Initiatives?

As originally conceptualized in conservative evangelical intellectual circles, the philosophy behind the faith-based initiatives was twofold. First, by "removing unnecessary barriers" to participation, small faith-based groups would compete in large numbers for federal and state money without having to give up their inherently religious character (Chaves 1999; Formicola, Segers, and Weber 2003; Wineburg 2001). Some conservative evangelical activists have argued that the current view of church-state relations in the United States has led to an unreasonable burden on religious organizations and discrimination against them by government agencies. For example, in *Renewing American Compassion*, Marvin Olasky (1996:162) argued that "the federal government's gradual entrenchment in America's public service sector has created an increasingly inhospitable environment for charity's religious elements." According to this view, it is only by fundamentally altering how church and state are seen that religious groups will be treated fairly and given the opportunity to compete with secular organizations for government funding. George W. Bush read Olasky's book when he was the governor of Texas, and it inspired his way of thinking about the initiatives and the potential for faith-based groups to change the social services sector (Aronson 2004). Texas was actively involved in pursuing these practices at the time that the first federal faith-based initiative, Charitable Choice, was being attached to welfare reform legislation by conservative evangelical movement leader John Ashcroft.

Second, supporters such as Ashcroft and Bush argued that religious groups would offer holistic services different from—and better than—traditional nonprofit and government social services. The hope was that after this legislation was passed, the "armies of compassion"[3] would be unleashed, and small religious groups would work side by side with government social services agencies in helping the addicted, the poor, and the needy (Colson and Pearcy

1999; Green and Sherman 2002; Loconte 2002, 2004; Olasky 1996; Sherman 1999). Supporters argued that the main goal of the faith-based initiatives was to give churches and other FBOs access to federal money so that they could offer these better, more caring social services (Ashcroft 1999; Olasky 1996).

While religious organizations had been providing social services all along, the goal here was something new. Large religious organizations, such as the Catholic Church and Lutheran churches, have traditionally provided services through separate nonprofit agencies e.g. Catholic Charities and Lutheran Social Services. Such agencies are religiously influenced and are separate nonprofit organizations largely disentangled from their churches' explicitly religious activities. This means that even though faith-based groups were always allowed to provide social services, the feeling among some in evangelical circles was that these separating mechanisms were too arduous for smaller groups to overcome. With the implementation of state and federal faith-based initiatives, the hope was that new organizations would become involved in contracting for social services; a further hope was that these new providers would be smaller and more sectarian in character. The initiatives also promised that these organizations would not need to "leave religion at the door" to obtain government money to provide social services—although faith-based groups that were already getting federal money were not required to completely remove religion from the equation, but had to disentangle their hiring practices and finances in specific and concrete ways (Monsma 1996). Charitable Choice blurred these boundaries; rightly or wrongly, policies were put in place to help alleviate the fears of some that these boundaries were too restrictive.

What these changes mean for religious groups is still uncertain. The proposed "new" idea was that "faith-saturated" groups should be able get federal money without giving up their inherently religious character, if they made sure that the religious aspects of the program took place either before or after the social services section or were otherwise made entirely optional. Additionally, in these cases the government would have to provide a secular social services option. In reality, neither of these stipulations is systematically regulated, and recent research has found that states accepting help from faith-based groups overlook religious activities that significantly blur these lines (Allard 2008). There is debate about how new this idea was, or how much change it could make. What tended to happen was that religious groups were allowed to believe religion could be integral to the services that they provide, usually with just a mention that groups could not proselytize or use the funds provided to buy bibles; the rules, however, are far more complex. This situation led to sanctions against some groups for integrating religion into their services. When this occurred, the federal government did not come to their rescue, even though some in the federal government had argued that religion would improve the character and quality of the services provided.

The rhetoric of supporters of the initiatives has often been taken as fact; however, some of the most crucial assumptions behind the arguments for the faith-based initiatives have not been verified. For example, faith-based groups have not been excluded from the social services sector: some of them have long been providing much-needed services (Chaves 2004; Wineburg 2007; Wuthnow, Hackett, and Hsu 2004). Further, there is no evidence that religious groups were ever discriminated against (Chaves 2001, 2004). Nor is there any evidence that FBOs are uniformly better at providing social services (Bielefeld and Seuss-Kennedy 2003; Sager and Stephens 2005; Seuss-Kennedy and Bielefeld 2006; Wineburg 2001).

Nonetheless, regardless of whether religious groups offer better—or even different—services, the overall impact of the faith-based initiatives is important in one critical area: Through their symbolic policies and practices, faith-based initiatives have the potential to reshape political alliances. Perhaps just as crucial, these faith-based initiatives are part of a larger cultural process involving Supreme Court decisions that are increasingly accommodationist (Flowers 2005), as well as federal and state policy changes that blur boundaries between religion and the public square.[4] This is, of course, a process that is dynamic and evolutionary, and one that is currently shifting toward increased interaction between religion and government.

From Federal to State Policies

These changes began at the federal government and in the state of Texas; from there, faith-based initiatives have spread widely among states, with 41 enacting some sort of faith-based provision into law or administrative policy and 39 creating faith-based liaison (FBL) positions to integrate religious groups into the social services sector. Enacted as part of the 1996 welfare reform bill, called the Personal Work and Responsibility Act (PWORA), Charitable Choice was intended to guarantee that small religious groups were not discriminated against in government funding decisions (Center for Public Justice 2006). States were not required to implement any part of the initiative other than to honor this guarantee. However, while some states have done very little or nothing to implement the initiative, most states have adopted faith-based practices that go well above and beyond this minimum federal requirement. States that act tend to rely on three common means of implementation. They may appoint the actors known as FBLs or create state Offices of Faith-Based and Community Initiatives (OFBCIs), or both; they may pass legislation; or they may present state-sponsored policy conferences. This new activity in the states exists despite the fact that all 50 states already worked with religious organizations to provide social services. One might expect that since working with religious organizations was really nothing new, states would not have had any impetus to add new and potentially costly policies to their agendas. That a majority of states have taken action in this situation suggests that there must be benefits that outweigh the costs of new policies. What those benefits might be and why they are being pursued at a growing rate are questions worth exploring.

A Child of Many Parents

While supporters argue that the faith-based initiatives are about solving problems of poverty and an overburdened welfare system—and I found that those I spoke with came to the table with nothing but good intentions—the reality of the initiatives is that their promises of substantial new help to the poor and needy have not been kept. The paucity of new help for the poor is ascribable partly to the complex and varied motivations for implementation of the initiatives; further, various constituencies hold multiple—and sometimes conflicting—goals, which dilutes the possibility of actually increasing aid for the needy. While the initiatives have their roots in the evangelical tradition, their appeal is much more far-reaching. They appeal not just to evangelical religious sentiments but also to the religious sentiments of a wider audience; further, they have instrumental appeal for those who want to create new avenues for help to the needy (especially since the advent of welfare reform). In addition, those with purely political motives see the initiatives as a possible way to attract some portion of the black religious population to the Republican Party. Finally, the initiatives appeal to conservatives who want to decrease the size of government and see the initiatives as providing an inexpensive alternative to government-sponsored social services.

Such multiple motivations and constituencies create a broader base of support, but they also create tension among supporters; in this case, those hoping for more money, rather than just less government (and, perhaps, more religion), are losing out. The result is an environment in which acting on the initiatives is often done in part from fiscal necessity, in part from true belief in faith-based social services and the power of religion, and in part because of politics and a desire to change cultural norms. In the latter case, the initiatives are part of a movement, reflecting the desire of some in power to reduce government by shifting the social services burden away from government and toward the nonprofit and private sector. For many, this wave of devolution made the initiatives a necessity—the best response possible in a time of fiscal crisis and uncertainty in the system after welfare reform; for others, it was also part of a call to change the world based on faith.

Many of those who helped found the initiatives and many of their earliest supporters are now those most bitterly disappointed by their shortcomings. Much research on the initiatives highlights the tension between those on the ground who want to do good works but need money to do them and those at the top who may have goals of a more political nature (Wineburg 2007). By

examining the politics, practices, and policies of state faith-based implementation, a picture begins to emerge of initiatives that promised much but delivered
very little. The continued presence of the initiatives in our political life suggests, however, that hope still persists—or that some other goals of politicians
or constituencies are being met. In many cases, fiscal need created the opportunity for success in passing faith-based policies, while belief in the fundamental importance of religion as part of the social sector created the original
motivation and political ties necessary to adopt early policies.

In examining faith-based politics at the state level, three steps in the policy
process became clear. First, rhetoric surrounding the initiatives was developed;
then there were responses to the rhetoric through implementation; and finally,
there was reaction to the implementation. Although this is simple in outline,
state implementation of the initiatives has been a complex interplay between
those at the top creating rhetoric about faith-based practices and those on the
ground trying to respond this rhetoric. Faith-based policy implementation was
then a result of multiple constituencies: the believers, the fiscally concerned,
and the conservative political ideologues.

Current Understanding of the Faith-Based Initiatives

Is Faith Better?

Although the role and importance of religious organizations in providing
social services has been long established (Cnaan, Wineburg, and Boddie
1999; Cosgrove 2001; Monsma 1996; O'Neill 1989), the debate regarding
whether their spiritual elements are advantageous to those in need has become
more critical because of the faith-based initiatives. While the notion that
religious groups offer services that are both different from and superior to
those offered by traditional nonprofits and secular social service agencies has
been a crucial part of promoting the faith-based initiatives, these claims are still
being debated. The question of which types of organizations are best suited to
help the poor and needy is an important one, addressed by numerous researchers (Bielefeld and Seuss-Kennedy 2003; Seuss-Kennedy and Bielefeld 2006;
Wuthnow, Hackett, and Hsu 2004). So far, asking whether faith-based groups
are better than secular ones at providing this help has yielded various answers,
and the debate has not found a clear winner.

On one hand, Wuthnow and his colleagues showed that clients of FBOs
found their workers more trustworthy (Wuthrow, Hackett, and Hsu 2004).
Studies related to health care and patient relationships have also found clients
more satisfied with the religious alternative (University of Missouri-Columbia
2007). Others have argued that collaborative relationships between government and faith-based groups nurture civic engagement and highlight the

benefits of recruiting efforts from the faith-based sector (Lichterman 2005; Wood 2002). On the other hand, however, some who have been studying these groups for years, including Robert Wineburg and Mark Chaves, have argued that while there are a great many benefits to engaging the religious sector, it is unrealistic and untenable to suggest that most religious groups (or even a significant minority) will be able to offer the types of long-term social services provided by the government (Chaves 1999, 2001; Chaves and Wineburg 2008; Wineburg 2001, 2007). They have both argued that the initiatives are less about changing the social services sector to bring in these groups and give them substantial money to carry out their work than about politics and religious ideology.

In addition, studies have found some FBOs to be less effective than their secular counterparts. This was the case in a multistate study of faith-based versus secular service providers by Wolfgang Bielefeld and Sheila Seuss-Kennedy (2003, 2006). In comparing job training programs, they found that faith-based job-training programs resulted in the same numbers of jobs, but the jobs had lower wages and fewer benefits than those found through secular programs. In another study, Laura Stephens and I found that the clients—both religious and secular—of faith-based services disliked the religious elements of a social service if they felt the religion was forced upon them (Sager and Stephens 2005). These results have led most in the field to conclude that sometimes faith-based groups are better at providing services and that at other times secular social services are preferable.

Do Faith-Based Initiatives Work?

In addition to questions about whether faith-based services are more effective than other types of services, there are questions about whether faith-based initiatives, designed to enhance participation of religious groups in social service delivery, have actually enlarged the pool of faith-based social service providers. In the most recent study of the willingness and ability of faith-based groups to offer social services, Chaves and Wineburg (2008) found that although those groups that were already active in providing such services may be doing some more work than before, the number of churches that are active providers has not increased at all since the initiatives were introduced in 1996. Additionally, John Green found that most congregations were unlikely to be able to become active players in the social services sector. Like Chaves (2004), Green found that many congregations did not have the capacity or the desire to get involved in the long-term provision of social services. In his survey results, Green noted:

> Relatively few congregations are applying for government funds to
> provide those services, or know about changes in federal law over the

last 10 years meant to ease the way for them to do so. Of those congregations that have competed for government funds, almost 80 percent report difficulty in applying for and managing the grants. Those that did not apply listed concern about external control and a lack of space for new grant-funded activities as their key reasons. The congregations surveyed represent the very types of religious groups targeted by the Initiative—smaller, grassroots organizations, as opposed to longstanding faith-based social service providers with established national reach. (2007)

As Richard P. Nathan, codirector of the Rockefeller Institute of Government, parent to the Roundtable, noted, "For many congregational leaders, the government contracting process remains daunting. And few have the organizational structure in place to manage such contracts. If government is to increasingly partner with such groups, there remains a lot of work to do" (quoted in Hughes 2007a). For example, Green (2007) found that the largest administrative challenges facing congregations that provide services were program evaluation, volunteer recruitment and retention, and new client recruitment; only about half of the congregations surveyed reported having in place the administrative practices (such as audited financial statements) that would be needed to receive and manage public money. Other essential practices were even less common, with only 24 percent having an evaluation of program outcomes and 19.5 percent reporting formal polices for overhead charges.

In addition to arguments about whether the original premise of the initiatives is tenable, critics have argued that current federal implementation of faith-based practices can be said to "ring hollow" (Singer and Friel 2007). The most prominent critic of the initiatives is probably David Kuo, once a strong supporter. While not an academic account, his recent analysis of the initiatives, *Tempting Faith: An Inside Story of Political Seduction* (2006b), is a comprehensive and critical insider's view. Kuo argues that the initiatives once had great promise, and that many of the early supporters, including John Dilulio (the first head of the White House OFBCI) and himself, had felt that the role of religious groups in the social services sector could be increased and that the religious groups would, indeed, have been able to offer improved services. Instead, Kuo found a world in which the initiatives did not live up to their promises: adoption of faith-based practices was a political tool used to get votes, and it promoted only the appearance that new religious groups were filling social needs.

Although there are many critics of the initiatives, the initiatives still have strong support from many at the federal and state levels. In his 2008 State of the Union address, President Bush reiterated the importance of the initiatives, arguing that the changes that Congress had failed to make in the previous eight years needed to be made now. In addition, state offices and laws keep springing up, and supporters of the initiatives, including Stanley Carlson-Thies and Stephen Monsma, argue that they have been beneficial insofar as they brought the faith-based voice back into the public square. Indeed, this is what I, too, argue has been the clearest accomplishment of the initiative: although it has not brought substantial new money or created sustained social service efforts or improved services for the needy, the initiatives have been successful in changing the laws, policies, and practices that define the relationship between church and state.

What Is Happening in the States?

Most research on the faith-based initiatives has focused on three main issues. In addition to the question of whether secular or religious groups are better providers of social services, as discussed above, research has also examined the implementation of the initiatives at the federal level (Bielefeld and Seuss-Kennedy 2003; Farris, Nathan, and Wright 2004; Formicola, Segers, and Weber 2003; Seuss-Kennedy and Bielefeld 2006) and studied questions about the relationship between church and state (Lupu and Tuttle 2003).

This leaves a significant facet of faith-based policy unexplored: namely, the role of state governments in creating faith-based policies and practices. While there has been a great deal of attention paid to changes at the federal level, little attention has been paid to how and why states are adopting the initiatives. The limited research thus far has focused on descriptive accounts of actions at the state level, nationwide, or within a single state. The most complete research on state implementation has been conducted by Mark Ragan, Lisa Monteil, and David Wright (2003) of the Roundtable for Research on Religion and Social Welfare Policy.[5] They found that states have been engaging in a variety of relevant activities, including creating advisory boards to research faith-based state social services and enacting legislation that includes faith-based language. Still, these studies have not accounted for many aspects of the initiative. Among the areas left unexplored are a detailed account of FBLs and their role in the implementation of the initiative, an account of legislative activity over time, and descriptions of various state practices. No research has gathered comprehensive data for all states in an attempt to understand and evaluate the various reasons underlying adoption of faith-based policies by states or to describe the on-the-ground reality of their implementation.

Why Are States Adopting the Faith-Based Initiatives?

States' adoption of the faith-based initiatives has increased greatly since the initiative's inception in 1996. For example, in 1996 there was no state legislation specifically related to the initiatives, and in 1997 there were only seven such laws, but by 2007, 271 laws had been enacted. In addition, state bureaucracies have grown: as I write, 39 states[6] have FBLs, and 22 states have an OFBCI from which the liaison works. Why the increase in interest? The extensive interviews, fieldwork, and data analysis I have conducted over the past few years can begin to explain what has happened, and why. While these data cannot show all the answers, they do begin to hint at a process of social movement access, bringing success by creating ties to others using large-scale meaning systems to attract attention (Lindsay 2008). The results also indicate that part of the initiatives' appeal for politicians has been the promise that the initiatives would help alleviate the burden on strained welfare systems. My study and others have shown this financial benefit has largely not occurred.

Desecularization and Devolution: A Hollow State

This increase in implementation of state faith-based policies reflects two larger battles in American politics: the growing devolution of government social services to the nonprofit and private sectors (Milward and Provan 2002) and the increasingly prominent role of religion in politics and policy (Gushee 2008; Hudson 2008). The first faith-based initiatives were part of the 1996 Welfare Reform Bill, which worked to shift the burden of social services to the religious sector of the nonprofit community, and was a mechanism by which the presence of religion in the public sector has been increased.

The twin processes of government desecularization and devolution—most prominent in conservative political philosophy—have significantly altered culture and politics in the United States. "Desecularization" can be defined as the increasing role of religious authority in aspects of society. Most American political institutions are largely secular in nature, and this has angered conservative political and religious leaders from William F. Buckley to Jerry Falwell and Pat Robertson. The movement to alter this secularization of the public square has led to inroads in creating a greater role for religious organizations within secular institutions (Belluck 2006; Henriques 2006). The promotion of faith-based initiatives is one of the ways that this is happening. In addition, conservative political advocates have been increasingly privatizing the government sector, effectively ending government as it has been since the New Deal, and resulting in the devolution of power away from government and toward the private and nonprofit sectors. The phrase "hollow state," or one in which the government plays an increasingly less active role in favor of private and nonprofit organizations, was first coined by Brinton Milward and Keith Provan (2002:1) after the welfare reform of 1996. They have defined the hollow state as "a metaphor for the increasing use of third parties, often nonprofits, to deliver social services and generally act in the name of the state." One aspect of this hollow state is that faith-based groups provide social services, either with or without public money. It is, in fact, welfare reform that creates both the supply and demand for the faith-based initiatives: welfare reform creates the mechanism by which religion can become part of the public sphere, while also driving the need for these social services to take up where government left off (whether the religious groups are willing and able to do so, or not).

Desecularization and the Role of the Evangelical Movement and Faith Constituencies

In the literature on public policy and social movements, changing the political landscape by creating new symbols and frames of understanding is considered a crucial way for movements to gain political power (Benford and Snow 2000; Brysk 1995; Edelman 1964, 1971; McVeigh, Myers, and Sikkink 2004; Miceli 2005; Pedriana 2006; Williams and Blackburn 1996; Wysong, Aniskeiwicz, and Wright 1994). Symbolic politics are important to social movement success because of the changes that those policies represent and the political alliances they create; and they also reassure anxious groups. In fact, the conservative evangelical movement is not the only religious constituency to believe in the initiatives or support their goals and the initiative has been able to reach other audiences. However, it was the first religious movement to back the initiatives. Furthermore, the conservative evangelical movement counts among its members a man who has been the initiatives' most important political supporter, George W. Bush.

The faith-based initiatives meet the instrumental political goals of the resurgent evangelical movement in at least several ways. They create a new role for religion in government, using symbols to change political culture in a way that brings religion into government through collaboration and cooperation; regardless of whether the actors have any real power or whether significant amounts of money are involved, the creation of new legislation and administrative positions signals support to the evangelical movement base and legitimizes a new role for religion within politics (Lindsay 2008). Of course the evangelical movement is not a monolithic set of people and organizations (Gushee 2008, Smith 2000); there has been much research and writing on the evangelical center and progressive evangelical movement, which is in many ways very different from the older generation of Christian Right activists who held power for so long, especially within the Republican Party (Conger 2008a, 2008b; Gushee 2008). However, the goals articulated in much of the research on the conservative evangelical movement and many actions the movement has taken in both politics and public policy are specifically geared to creating a larger space for religion within the public sphere (Green 2007).

THE GOD STRATEGY. This movement to create a larger space for religion in the public square is documented in several new books including David Domke and Kevin Coe's *The God Strategy* (2007). Domke and Coe chronicle how the original goal of the evangelical movement—to create a large role for religion in public life—has turned into politicians relying on what they call a "God strategy," or a strategy of using the language of faith to win support. When looking at the role of the faith-based initiatives, one can see that although they are part of a political strategy, they are also creating a cultural shift through the implementation of symbolic policies and practices that reframe the debate surrounding church and state to one about cooperation, collaboration, and institutionalization rather than one about separation. Even if politicians do not believe in the goals of the evangelical movement, they can benefit from using the policies the movement has created for their own benefit. Faith-based policies are not just about the tangible effects of legislation and administration; they are symbols that some people respond to, mechanisms that alter how the culture of government operates.

In addition, because of these symbols, the initiatives also have the potential to generate support within other religious communities including among some Catholics and, most significantly, many in the black religious community. In his research on evangelical elites, Michael Lindsay (2006, 2008) argues that the involvement of the evangelical movement elite was successful because they were able to make bridges to other organizations through activities that reach out to people with similar meaning systems. Although the evangelical and black religious communities have many differences in outlook, both among themselves and with each other, and have not traditionally worked closely together, they tend to have similar feelings regarding the role of religion in government. Seeing members of black religious groups as potential allies, supporters of faith-based polices and practices have focused on wooing them in two ways. First, a large proportion of those appointed as FBLs are black clergy members, who clearly have connections with their religious communities. Second, state-sponsored faith-based conferences have specifically targeted the black religious community, using tools found in black churches to promote social action based on the faith-based initiatives. As is explored in Chapter 5, these attempts at creating new political alliances with the black community have not always succeeded.

THE SHIFTING TIDE OF CHURCH-STATE SEPARATION. Over the last 50 years, evangelicals have moved away from the traditional understanding of the relationship between religious groups and politics. Instead of taking an entirely otherworldly perspective that some thought to be the perspective of conservative religious groups,[7] the resurgent conservative evangelical movement has now focused on bringing religion into *this* world by entering the realm of politics and government in an attempt to confront what they see as the collapse of traditional values and mores in society (Lindsay 2008, Monsma 2006, Olasky 1996, C. Smith et al. 1998). Some in the movement believe that the absence of religion—in this case, conservative Christian religion—in public life is creating a social downfall, and that religion should return to the forefront of American life through the reshaping of church-state relations. Further, some evangelicals believe that the secularization of the public sphere—for example, by means of court cases that made prayer in school illegal, allowed the teaching of evolution, and made abortion legal—must be stopped. As Randall Terry, a controversial, conservative evangelical movement activist and the head of Operation Rescue (a conservative pro-life organization), said, "Our goal is a Christian nation. We have a Biblical duty and we are called by God to conquer this country. We don't want equal time. We don't want pluralism" (1993, quoted in Boehlert and Foser 2005). While there are many evangelicals who would not see Terry as representing their goals, his statement reflects a more subtle sentiment that they would agree with: that the relationship between church and state has become too separate and that religion has for too long been banished from the public square. Faith-based initiatives are seen as a means of changing this situation.

REFRAMING THE QUESTION. As Edelman (1971:7) argues, "Political actions chiefly arouse or satisfy people not by granting or withholding their stable substantive demands, but rather by changing the demands and expectations." One part of the strategy of the conservative evangelical movement has been to increase the role of religion in all aspects of state government, including social services. And one of the ways of doing this has been to create a new metaphor or story about church-state separation and how it affects social services and government. Instead of separation, the movement's argument goes, government should seek collaboration and cooperation between faith-based groups and government-funded social services. This new relationship would bring new and better help to the poor and needy; further, such collaboration would help the poor and needy more cost-effectively than the government working alone can. In short, everyone would win in this new, cooperative atmosphere.

Unfortunately, there has been no oversight or review to ensure that these new policies are fulfilling their promise, and, as I said above, there is little evidence to indicate that the initiatives have made anything but modest gains in this battle (Green 2007, Kuo and Dilulio 2008). Instead, the data show that the main success of the initiatives has been in creating institutions and policies, a new "faith-based bureaucracy," that links state governments and religious organizations and potentially creates new political alliances.

Sociological Importance of the Faith-Based Initiatives

Symbolic Politics as Cultural Goods

In his work on the role of evangelical elites in changing culture and social structure, Lindsay (2008) argued that by articulating a vision for the future, then fueling that vision through individual agency leaders and collaboration of overlapping networks, this vision for the future could be realized in cultural goods. When examining the faith-based initiatives, one can see how the articulated vision for society was transmitted through its specific goals of bringing religion closer to the state. While the collaboration among various groups for its implementation was almost certainly not done in a colluding manner, the result was the same as if it had been: states have increasingly created faith-based policies and practices that confirm the original vision for the initiative and potentially influence society through laws, offices, and practices. These practices are the "goods" produced by the rhetoric and leadership begun by the evangelical movement. That it has appealed to other constituencies is certainly a reason for its success, but it is important to understand how these processes occur and how this cultural production that is their end result enables further movement action—even if that is not the goal of most of the supporters of the initiatives (Lindsay 2008). Again, what these policies do in concrete fiscal terms is not necessarily important; that they *exist* in a framework that appeals to the values of their constituencies—and, it is hoped, new allies—is what is important. The faith-based initiatives, when looked at through the lens of symbolic politics, cater to the ideological concerns of the evangelical movement; they act as a political tool to reach out to new groups who view the world similarly, and they become part of the hoped-for larger cultural change.

Social movement theorists have argued that by gaining access within the political system, social movements can begin to implement their goals through policy changes (Zald 2000). Through inside access to state politics, evangelical movement actors are able to gain legitimacy within state government, and they are thus better able to pursue their various goals. In their study of evangelical movement access to government, Green, Guth, and Wilcox (1998) argued that the movement can gain much from its influence in state Republican parties: legitimacy, access to organizational resources, and a key role in nomination and platform politics. I have found that faith-based policies and practices were more likely to be created in states where this evangelical presence was greater. While this may not be the only motivator of state action regarding the initiatives, it is undoubtedly a significant one.[8]

A Path Previously Traveled

The evangelical movement is not the first movement to begin to gain political access by making inroads through largely symbolic policies. Other movements have gained slow but steady access to government by taking small steps that eventually led to stronger and more concrete legislation. One of the best examples of this is the Civil Rights movement. The original policy implementation of the Civil Rights movement began with the appointment of directors who worked from offices similar to OFBCIs. Although the directors worked without support staff or any real funding or organizational structure, those appointments were the first steps in the implementation of policies destined to meet the goals of the Civil Rights movement (Bullock and Lamb 1984; Lockard 1968). From those largely symbolic displays of agreement with the movement's efforts, real policy changes at the state level, such as the creation of Equal Employment Opportunity councils and Affirmative Action programs, soon followed. Such policy measures were able to succeed because of the groundwork laid by their predecessors, the state civil rights directors.

By examining this increase in the legitimization of the Civil Rights movement in state politics over time and the increase in the strength of social policy supporting it, we can enhance understanding of the evangelical movement's tactics and the symbolic policies that begin to meet its goals. While present faith-based policies act mainly to weaken the separation of church and state without necessarily offering direct material change or resources to faith-based groups, some evidence indicates that future policies may be more concrete. For example, the number of states that are funding OFBCIs has increased over the years. While no state OFBCIs or faith-based efforts received faith-based appropriations in 1997, now 16 states have faith-based appropriations. In addition, the number of state laws pertaining to FBOs and other aspects of the initiatives now numbers over 270. Thus, FBLs, like civil rights directors, may have been the first step in the policy process—a process that increases in substance over time. Even so, the future direct material results of these policies are not necessarily the only important facet of these practices. The crucial and simple fact is that these policies, positions, and practices exist in a framework that changes the political, institutional, and social culture in ways that alter the relationship between church and state that was the norm for much of the twentieth century.

New Understandings, New Allies: The Creation of a Faith-Based Movement Political Platform

Research in public policy has found that policy creates politics, with new social policies altering the political landscape (Lowi 1964, 1969; Mooney and Lee 1995; Stone 2005). Policies based on beliefs and ideas shared with other groups can also create new allegiances and political allies. Green, Rozell, and Wilcox (2003) found that the evangelical movement's access to state Republican parties was important for several reasons, but they also argued that to move beyond their base and gain influence in other states, the movement would have to access black churches. Faith-based initiatives are a means by which these allies might be sought.

I have found three ways in which faith-based initiatives are creating new politics. First, FBLs operating as policy brokers bring a new understanding of church-state separation and the new language of the faith-based initiatives to both religious groups and to state government, expanding the means of communication among them. Second, state faith-based policy and institutional changes are creating new state bureaucracies that appeal to the fiscal needs of states and to political allies that see this as a greater part of a much-needed devolution of government to the private sector. Finally, two faith-based practices appear to be specifically aimed at creating new allegiances with black religious communities—the recruitment of members of black churches as liaisons and the creation of faith-based conferences that rely heavily on symbolic cues from black churches. The role of faith-based liaisons as policy brokers, faith-based legislation as symbolic politics, and faith-based conferences as political rallying grounds are discussed in Chapters 3, 4, and 5 respectively.

A Triangulated Approach to Research

How have states implemented the faith-based initiatives? Why have states implemented these practices? These questions have driven my research, and I compiled data by three means to begin to answer them.[9] Using LexisNexis, an online legislative database, I collected data on all state legislative changes related to the initiatives for the years 1996 to 2007. I also interviewed state FBLs, the main actors responsible for carrying out the faith-based initiatives at the state level, and several other key players. Together, my research sources outlined both a fairly complete historical record of policy changes made at the state level and some of the concrete details about the on-the-ground efforts and the actors who are in charge of carrying them out. Finally, I conducted field research, which gave me an unfiltered view of what some states' implementation efforts look like in actual practice. My experiences in the field also gave me the background and means needed to speculate on what their potential effect may be.

LexisNexis Data on Legislation

The LexisNexis database includes legislative activity in all states; from this I collected data on nine types of legislation passed over the last 11 years, using key words such as "faith-based" and "Charitable Choice" to determine how many such practices had become incorporated into legislation. Data for each piece of legislation included the date of passage, its sponsor, and the complete text of the bill. For purposes of analysis, I coded legislative acts by category and year of passage. LexisNexis was also a source of information on liaison positions that were created by law or an executive order from the governor. This data included the date of appointment, an official description of the position, and the means by which each FBL was appointed.[10] I found that states varied greatly in the number and types of laws enacted over the time period covered;

discussion of this means of implementing the faith-based initiatives is found in Chapter 4.

IN-DEPTH INTERVIEWS WITH KEY PLAYERS. Using data on liaisons compiled by the White House OFBCI, the Roundtable for Research on Religion and Social Welfare Policy, and the Center for Public Justice and LexisNexis data, I compiled a list of all liaisons and categorized each state's appointment of a liaison as being by legislation, by the governor, or by a state agency head. The list of state liaisons used for this research was in congruence with those of the White House and the Roundtable in late 2005.[11]

In-depth interviews were then conducted with liaisons in 30 of the 34 states that had an FBL; efforts to reach the remaining four states' liaisons by telephone and e-mail were unsuccessful. In their analysis of the use of interviews in studying social movements, Kathleen Blee and Verta Taylor (2002) argue that there are several distinct advantages to this methodology over other types of data collection. Interviews are important because they may offer insights that are not available from other sources. Unlike surveys or written data on legislation, interviews offer firsthand accounts of social movement actions and policy implementation. Only through interviews could I pose questions about the motivations and perspectives of the liaisons; this dialogue was crucial to my understanding of why liaisons took this position and how their own religious beliefs and ideas affect their work. Interviews also yield information about the contexts of action and the identities of participants. Through these interviews I was able to explore why these policies and positions were being created and what the liaisons themselves thought about the faith-based initiatives. Finally, it was only through interviews that an analysis of the actual power and agency that FBLs were able to exercise was possible.

For almost half of the interviews conducted, I was able to meet with the liaisons in person and spend time with them during their day-to-day activities. This kind of access to the liaisons helped me gain an understanding of the people behind the initiatives that I could never have gained otherwise. When I was not able to meet with liaisons in person, interviews were conducted by telephone. The interviews with liaisons were conducted in a confidential manner. This was to ensure that the liaisons would speak openly to me not only about their specific roles as liaisons and the exact duties of the job, but also about their feelings regarding implementation of these policies and practices. Without anonymity many of the liaisons may not have granted interviews, or would not have felt free to be as forthcoming and candid about their hopes and fears for an initiative with which many felt emotionally connected.

Whether in-person or by telephone, the formal interviews lasted between 20 minutes and two hours and were designed to elicit information on the actual practices of the liaisons, particularly those that would not show up in the official job descriptions found in the LexisNexis data. All interviews were taped and then transcribed into Word documents for coding. The interviews were made up of two parts: closed-ended survey questions asked about specific state-level activities, such as whether the state had a Web site or e-mail listserv and whether the state offered conferences for FBOs; these questions were designed to elicit easily comparable data on exactly what state liaisons and state Offices of Faith-Based Community Initiatives were doing to incorporate faith-based practices into state policy. The other part of the survey consisted of open-ended questions regarding such things as their reasons for becoming FBLs, their relationships with religious communities, their personal religious backgrounds, and various aspects of their duties. These qualitative questions were useful for gathering information about FBLs that did not come up in quantitative data collection and were especially important in informing my work on the role of state liaisons in social movements and public policy.

I also collected information on liaisons' relationships with one another and with the White House OFBCI. Liaisons were asked how many other liaisons they knew, whether they communicated with the White House office and, if so, how much and how often. Information on this networking was designed to yield a picture of how interconnected—or disconnected—FBLs were with one another and with the White House.[12]

Supplemental Interviews

In addition to speaking with current liaisons, interviews with eight additional state actors were conducted. These interviews used the same general format as the liaison interviews, but they also included questions about previous state activity involving the faith-based initiatives. For example, in Texas I spoke with the state's first FBL, who had worked for Governor George W. Bush and then followed Bush to Washington for his first term as president. Under President Bush, he helped create the White House Office for Faith-Based and Community Initiatives and worked with John Dilulio, the first head of the White House OFBCI. He discussed with me not only what originally occurred in Texas regarding the faith-based initiatives but also what happened once George W. Bush became president. In several other states in which there was no one currently occupying the position of FBL, I spoke with the person who had previously filled the position. Other interviews were conducted with past liaisons and with actors who worked closely with state liaisons, such as faith-based directors in other state agencies.

In addition to these state actors, I met with two federal officials. Both were the coordinators of state activities in the White House OFBCI. During these interviews I gathered information on the role of the White House in encouraging faith-based practices by states and on its connections to state OFBCIs and

FBLs. The first of these interviews was conducted in 2004, and the second, with an interim director, in 2005.

After the qualitative data were collected and coded, I identified patterns that emerged using grounded theory. For example, I examined how many FBLs had worked with religious groups, or how many saw their job as part of their personal religious mission. These qualitative data were then used both on their own to describe in detail what is happening with the faith-based initiatives and in support of the conclusions derived from the quantitative data.

The Bounds of My Research of This Study

Needless to say, my research thus far was unable to cover all aspects of the faith-based initiatives. Perhaps the most important omission is that I was unable to measure the impact of the policies of the faith-based initiatives on the numbers of FBOs receiving state money to provide social services—exactly that which the initiatives were supposed to do. There are several reasons for this. First, no state had any baseline measurements of the numbers of FBOs it funded for this purpose. Second, even with the policies in place, almost no states collect these data; gathering or estimating this information on state funding streams from state budget data would be a worthwhile extension to this study. Fortunately, I was able to assess whether any new funds had been created for these purposes through the FBLs or OFBCIs. Only New Jersey has created significant new funding through these organizations, and the CCF is the only new funding source in the federal government. So while money may be shifting from one group of service providers to another, the initiatives have not produced the amounts of new money promised in early rhetoric by the founders of the policies and offices.

Third, these data are limited in the time period in which they were collected, with data on liaisons ending in 2005 (see Winston, Person, and Clary 2008 for an update on eight states). Interviews with liaisons were conducted toward the beginning of the initiatives, so there is good reason to suspect that there have been and will be changes along the way, with some liaisons leaving, others coming in, and states expanding or contracting their operations. However, this study does paint a picture of the early time period of the initiatives and explains the history, complexity, and dynamic nature of faith-based policy. This is a snapshot of how the faith-based initiatives were practiced in their early years, and further study of how it progresses after this time will be a productive future avenue of study. When thinking about the initiatives and how they have changed over time, it is important to remember the great variance in original state reaction. The faith-based initiatives are not like most other policies; according to Michael Gerson, they have their roots and justification in evangelical political activities that ebb and flow over time (quoted in Hagerty 2008), so future study on these dynamic processes can lead to a better understanding of how some states that have strong conservative political and religious traditions vary compared with those without these actors.

Although this study that forms the basis for this book is limited in several respects, the data collected and analyzed here have allowed me to examine the faith-based initiatives in enough depth to see that they represent a fundamental shift in the way some Americans would like the relationship between church and state to look. These data illustrate how states have begun to embrace faith-based practices in a way that indicates a shift away from church-state separation and toward a norm of cooperation and collaboration between church and state.

Summary and Conclusion

As a matter of policy, faith-based initiatives are both a success and a failure. Their success—in the eyes of some—has come in the form of creating new institutions and public policies that bring church and state closer together, allowing for a new conversation and partnerships between the two to emerge. On the other hand, they have failed in that most of their promises to spur a social services revolution have not been fulfilled to a noticeable degree (Green 2007).

Faith-based practices at the state level have resulted in new laws and institutions as part of a continuing devolution of state government to the nonprofit and private sectors. While ideological concerns about religion have guided state implementation for some, state faith-based policies have also arisen in response to genuine fiscal concerns and political ideology about the overall role of government in society. The faith-based initiatives have appealed to these instrumental and affective concerns because they have promised not only to alleviate the fiscal burden on states by offering more services through the faith-based sector but also to further a hoped-for shift to a smaller role for government. Thus, the initiatives become one step in a process of moving away from government-run social services toward the creation of a system that relies more heavily on nonprofit organizations and the private sector.

This tangle of ideological reasons for backing the faith-based initiatives has resulted in myriad policies and practices stemming from the initiatives. While for some the goal was to bring novel resources and renewed hope to those in need of social services, for others it was a response to fiscal necessity; it represents hope for a revolution in some faith-based circles, while for others it is simply a matter of politics. Regardless of the reasons behind them, faith-based policies legitimize a new role for religion in the public sphere and blur the line between church and state.

2

The Historical Role of Religion in Government Social Services and the Development of the Faith-Based Initiatives

You always hear that it is impolite to discuss religion and politics in polite conversation, but when you combine them, it's a pretty combustible mixture.

> —Former advisor to George W. Bush, interview
> with the author, March 27, 2005

In this chapter, I examine the historical role of religious groups in the provision of social services and how faith-based initiatives are redefining this role. Since 1996, federal and state governments have, with increasing frequency, adopted a variety of policies and practices related to the initiatives. Such action by the federal government and a majority of the states is surprising, considering that—as one liaison noted—the combination of religion and politics can be a combustible and controversial mixture. To understand why the initiatives have garnered so much public policy attention, I will begin by examining the historical development of these policies and practices.

The Texas Experience

Though this chapter contains a broad overview of faith-based implementation over time, I also examine in detail the historical development of faith-based practices in Texas. The history of the faith-based initiatives in Texas is crucial to understanding the faith-based initiatives in the United States. It was the first state to create extensive faith-based practices, having started in 1996 some months before Charitable Choice was passed as part of federal welfare reform. Other states soon followed Texas, often relying on its models of implementation, which coupled legislative implementation with administrative attempts at changing government culture. After initial successes in implementation under Governor George W. Bush, however, the drive to create lasting and cohesive faith-based policies and practices faltered in Texas. Since aspects of the history of the initiatives in Texas were repeated later in other states around the country, the Texas story encapsulates much of the initiative's potential and its pitfalls. In Texas and in each successive state, the role of religious groups in the provision of social services was broadened and redefined, sometimes with some lasting success and sometimes not.

The Role of Religion in Social Services

In the late 1990s, the faith-based initiatives brought the role of religion in the provision of social services into the public eye; however, churches and religious groups have long played an integral role in helping the disadvantaged. Michael O'Neill (1989: 20) has referred to religious groups as the "Godmother of the Nonprofit Sector," because they are the "oldest, largest and most generously supported" segment of the nonprofit world, and have given birth to many other nonprofit institutions.[1] About half of all private charitable donations in the United States are directed to religious congregations and other religiously affiliated groups; a substantial portion of private schools, day-care centers, and international aid and relief organizations are also affiliated with religious groups; and 57 percent of U.S. religious congregations report being involved in at least one social services program (Chaves 1999; Monsma 1996; O'Neill 1989).

In the context of recent debate over the faith-based initiatives, many claims have been made about the desirability of faith-based social services. One advocate of faith-based initiatives described the use of FBOs as service providers as "unleashing the cultural remedy to societal ills," because "churches have been transforming shattered lives for years by addressing the deeper needs of people—by instilling hope and values which help change behavior and attitudes" (Ashcroft 1999). This claim contains two important assertions regarding FBOs. The first is that faith-based service providers seek to transform the lives of their clients. The second is that faith-based groups are successful in attaining this goal. While this study does not attempt to assess whether these assertions are true, it does examine how states have been attempting to engage the faith-based sector, a goal that is clearly based on the premise that this sector offers something more desirable than other social services providers. Even though faith-based social services have always been part of the social services sector, the faith-based initiatives claims something new. They assert that these groups should not only be a part of the sector but that they should be incorporated into key aspects of social services delivery from the government because they are better suited to the task.

A New View of Church-State Relations

The faith-based initiative is one policy among many that is shaping a new norm for church-state relations (Henriques 2006). Over the past century, the legal doctrine of these relations in the United States has held to the Jeffersonian ideal of a wall separating church and state. Recently, however, many people—particularly evangelicals and other conservative Christians—have pushed for a new relationship, based on cooperation and collaboration rather than separation. As Chief Justice William Rehnquist (1985) articulated in a dissenting opinion, "The 'wall of separation between church and state' is a metaphor based on bad history, a metaphor which has proved useless as a guide to judging. It should be frankly and explicitly abandoned." This new view of church-state cooperation is inherent in the faith-based initiatives as they are being adopted at both the federal and state levels, where laws and policies that give religious groups an expanded role in government and public life are being created.

Faith-Based Initiatives at the Federal Level

The Birth of the Faith-Based Initiatives

The earliest version of a federal faith-based initiative, Charitable Choice, was signed into law by President Bill Clinton but was implemented primarily through a variety of executive orders issued by President George W. Bush. In particular, Executive Order 13199 called for eliminating "unnecessary legislative, regulatory and other bureaucratic barriers that impede effective faith-based and other community efforts to solve social problems" (Bush 2001). Charitable Choice also provided that private faith-based groups receiving government contracts "shall retain their independence from [government], including such organization's control over the definition, development, practice and expression of its religious beliefs" (Stern 2001: 174). As one of Governor Bush's former advisors told me in an interview (March 27, 2005), Charitable Choice was a little provision with a potentially big impact: "In August of the year they [Congress] passed the 1996 welfare reform act Charitable Choice provisions. It was pretty revolutionary, landmark, buried in a gigantic bill." This small provision, buried in a gigantic bill, was the way a small cultural revolution regarding the role of religion in the public square got its start.

Although President Clinton enacted Charitable Choice, he favored a narrow interpretation of it because he felt that it came dangerously close to violating the principle of separation of church and state (Formicola, Segers, and Weber 2003). He stated that the establishment clause of the First Amendment would guide interpretation of this legislation, assuring the nation that "this provision will never be implemented in any way that jeopardizes the religious freedom clauses in the Constitution" (Aronson 2004). Therefore, although Clinton was the first president to sign a faith-based initiative into law, he did very little to support it.

The Early Blossoming of the Faith-Based Initiatives

A CHAMPION. The situation changed dramatically when George W. Bush came into office as president. During his tenure as governor of Texas he had incorporated the provisions of Charitable Choice into Texas policy and politics, supporting legislation that limited licensing requirements for religious groups and creating the first state FBL positions. As governor, Bush believed it was important to create opportunities for faith-based groups to provide social services, according to the former advisor cited above; as president, he chose to expand the original faith-based initiative, turning a single piece of legislation into a series of executive orders and a number of faith-based offices within departments. He made faith-based initiatives his top-priority domestic policy, a point he has reiterated in his State of the Union addresses. As he said in a speech on the faith-based initiatives:

> Government can hand out money—and I'm going to talk about
> some of the money we're trying to hand out—but government can't
> put hope in a person's heart, or a sense of purpose in a person's life.
> That is done by loving individuals who spread their love. That's
> what happens. And it seems like to me it makes sense for those of us
> who are honored to hold office to gather that strength, rally that
> strength, call upon that strength, and, most importantly, support that
> strength from the halls of government. (Bush 2006)

This clearly illustrates the president's views on the ideal relationship between church and state—it should not be one of separation but one "characterized by collaboration" (Formicola, Seger, and Weber 2003: 7). President Bush's concept of how church and state should interact is also revealed in other ways, for example in his Supreme Court nominations of religious conservatives John Roberts and Samuel Alito. His first use of the presidential veto—blocking federal funding of stem cell research, an issue that caters to the conservative evangelical movement and not the majority of the population—also suggests that he considers government and religion as interrelated spheres.[2] His stands on numerous other policy issues, including signing the "partial birth abortion" bill into law, also indicate this wish for a closer relationship between church and state, a position with great appeal to his evangelical base.

Several of Bush's executive orders have expanded the faith-based initiatives significantly. From establishing the White House Office of Faith-Based Community Initiatives, which is responsible for the federal management of the initiative, to creating separate faith-based centers in 11 agencies and departments of the federal government,[3] the Bush administration has actively sought to increase the role that religious organizations play in the provision of social services. As with state efforts, the vast majority of this implementation has been about changing government culture and creating a new "faith-based bureaucracy," rather than creating new funding streams for religious groups.

THE COMPASSION CAPITAL FUND. There has been one exception to this general rule, however: The Department of Health and Human Services offers funding specifically to religious groups through its CCF. The rhetoric surrounding this funding has been about including all varieties of religious groups and small community-based organizations in the funding process; however, was not always what occurred. Since its inception in 2001, the CCF has granted more than $200 million in contracts to faith-based groups. Recent reports argue that the vast amounts of this funding went to Christian organizations and to friends of President Bush. For example, in a recent report in the *Washington Post*, Thomas Edsall (2006) found that "beneficiaries of more than $2 million each from the Compassion Fund include five organizations run by black and Hispanic leaders who endorsed Bush and Operation Blessing, a charity run by television evangelist Pat Robertson. It has received $23.5 million, which includes $1.5 million from the CCF and $22 million in surplus dry milk from the Agriculture Department." This bias favoring political allies and certain faith groups is an example of how the faith-based initiatives, as they were employed especially in the early years of the initiative and at the federal level, appear to be aimed at increasing the presence of a certain brand of Christian religion in government and reinforcing political ties rather than at ameliorating the problems of poverty (Kuo 2006a; Kuo and Dilulio 2008).

PERMISSION TO DISCRIMINATE—PERHAPS. President Bush has made religion an even more salient issue by issuing executive orders that would allow religious organizations to discriminate in their hiring practices, making it possible for them to hire only those who share their religious beliefs, despite their receipt of federal money. While early support for the initiatives was drawn mainly from evangelical circles, provisions like this soon caught the attention of others, who saw the potential of the initiatives and began supporting these efforts. This support came from a variety of black churches (Chaves 1999), which I discuss in detail in Chapter 5, and the Catholic Church, groups that had long been running social services under the old rules that required a brighter line (usually a separate 501[c]3 organization) between secular social services groups and the religious arms of these organizations. However, after

Charitable Choice, some of these groups began making changes in their longtime secular social services agencies, taking on a more religious flair.[4]

The Catholic Church, in particular, felt that this aspect of the initiatives was important to the work that the church was doing and would allow it greater religious freedom while performing social services. Members of the church and the church's main social services arm, Catholic Charities, viewed the proposed rule change as one that would better allow them to fulfill their mission of providing Catholic-centered social services. In a recent press release, Bill Donohue, the president of the Catholic League for Religious and Civil Rights, argued that Barack Obama's proposed revisions to the initiatives that he stated during his 2008 presidential campaign would not and should not satisfy Catholics, since they lacked the religious hiring provisions key to the initiatives:

> Any church or religious agency that agrees to take federal money on the condition that it must operate in a secular fashion—in hiring and in disseminating its values—is selling out. If Orthodox Jews running a day care center are not allowed to exclusively hire Orthodox Jews, there is nothing kosher about it. If a Catholic foster care program cannot place Catholic children with Catholic parents, it is doing a disservice to the children. If an evangelical drug rehab program can't deliver a Christian message to its clients, it may as well close up shop. But that's what Obama wants—he wants to secularize the religious workplace.
>
> The whole purpose behind funding faith-based programs is that they are, in fact, superior to secular programs. And the reason they are has everything to do with the inculcation of religious values disseminated by people of faith. No matter, Obama wants to gut the religious values and bar religious agencies from hiring people who share their religion. Hence, his initiative is a fraud. (Donohue 2008: n.p.)

Religious groups that at one time provided religiously based but overtly secular social services are now mired in controversy about these services, with the unspoken consequence of leaving less time and money to care for those whom the initiatives were supposed to help in the first place. In the end Obama may have realized the potential political ramifications of eliminating the hiring provision Bush enacted and has kept it largely intact in his current version of the faith-based initiative; this will be discussed further in Chapter 7.

THE BOTTOM LINE. Even though President Bush had some success with his executive orders and bureaucratic implementation, his inability to get significant funding measures passed through legislation generally parallels the history of the faith-based initiatives at the state level. At the beginning of his presidency, Bush attempted to create new legislation and funding for these organizations, but he was largely unsuccessful. His lack of success in allocating large amounts of new government money to religious groups or in clearly allowing religious discrimination in hiring practices frustrated him. In his final State of the Union address, he called for renewed efforts at implementing these provisions of the initiative; however, with a Democratic majority in Congress, this did not come to pass in the final year of his presidency. This leaves the Bush legacy of federal faith-based policy implementation similar to the one he left in Texas, one in which eliminating the initiative is not politically viable, but retooling it is. Obama has indeed paid some cursory attention to the initiative and changed it as he sees fit.

The Historical Development of Faith-Based Initiatives at the State Level

While the support of the Bush administration explains federal enactment of the faith-based initiatives by means of executive orders, it does not explain why numerous states have adopted a variety of practices related to the initiatives. This generally ignored and unnoticed world of faith-based initiative enactment at the state level is the focus of this book. As noted in the previous chapter, states are not required to implement any part of the initiative other than guaranteeing that FBOs will not be discriminated against in funding decisions. Nonetheless, states have faced pressures to do more—pressures from within and from the federal government. Letters sent by the White House OFBCI to governors in 2002, 2004, and 2006 encouraged them to create their own OFBCIs; however, these letters did not provide any guidelines on how to establish the offices or on how to fund them. In the end, without specific federal guidelines, states were left to choose whatever action seemed appropriate. As a result, some states made no policy changes, whereas others actively embraced the initiatives. Most states chose a middle ground and relied on administrative changes to encourage faith-based groups to apply for and receive government money. As I explore in Chapter 6, states that adopted the initiatives were motivated by reasons religious, political, and fiscal in character.

Regardless of the type of implementation occurring at the state level or the reasons behind implementation, a pattern has emerged: there is a continued and growing effort at the state level to increase the presence of religious groups in the social services sector by specifically encouraging their participation and by encouraging government employees to work toward the inclusion of such groups in government-funded programs. Specific efforts range from the administrative appointment of FBLs to the passage of legislation that exempts faith-based groups from the licensing requirements imposed on other types of organizations. In this book, I focus on the three primary means by which states have implemented the faith-based initiatives—the creation of liaison positions and/or offices, the passage of legislation, and the sponsorship of conferences—and on what those practices look like on the ground. It is crucial to understand that nearly all state-level implementation is not about new funding for FBOs; instead, it consists of laws, policies, and practices that symbolize and create a new relationship between church and state.

Texas: The First State

As I indicated above, if there is one state that embodies the faith-based initiatives, it is Texas. Stemming from a governor's belief in the power of religious groups to help the needy, the story of state implementation in Texas foreshadows the story of other states and their adoption of faith-based practices.

THE FIRST FAITH-BASED LIAISON. To understand the history of faith-based policy implementation in Texas, I spoke with one of the early advisors to George W. Bush during his tenure as governor of the state. This advisor, who advised Bush on a wide range of legal and policy issues beyond the faith-based initiatives, was in effect the first state FBL; although this terminology did not exist at the time, the job position was essentially the same as that of liaisons across the country now. In addition to speaking with this advisor, I also spoke with the most recent Texas FBL. Though the current liaison was able to describe recent activity in the state, the early advisor was there from the beginning and knew about the early implementation of the initiatives and their historical roots in the state. His recollections form the basis of the sections that follow.

Crucial to the early implementation and success of the faith-based initiatives in Texas was the close relationship that Bush's gubernatorial administration had with the intellectual branch of the resurgent evangelical community. Working with early faith-based supporters such as Joe Loconte, Marvin Olasky, Stanley Carlson-Thies, and Carl Esbeck, the Bush administration created far-reaching changes in state government policy and administration. The story of Texas illustrates how complex, varied, and personal implementation can be at the state level, with policies and practices coming from the governor's office leading to laws being enacted.

TEEN CHALLENGE AND THE BEGINNING OF THE STATE FAITH-BASED MOVEMENT. To understand faith-based implementation in Texas, Bush's advisor told me we had to go back to 1995, the governor's first year in office, and the story of Teen Challenge. Teen Challenge is a Christian-based drug treatment program offering drug rehabilitation through Christian scripture. In 1995 their Texas offices were threatened with closure by a state regulatory agency. Although Teen Challenge did not receive any government funds, it did offer treatment to drug users and therefore fell under the state's regulatory powers. The Texas Commission on Alcohol and Drug Abuse threatened to close the doors of Teen Challenge for violations of its regulations. The supporters of Teen Challenge viewed this as infringement of their rights as a religious organization, so the shutting down of the organization by the government offered a ripe opportunity to question the rightness of church-state separation. The story of how the faith-based initiatives got started as a response to the Teen Challenge shutdown highlights two common themes present in the discourse surrounding justification of implementation. First, it is stressed that the government cannot do all that is needed to help the needy. Second, supporters argue that the government needs to allow religious groups that can help fill this need to do their work without any interference.

Describing his understanding of implementation in Texas, the early advisor I interviewed discussed Teen Challenge and how the backlash against its shutdown was the impetus for the creation of the broader faith-based initiatives:

> I joined Governor Bush's office in April 1996. At that point, there had been a recent incident involving a group called Teen Challenge, which was a faith-saturated drug treatment program that boasted strong results. There was a state agency in Texas, TCADA, the Texas Commission on Alcohol and Drug Abuse. There was a well-meaning, I'm sure, but overzealous regulator at TCADA that was going to shut down Teen Challenge. There was a laundry list, probably the thickness of a Manhattan phonebook, of ways Teen Challenge had misstepped and run afoul of myriad state regulations. Whether it was a frayed carpet or a torn shower curtain, all the way to counselors' not having the TCADA-preferred degrees and clinical bona fides, TCADA was enforcing one government-approved way to tackle addiction. Under Texas law, if you whispered the magic word "treatment," then you had to do it the government-sanctioned way, which meant hiring counselors with a certain academic pedigree and a certain amount of clinical expertise.

The advisor then discussed how Teen Challenge was important because it offered something government groups could not. He argued that if groups like Teen Challenge were subject to one-size-fits-all regulation by state agencies, it would impede their ability to do the good work they needed to accomplish:

> At Teen Challenge, they have a sharply different view. They view addiction as sinful behavior prompted by the lack of religious commitment, and they tackle it from that direction. And the results they claimed were pretty spectacular. Governor Bush was unshakably focused on results and performance. His view was, if we can cure people from addiction, then we ought to cheer success and applaud it, and not short-circuit success by force-feeding a too-narrow government-approved model that robs faith-based charities of the very things that make them so uncommonly effective.

This statement illustrates a larger understanding of the faith-based initiatives, which is that what makes these groups work is something that government cannot provide; further, for such groups to be properly effective, the government should be supportive—or at least not intrusive. The advisor went on to discuss how this view of government and religion was translated into government action in Texas, saying that the faith-based initiative "was garnering national attention. The Teen Challenge episode included a rally at the Alamo, which is a great venue if you're claiming that you're besieged and trying to struggle against tyranny." Again, this attachment to an understanding of religious and government cooperation was consistent with the public policy views of Bush's advisor, but like that of other liaisons (see Chapter 3), his professional commitment was augmented by personal beliefs:

> I joined the Governor's office in April 1996, but I was actually pretty settled in my private law firm life, about to write a policy piece for the Texas Public Policy Foundation on how clumsy and burdensome government regulations affected faith-based ministries. So it was serendipitous because the Teen Challenge episode had sparked me to write a paper about sacred-secular policymaking more broadly. I was a full-time lawyer, but in what precious little time you have as a young associate at a major law firm, the firm was good about indulging my extracurricular policy musings. I was preparing to tackle this topic, and then I got this invitation to join the governor's team.

Part of the reason for this personal commitment to the initiatives was the feeling that Teen Challenge was not the only group that was being harmed by too much government interference. Although several studies have shown that there was no systematic or large-scale discrimination against faith-based groups (Chaves 2001, 2004), the feeling among many involved in the initiatives and in evangelical circles was that battles of the sort that Teen Challenge was facing were widespread:

> As I was coming on board in April 1996, they were already putting together an advisory task force of Texans from across the state, about 15 or so, to look at this topic in the wake of Teen Challenge, which the governor rightly thought was the tip of a very large, submerged iceberg. How many more faith-based helpers and healers were being threatened, even if inadvertently, by government or pressured to secularize? So that process was under way as I came on board. That advisory task force was given to me, and I was tacked with shepherding their deliberations and helping them craft their recommendations to the legislature and other state policy makers.

I asked how others ended up on this committee. He explained that "it was a very eclectic assortment of folks, diverse in every possible way, racially, theologically, denominationally, geographically—from all over Texas. Some were in ministry day-in, day-out. Others were more nonprofit leaders. Others were laypeople with a heart for effective poverty-fighting. One was a federal prosecutor." He went on to discuss how this task force, the Governor's Advisory Task Force on Faith-based Community Service Groups, changed the course of faith-based public policy by creating a redefinition of faith-based practices in Texas, one that has been echoed in other states:

> [The advisory board] met probably four times, once every other month or so. They released their blockbuster report in December 1996, called "Faith in Action: A New Vision for Church-State Cooperation," and the governor announced it personally with enormous fanfare at a ministry in San Antonio. The report contained a range of topics; under each topic were a number of concrete policy recommendations and policy options for consideration. . . . The recommendations that were legislative in nature we turned into bills that were proposed and enacted in 1997. A few others were enacted in the next legislation session in 1999.

The first of these recommendations resulted in legislation that would specifically aid Teen Challenge:

> We passed a number of bills in 1997, including the so-called Teen Challenge Bill, which exempted exclusively religious treatment programs from state licensure and oversight. We did require that such programs register with TCADA in a simple, one-page document: here's who we are, where we are, what we do. But there was no requirement of formal TCADA approval. But these programs had to be exclusively religious; they couldn't be a blend of religious and medical-model treatment. If they were a medical-model program replete with all the therapeutic ins and outs of that, they had to do it the government-approved way. So to qualify for the exemption, these had to be purely religious ministries that aimed to help people kick addiction via religious devotion. From all accounts, the Teen Challenge law, now a decade or so old, has apparently been a great success.

In addition to this direct intervention, the advisory board also moved Texas toward a faith-friendlier environment, and started a new dialogue between faith-based groups and state actors. The board's recommendations resulted in legislation that included creating official state liaison positions in several key government entities and limiting certain licensing requirements for FBOs. In Chapter 4, I discuss the outcome of this legislation after Bush left Texas.

FURTHER BUREAUCRATIZATION OF THE FAITH-BASED INITIATIVES. Not only was Texas the first state to create an advisory board and liaisons to implement the initiative, it was also the first state to create a formal OFBCI. Creating an OFBCI, as well as appointing liaisons in various sections of government, was part of a larger cultural and structural shift that changed how church and state were understood by those in Texas government. As Governor Bush's advisor put it,

> I was tasked with bringing to reality all the recommendations, both legislative and nonlegislative, from the December 1996 report, which preceded the opening of the next legislative session by only a few weeks. . . . During that session, we successfully passed all our proposals. Then, after adjournment, I focused on working with key agencies to overhaul their regulatory machinery to make them more hospitable and welcoming to faith-based programs.

This type of effort, creating change in government culture from the inside out, has since been repeated in states across the country, with actors in various states concentrating on creating a new understanding of the role of religious groups in government social services; it has been done with various degrees of success. This new cultural understanding often starts in the governor's office and is directed toward state agency heads and workers. In Texas, as the advisor described later in the interview, these changes were fortified by appointing people to serve on agency governing boards who were not only qualified but also receptive to the policies:

> As the governor often said, he welcomed faith-based charities as partners instead of resenting them as rivals. There was a woman . . . on our task force, she was from a religious nonprofit background on a volunteer level. She was the MVP [most valuable player] of the task force. . . . We later named her to the Department of Human Services board, where she could more consistently and in a more formal agency-specific role push the agenda, kind of get it deeply embedded into the culture of that agency. She was fantastic and ultimately became the vice chair of that board.

The importance of an individual who believes in the goals of the initiatives and pushes cultural change in a bureaucratic environment is a theme that is repeated throughout the states, with the greatest burden of implementation falling on the heads of single state liaisons. Bush's advisor elucidated this goal of creating a more hospitable environment for religious groups, using words similar to those found in the original discussion regarding implementation. When I asked him what he was hoping the state agencies would do, he stated that the goal was "to overhaul the state's regulatory machinery to make the landscape more benevolent, more outcome-focused, and more reflective of the Charitable Choice principles that Congress enacted in August 1996 as part of federal welfare reform."

CHARITABLE CHOICE, STRATEGIES, AND MOTIVATIONS. Governor Bush's advisor said that he and his colleagues carefully followed federal developments on faith-based initiatives while also creating legislation of their own to allow for greater public participation by religious organizations in Texas:

> We knew about [Charitable Choice], and we were following it. One of the bills we passed in that 1997 session, it was done very quietly, because we didn't want to draw undue attention to it or spark a bitter church-state debate, but we inserted a short provision that required local workforce development boards, the primary welfare-reform engines in Texas, to carry out their myriad duties in a manner that reflected the nondiscrimination principles stated in federal Charitable Choice legislation. We didn't use the phrase "Charitable Choice," [and] we didn't say the word "religion" or "religious"—we just used the word "nondiscrimination" or "neutrality" and cited the federal statute—just to make sure as state welfare officials went about their day-in, day-out jobs, they did so in a way that honored those principles of evenhandedness and neutrality and pluralism, but we did so in a way that was very innocuous. This state provision was legally unnecessary given the passage of federal Charitable Choice, but it served as strong reinforcement of those principles.

This tandem approach to creating Charitable Choice–like provisions at the state level while such implementation was happening at the federal level, put Texas in the forefront of the faith-based debate. Relying on the central principle of nondiscrimination, Texas was the first state to enact the faith-friendly principles that would be the most common manifestation of the initiatives at the state level. Even though much of this type of legislation is common now, at that time creating bills that would allow for "nondiscrimination" was tantamount for many to allowing religious groups to hire only coreligionists even when they received government money to provide social services. Therefore, creating these types of laws, especially in 1997, could have led to a showdown between state governments and various watchdog groups such as the American Civil Liberties Union, the Freedom from Religion Foundation, and Americans United for the Separation of Church and State.

Later in that interview, the advisor discussed why this legislation was introduced with such circumspection:

> With the Charitable Choice provision we inserted in 1997, we did so quietly with no fanfare; we didn't want to invite a full-on battle. We didn't want it to morph into a fight as to whether Texas was going to implement Charitable Choice or not. Congress already settled that fight, and it wasn't subject to state-by-state rematches. Charitable Choice is the law of

the land. You don't need a state legislature to ratify it or agree with it, whether they like it or not. . . . So this was not a bill that went through the committee; it was a simple and benign floor amendment by Senator Fraser that he described in the most colorless fashion. It was legally pointless to fight about Charitable Choice on the state level, but it helped that state lawmakers affirmed their support of Charitable Choice in state law.

While some may disagree with his interpretation that a battle was pointless, he was correct in assuming that Charitable Choice was the law of the land and that states would have to follow its provisions. The passage of specific nondiscrimination, or Charitable Choice–like, language was a way to create a new understanding of how relationships between religion and government should work. The advisor noted that some of the people the Bush administration worked with in creating this statute were, perhaps not surprisingly, at the forefront of the faith-based movement:

> After [Charitable Choice] passed, we then worked with Stanley
> Carlson-Thies and Carl Esbeck. They were the chief architects of
> Charitable Choice as it passed through Congress. There were few if
> any people who knew more about it than they did. Carl's a law
> professor and one of the country's foremost church-state legal
> scholars. Stanley's a Ph.D. and a bit more focused on the gritty, under-
> the-hood mechanics of government contracting and grant-writing.

After meeting with Carlson-Thies and Esbeck, they brought the men to Texas to meet with state agency heads to help them understand and get on board with the new law of the land. The advisor described how this meeting helped create Texas's faith-based policies, which met with little resistance because those who supported a separationist, rather than accommodationist, interpretation of the Constitution were not effective in voicing their concerns:

> We brought them down to meet with the executive directors and the
> certain key board members of various agencies, TWC [Texas
> Workforce Commission], DHHS [Department of Health and Human
> Services], TEA—the Texas Education Agency. So they came down. It
> was wholly uneventful in terms of controversy. There are some groups
> in Texas, as there are elsewhere, who are very pro-separationist, who
> simply don't like the principles underlying Charitable Choice. They
> would speak out on occasion, but frankly, not too often, not too loudly,
> and not too effectively. We didn't really encounter a lot of head-on, dug-
> in, entrenched resistance to enact the agenda. We spent the interim
> between 1997 and 1999 session meeting with different agency heads
> and trying to help them think through ways to overhaul the way they
> interact with religious charities, to make the Lone Star State a beacon
> state in terms of charting and blazing this trail.

In fact, Texas did blaze the trail, and the effectiveness of groups that were wary of greater cooperation and accommodation was even more limited over time. Supreme Court decisions such as *Hein v. Freedom from Religion Foundation*, which found that these groups could not in many cases bring lawsuits on behalf of taxpayers if they felt the First Amendment was threatened, along with the largely quiet and subtle nature of most state policies, has resulted in a slow change in these relationships that is largely unnoticed. Texas began this quiet revolution, but it has by no means ended it.

Near the end of our interview, the advisor summed up how he sees the new church-state relationship: as one with clear rules that ultimately reshapes both how government sees religious groups and how religion views government. As he explained, these rules were not just about changing the nature of government, but about ameliorating real or perceived fears among religious groups so that they would feel more comfortable interacting with state agencies.

> We really just focused on regulatory reinvention and on making the landscape a lot friendlier so that effective groups that want to partner with government can do so without thinking that if they get in bed with government that they'll never get a good night's sleep. There are a lot of groups that still say, "Look, I wouldn't touch government money with a proverbial ten-foot pole," and they believe government sheckles comes with government shackles, and they just throw their hands up and say, "Why bother?" That's fine, but we wanted to level the playing field for those who would be interested in joining government poverty-fighting but for restrictions they believe are too suffocating or secularizing, restrictions that don't permit religious charities to maintain their distinctive religious identity or character or integrity—which is why the Charitable Choice principles were so critical, just reassuring programs that linking with government doesn't require them to surrender what makes them so distinctive and effective. Heaven knows, there are countless examples of faith-based groups partnering with government and then beginning to drift in terms of philosophy and such. But while there are certain legal bright lines—you can't proselytize on the government dime—wall-to-wall secularization shouldn't be the price of helping government render effective compassion.

Thus, these policies came to be political symbols and signals to various groups and constituencies and in Texas, and the passage of new laws and policies reinforcing the initiatives continued, without much resistance, through 1999.

UNDER A NEW GOVERNOR. After the end of the Bush administration in 1999, there was some leveling off in efforts at implementation, but most of what was around persisted. Even if the new governor did not have the faith-based initiatives as a personal cause, he had no reason to want to undo them, and undoing would probably have been cause for greater problems than the original implementation. As in many of the other early-adopter states, there was some negative reaction to these efforts, both from within government or from external organizations. However, this negative reaction was limited for several reasons. Some of these activities were just too new, and by design very little press or fanfare was given to their passage, so creating new principles, laws, and bureaucracies got by without much notice or concern. In addition, state agencies appeared to react in a positive fashion, although little is known about whether they took these institutional changes to heart or simply did their jobs as they always had. I asked how state agencies had reacted, and the liaison argued that the changes had created a state government that went along with the spirit of cooperation and accommodation:

> You can't really pick up the phone and bark orders and unilaterally control things. So, it's really just a matter of persuasion. . . . There were really no hiccups. I never really encountered any deep-rooted resistance. But we were deliberate that this not be a heavy-handed, top-down thing we dictated. It was something we really went out of our way to explain and try to bring people on board via persuasion.

In short, the advisor said that he thought the introduction of the initiatives went smoothly for several reasons:

> Number one, Texas as a whole has an overall receptivity to faith-based approaches to tackling social ills. We had a very popular governor who was very persuasive and extremely talented at wooing and courting legislators and the broader public. There was not the sort of entrenched, shrill pro-separationist rhetoric here. We are among the reddest of red states and helping religious charities serve their needy neighbors doesn't drill into such a raw nerve here.

The importance of the specific conditions in which faith-based initiatives thrived in Texas meant that it was unclear that other states would be so amenable to these types of changes or as capable of accomplishing them.

GOING NATIONAL. This appeal of the initiatives to those in states where conservative religion and politics mixed meant that Governor Bush's goals were able to be transmitted to the national level when discussion of his run for president came around. This original appeal of the initiatives to those who were both conservative in their religious beliefs and in their politics was mirrored across the American landscape; Governor Bush saw that an appeal to these sensibilities could be politically beneficial. According to the advisor,

> I think 1999 is when presidential rumblings began to surface publicly, and [Bush] delivered his first major policy address as a presidential

candidate that July in Indianapolis. The topic was intentional and deliberate; it was what he would do on a federal stage to carry that pro-faith-based agenda to DC and what steps he would take as president to overhaul the federal legal and policy landscape. It was really an audacious message, and a really bold selection as a topic of your first major policy speech. This was no rote recitation of conventional GOP views on education reform or lawsuit reform or tax reform or national defense. It really set him apart as a different kind of Republican; this was the bold unveiling of compassionate conservatism on the national stage.

The faith-based initiatives then became synonymous with a new "kind of Republican," one who was compassionate and would use faith-based groups to help those in need, but one that was also politically conservative, so fiscal conservatives could hope that this help would come with relatively little government spending.

After Governor Bush's departure to the national stage, the faith-based initiatives in Texas stagnated. This pattern of original high levels of interest and implementation at the state level, and then either a stalling or ebb in faith-based implementation after original champions leave, has been followed in many states. Original state faith-based actors who have a strong connection to the initiatives and their success are replaced, and some of these governors, liaisons, or others are replaced by those who do not have the same goals and ideas in mind. This was the case in Texas until 2005, when a new state OFBCI was created to deal with the initiative. This process of ebb and flow based on the people in charge bears further examination in the future. What I found in Texas was that the new office and new liaison brought in a rejuvenation of and commitment to the initiative. The original liaison I spoke with had some advice for this new liaison: he argued that the office should remain outside of legislative control to keep its freedom to do what it needed to do without unnecessary interference. So far, the office in Texas has indeed remained fairly freewheeling.

It bears repeating that implementation of the initiatives in Texas was strongly affected by the personal beliefs of the actors involved. This is a common theme: more often than not, the sentiments about the initiatives expressed by the advisor I interviewed were reflected and repeated by others in other states. When talking about the piece he was going to write about the Teen Challenge episode before taking on his role in government, the advisor summarized the sentiment nicely:

> It was going to a piece on urging government to be a bit less antagonistic and a lot more benevolent. Religious groups, they were doing a lot of heavy lifting and helping people transform their lives from the inside out. We ought to applaud them, not bark at them for having frayed carpet. This is a byproduct of my fundamental belief

about the role of government, that it should understand what works and not be so blindly process-oriented that it impedes programs, religious or not, that produce impressive outcomes.

Nationwide: Patterns of Action and Inaction

The Texas liaisons, offices, and legislative requirements were the precursors to similar policies and practices now found across the country. Since Texas began its policies of legislative reform, bureaucratic implementation, and cultural change through networking and rhetoric, other states have followed.

FAITH-BASED LIAISONS. The most common way for states to implement new faith-based policies has to been to appoint an FBL. Like the Texas liaisons appointed in 1996 in their various government agencies, they are generally charged with making administrative changes in state bureaucracies that interact with faith-based groups, to ensure that there are no barriers to these groups receiving government grants. The Texas FBLs were the first administrators of this public policy—one that had little prior background, direction, or network of support. Instead, FBLs were given a broad policy goal—to create a state social services system in which FBOs would be more involved, then put in charge of figuring out some way to further define and then carry out this goal (Loconte 2002, 2004; Sherman 1999). It would seem reasonable that liaisons in other states would then have had the Texas experience to refer to in implementing the initiatives in their own states. Because of poor communication among liaisons from different states in the early days, however, most liaisons resembled those in Texas in this aspect as well: they had to define their own jobs as they went along.

After Texas, FBL positions were created in New Jersey and Oklahoma. However, there were some important differences between the liaisons in New Jersey and Oklahoma and those in Texas. First, whereas Texas created only part-time administrative positions in existing state agencies, New Jersey and Oklahoma appointed full-time liaisons. Second, unlike Oklahoma and Texas, in New Jersey the liaison position was created under a separate, new OFBCI. This office was designed to create a positive and cooperative environment between religious groups and government officials; it was given the responsibility of integrating small FBOs into the social services fold. Established under the lieutenant governor's office, the New Jersey OFBCI was created to act as a single authority overseeing faith-based policies at all levels and in all branches of state government. In contrast, while Oklahoma had a full-time liaison position, it was located within an existing administrative branch of the state government, the Department of Children and Families; being embedded within an existing agency limited its ability to communicate with and affect other state agencies' relationships with FBOs.

THE SPREAD OF FAITH-BASED LIAISONS AND OFFICES. The fact that the initiatives spread from Texas to these two states is perhaps not surprising. In New Jersey, the state OFBCI was established under Governor Christie Todd Whitman, a close friend of George W. Bush's. Employing faith-based policies in New Jersey was politically savvy, as well. With a large and active black religious population, creating an OFBCI was a way for a Republican governor to reach out to this mainly Democratic African American constituency. In Oklahoma, the story was similar. The governor was also close to Governor Bush, and his advisors were very close to evangelical movement activists in the state. Therefore, when they came to him with the idea of creating an OFBCI in Oklahoma, the idea quickly found a supportive audience.[5]

Florida was the next state to embrace the faith-based initiatives. The governor, Bush's brother, Jeb Bush, made the faith-based initiatives a high priority, calling for increased legislation, new faith-based prison wings, and a new office for the initiative. Although an OFBCI in Florida did not come about until 2004, the state made substantial legislative and administrative efforts to implement various practices from an early date (see Chapter 4 for more on the legislation). Further, unlike governors in other states, Jeb Bush extended his power of executive order to state government branches, assigning someone in each office to be the point person for the faith-based initiatives. These state employees were then responsible for overseeing the faith-based initiatives in their departments and ensuring that new religious groups were brought into the social services fold.

Chapter 6 explores how similar patterns in early implementation were seen throughout many states. Although implementation of the initiatives has also had fiscal motivations, these religious and political ties remain important to understanding state implementation of the initiatives.

LEGISLATIVE CHANGES. The history of faith-based legislation is also one of an increasing emphasis on enacting laws that create an underlying administrative system to give religion and religious groups a greater role in public policy—but without offering new money to provide social services. Like the laws in Texas described earlier in this chapter, the vast majority of state legislation is focused on "leveling the playing field" for religious organizations. Instead of providing new money, the history of state legislation has been by and large to provide encouragement and nonmonetary assistance to faith-based groups, thereby increasing the number of such groups providing social services. I should note, however, that there is some evidence (see Chapter 4) that points to growing state appropriations; this lends support to the conclusion that these measures now aimed at changing culture may in the end have more material effects.

FAITH-BASED CONFERENCES. Similar to the history of state FBLs and legislation, state faith-based conferences have also played a historically important role in faith-based initiatives. The conference described at the beginning of Chapter 1 is representative of these conferences, which are, in effect, state-sponsored religious events that are being used as political tools. Conferences on the initiatives have been held in at least 23 states (see Appendix C), including Arizona, New Jersey, and Texas; regardless of where a conference was held, the form and content have been similar. Religious leaders praise the faith-based initiatives and their political supporters at the state level and use various religious symbols to indicate the state's support for the integration of religion into state activities (see Chapter 5).

WHERE'S THE MONEY? As noted earlier, the White House has encouraged formation of OFBCIs but has not offered real help in the form of structural support or funding; these new bureaucracies have had to figure out both their jobs and their funding, more or less on their own. In addition, congressional support for the initiatives is essentially nonexistent; the many interested parties have not been able to agree on how to fully implement the initiatives at the federal level, let alone decide what to do with the states. When looking at the initiatives through the lens of symbolic politics, this emphasis on new bureaucracies and new appointees—and de-emphasis on funding them—is not surprising. Instead of having to expend money on new services, these symbolic policies create an environment in which religion has greater acceptance in public life; the material changes inherent in the policies themselves are of far less importance to many of the politicians who claim to support them.

Summary and Conclusion

The history of the faith-based initiatives is one of symbolic politics being used to usher in a greater presence of religion in state government. A number of scholars argue that symbolic politics is crucial in shaping government activity and society because it activates new support for various political groups and eases the way for more concrete measures in the future. The faith-based initiatives function admirably in both of these capacities. By creating new offices and bureaucratic appointments, the initiatives energize supporters and open new opportunities for the redistribution of money and for significant changes in church-state relations in the future.

The government has already been working with faith-based groups in various capacities for many years; from the Freedmen's Bureau working with the American Missionary Association to help former slaves by cooperating to build what are now historical black colleges, to the District of Columbia providing funds for a Catholic Charities Hospital in 1899,[6] there is a robust history of government and faith cooperation (Buckley 2002, Chaves 2004). In many ways the faith-based initiatives are merely a continuation of the battles over religion and politics that crop up from time to time in American history. The skirmish over the faith-based initiatives is another chapter in this history, with states creating policies and practices that seek to alter the relationship between religious groups and government and further this debate.

In the following chapters, I explore how and why faith-based initiatives have become a part of the political landscape in most states at this time. Though the argument can be made that the initiatives are an epiphenomenon that will pass now that President Bush is out of office, I argue that, once in place, the actors and offices empowered by the initiatives will become part of the political landscape and be taken for granted, changing the culture of understanding regarding church-state relations for years to come. The debate about the role of religion in government and the public square is one that not only extends back well beyond our recent history, but is likely to continue far into the future as well.

3

Faith-Based Liaisons

Finding Faith in the Faith-Based Initiatives

What I deal with is that most congregations feel like we should take care of our own. And those pastors feel that they can take care of their own. And that you still have the thought and the belief that prayer heals and that if we pray hard enough, you know, we don't need services . . . we need to try to deal with it first.
>   —Faith-based liaison, interview with the author,
>   Dec. 14, 2004

We have a lot of these small organizations [and] all they want is money. All they want is the means to carry out the good work that they do
>   —Faith-based liaison, interview with the author,
>   Nov. 8, 2005

Faith-based initiatives are a series of policies and practices that aim to forge stronger relationships between state governments and faith communities. But this has not been a smooth or uniform process, and many states are still searching for the most efficient and effective way to foster better connections with faith communities and a larger social services presence from religious groups. Although states have come up with myriad ways to create faith-based initiatives, by far the predominant means has been to create state-funded positions called faith-based liaisons. These positions are designed to create and enhance connections between state government actors and faith communities; the individuals holding these positions have the primary responsibility for shaping the state's faith-based initiatives.

In this chapter, I focus on the role of these liaisons, the challenges they face, and the personal perspectives they bring to state implementation.

Increasing Implementation

Over the past ten years, state implementation of the faith-based initiatives has increased in a number of aspects, but by far the most important change has been the increase in institutionalization and bureaucratization of the initiatives through the creation of liaison positions and, in many cases, new offices in which they serve. In 2000, only four states had liaison positions: New Jersey, Oklahoma, South Carolina and Texas. However, since then an additional 35 states have created these positions in various forms.[1] In addition, by 2008, 22 states had created an OFBCI. Modeled after the original faith-based offices in pioneering states such as Texas and Oklahoma, as well as the White House OFBCI, these offices increase the reach and scope of what a liaison may accomplish. Varying widely in their funding, background, and level of institutionalization, state FBLs—sometimes acting as part of an OFBCI—have attempted not only to reach out to FBOs in the hope of increasing such organizations' ability to provide social services to those in need, but have also focused on creating a government culture that shifts the understanding of religion's place and influence within the public sphere.

The Role of Faith-Based Liaisons

When implementation of the faith-based initiatives first began in 1996, liaisons became the administrators of a public policy that had little prior history, direction, or network of support. Unlike most major policy changes, which typically result when professionals working in the field identify a social need and then network to create specific rules and guidelines, there was little infrastructure in place at the state level to support the implementation of the faith-based initiatives. Instead, states and liaisons were given a policy goal—linking FBOs to the public social services sector—and instructed to figure out some way to carry it out (Loconte 2002, 2004; Sherman 1999).

Faith-based liaisons have two main functions. First, states have largely focused on creating a system of faith-based policy implementation by using liaisons to provide FBOs with information about existing funds that are available to support social services programs, helping those FBOs to assess their capacity to receive government grants and working to change attitudes within state bureaucracies about partnering with FBOs. Second, liaisons act as symbols of a growing trend of church-state cooperation. Contrary to the reasons some supporters give for faith-based policies—that new money for faith-based groups will lead to new help for the needy—faith-based policies and practices are often more symbolic in nature and rely on changing culture to "level the playing field," rather than increasing monetary support. Instead of creating significant funding opportunities, the liaisons became policy brokers and agents of cultural change rather than material change.

Because they have few resources and limited authority, liaisons' work in the political system consists largely of mediating concerns between groups and networking among various coalitions (Fischer, Miller, and Sidney 2006) while advocating for the initiatives and their continued implementation. By doing so, they bring attention and legitimacy to state faith-based policy efforts, increasing awareness about the faith-based initiatives. While lack of appropriations has greatly frustrated some liaisons, the concrete and material changes faith-based policies are creating can be less important than the normative changes they represent (Edelman 1964, 1971).

In Their Own Voices: Interviews

In this chapter, I rely on information from interviews, field research, and documents collected at the interviews. The interviews are especially important because they allow the liaisons to speak in their own voices; the liaisons are the face of the movement at the state level, running the policies and programs day to day. During my research I was able to talk with most of these liaisons and hear about their practices, problems, and reasons for perseverance. Between 2004 and 2005, I conducted interviews with 30 state liaisons (in two of the interviews more than one person from the state OFBCI was present); I also conducted eight interviews with former liaisons, advisory board members, and federal officials who were responsible for oversight of state implementation. The liaisons interviewed included 15 men and 15 women, with an average age of 39. While the conditions in many of these states have changed, these interviews provide an important glimpse into the history of the faith-based initiatives at the state level and some insight into the consequences of this history for the future. It became very clear in the interviews that these liaisons are working in a truly new area of government. They are not simple government employees; instead, they are policy entrepreneurs who have to find their way through the often muddied waters of the faith-based initiatives.

I focus on four areas of interest in this chapter. First, I explore the levels of resources, institutionalization, and position longevity by state. Next, I provide an overview of state faith-based policy implementation as it has been created by these liaisons. Third, I examine the problems and pitfalls facing these liaisons. Finally, I look at the liaisons, their own personal reasons for taking these jobs, and their connections to the faith community. This overview of liaisons is the first step in creating a complete picture of faith-based activity in state government.

Resources, Institutionalization, and Stability

Before I analyze specific aspects of liaison activity, there are several pieces of the larger picture regarding FBLs that are important to explore. First, while I do find that the amount of money going to state faith-based appropriations is increasing somewhat (see Chapter 4), at the time of the liaison interviews the vast majority of them—29 of 34 that were in place at the time of interviews—had no fiscal support outside of their salary (or often only a portion of their salary) and basic operating expenses. This meant that the range of activities they could carry out was severely limited.

The Scope of the Position

Funding is not the only resource that has often been in short supply as the faith-based initiatives have been implemented. The longevity, stability, and potential effectiveness of state liaisons are strongly conditioned by their level of institutionalization and by their level of authority to carry out their responsibilities. Of the 30 liaisons with whom I spoke, only 12 were full-time. Some states without a full-time FBL were in the process of increasing their emphasis on the initiatives or had just created the position, but at the time of my research, this left 18 states with only a part-time FBL. These part-time FBLs also had to attend to other responsibilities, such as working as the governor's chief of staff or working in other state agencies, such as the Department of Children and Family Services. These constraints greatly affected what the liaisons were able to accomplish, with some state liaisons spending less than 10 percent of their workweek on tasks related to their liaison position.

The Creation of FBL Positions

Most appointments of liaisons have been by administrative fiat, either through an executive order of the governor or through individual agencies such as the state's Department of Health and Human Services. Some argue that this allows liaisons flexibility in the performance of their jobs; however, others worry that any change in governor or state agency leaders, any change in political leaders, could lead to the dismantling or significant alteration of the liaison position or OFBCI. To remedy this precariousness, some states have turned to legislation to create OFBCIs or liaison positions. Currently, only six states—Alaska, Louisiana, Maryland, North Dakota, Ohio, and Virginia—have legislatively created OFBCIs, and only Iowa, Missouri, and Texas have created liaison positions by that means. Creating the position through legislative action has positive and negative aspects. As mentioned in Chapter 2, Governor Bush's advisor in Texas felt that although appointing a liaison by legislative means led to stability, it also decreased the liaison's ability to maneuver effectively within state government. In the interview

(March 27, 2005), he stated that he had spent some time discussing what steps to take next with the current FBL:

> I spoke a couple months ago about some legislation they [the state faith-based office] were considering this session to further their cause. I think they were thinking about seeking legislation to structurally fortify their agency. Right now, they are kind of an executive order creation, at the benevolence of whoever happens to be in office. They were hoping to get something that would anchor them a little more firmly for the long term. I understand that impulse for sure, you don't want to be hostage to whoever happens to occupy the governor's mansion.
>
> At the same time, if you are going to set yourself up to be just another government agency with legislative approval, you're going to open yourself to legislative tinkering to becoming an agency at the beck and call of individual lawmakers or key lawmakers, who want you to look at their pet hometown project, and it becomes a parochial football to some degree. You want to remain above that fray and be unencumbered by legislative powers and pressures. I just felt like the peril outweighed the promise, and it's probably better to be more free-wheeling.

For good reasons, most states have struggled with determining how best to establish an OFBCI or liaison position.

Institutionalizing a liaison position through legislation was one way states gained stability for the position and, potentially, more access to resources (because of the position's better chances of longevity). However, the ability of an FBL to conduct activities ranging from creating technical assistance funds for FBOs to running grant-writing workshops was also often directly tied to whether there was a formal OFBCI in the state. When I conducted this study, there were OFBCIs in 19 of the 34 states that had FBLs; since then, three more states have created an office. OFBCIs are more formal in structure than are FBL positions: they tend to have budgets, more than one person working on the initiative, and a clearer picture of how to implement the initiatives at the state level. Also, they are more likely to have the power necessary to get the attention of state officials because they usually have the support of their governors, a key ally. Even so, whether this extra effort and structure actually leads to significant changes in how the faith-community interacts with government and the social services sector remains to be seen.

Building a Faith-Based Bureaucracy

The types and range of activities that state liaisons can engage in have varied greatly, from funding large-scale new projects in New Jersey and Ohio to simply sending e-mail messages to tell groups about outside funding opportunities, which was the situation in Kansas, North Carolina, and North Dakota. Because of this variety and because of the lack of instruction and support from the federal government, liaisons have created numerous strategies to integrate the religious and public sectors.

Goals and Game Plans

As state policy brokers, liaisons have a complex job; some have relied on a specific game plan to create greater involvement by FBOs in their state and greater acceptance of that involvement by government actors. In my conversations with liaisons, I asked them about what they did as liaisons. The liaison from one of the states most prominent in creating new policies and outreach programs related the three-part strategic plan for implementation that had been determined by the governor's wishes and the state's particular needs:

> Let me start by saying, in January 2003, the governor created the Office of Community and Faith-based Initiatives. The office was created to do three specific things.... The first area is to create an avenue in which faith leaders and community leaders can address issues and concerns and make recommendations without going through a bureaucratic maze. They can utilize the Office of Community and Faith-based Initiatives as a conduit between themselves and their respective organizations, and the governor, and the governor's executive staff, or state officials who are representing the various departments that religious- and community-based organizations might have to interact with. Our role would be to cut through that red tape, to put issues front and center, and to get them addressed in a timely manner, or in a case of recommendations for consideration by the governor or state officials.
>
> The other thing, in terms of this avenue of dealing with issues and concerns, was part of our responsibility is to help develop clergy leadership advisory committees and community leadership advisory committees in those cities. The idea is to bring these committees together on a periodic basis so they can sit down with the governor face-to-face to address issues and concerns and make recommendations that are tailored to their cities, [those] that they reside in. We have a number of major cities in this state that have recommended these committee members that will meet with the governor and our state on a periodic basis throughout the year.... We have formed among these individuals a statewide interfaith steering commission for special projects, so that when we look at putting together a prayer breakfast, or that when we look at putting together a symposium or a forum, we bring this committee together to solicit

their ideas and get input, then recommendations in order to formulate whatever that event or program might be.

The second half is to create an avenue so that faith- and community-based organizations can have access to information relative to grant opportunities that are available through state government. Also, to serve as a conduit between the federal agency center for faith-based community initiatives, to help provide that same information and access, so that faith organization that are interested in augmenting their programs, be it housing programs, teenage pregnancy programs, be it positive youth development programs, be it senior programs. We want to be able to provide access to information so that people are aware of what is available, they are aware of the process or the criteria for applying for grant opportunities. (Feb. 9, 2005)

Liaisons from other states such as Indiana, Michigan, and New Mexico also mentioned creating a strategic plan before beginning to work on their faith-based initiatives. States that were more developed in their activities often told similar tales, both of the strategy they used and reasons that strategy was devised. These states were also those in which the liaison was full time and could spend the time to develop a plan that was relevant for the area.

One liaison said that the plan they [the state OFBCI] were creating came about after taking a survey of local religious organizations. This step was crucial to finding out the lay of the land. Without an understanding of the services and connections out there, a liaison might repeat steps already being taken or unwittingly step on toes.

So the governor did a special leadership roundtable breakfast where we gathered input and information [from local churches]. But while we were there we distributed surveys and gathered information from the [state] contingency. And so I forget exactly how many surveys we got back, but we asked [for] information about. . . . "What type of program do you have? How is your program organized or structured? You know, is it a 501(c)3? Is it just part of the ministry? What's your budget? Do you get federal funding now? Do you currently get any state funding?" So we could get some type of perspective of what FBOs are doing in the state and what kind of money they are currently bringing in. And then we were able to take that kind of information, like when we did the Children of Incarcerated Parents Grant—I could then go to the database and say, "Who does mentoring?" And then we could follow up and say, "Well, you do mentoring. Do you mentor this specific population?" This allowed us to put together a great collaborative effort for that application. Or we'll have people call, like someone called from the District Office of U.S. Small Business

Administration saying they want to work with community
development corporations that are faith-based. So we can go to the
database since we have the information to determine what we can get
out to them. (Oct. 10, 2004)

Regardless of whether a state could spend the time to create a strategic
plan, for most liaisons, the majority of their effort emphasized creating connections and cutting through the red tape for FBOs. Like the early advisor from
Texas quoted in Chapter 2, many liaisons expressed concerns that government
action and oversight were a hindrance to faith-based groups that needed to be
eliminated for the groups to be able to provide effective social services delivery.

Another liaison outlined his role, as well as the governor's vision for the
state, describing part of the state's game plan, which was intertwined with the
governor's larger social vision and personal faith:

The third part is a call to action to faith organizations, in particular, to
engage in what the governor likes to call citizen volunteers, tapping
into the volunteerism spirit of the citizens of [the state], and engaging
them in one of her most important initiatives which is called Mentor
Program. Mentor Program is an initiative . . . to increase the number
of adults that are mentoring children and young people in [the state].
Mentoring kids, as we know a number of children, especially young
boys are growing up in single-parent homes, and sometimes they
need a positive role model.

We place a heavy emphasis on working with the faith community,
to get them involved and engaged in Mentor Program. We have a goal
of increasing the number of mentors in [the state] by the year 2006;
we want to have at least 10,000 new additional mentors mentoring
children in need. We work closely with the faith community. The
governor goes out once a month, on the third Sunday of each month.
We call that Mentor Program Sunday, which they go to two churches
separately, and they encourage and they advocate on behalf of Mentor
Program, and work with local mentoring agencies to get those
parishioners and congregates to join after hearing the message from
the governor or the first gentleman. (April 30, 2005)

This illustrates how a specific target can be created for an OFBCI, while the
target is part of a larger goal of increasing the presence of religious groups in
the social services sector. It is important to note that to accomplish the rather
ambitious goal mentioned above—recruiting 10,000 new mentors—the
OFBCI in question had only one full-time employee, the liaison, and a budget
that covered only office overhead. While such a goal is certainly admirable and
might be met without significant funding, it represents a shift of the service
burden to care for those in need away from government programs and onto the

nonprofit and religious sector. The new mentors themselves would have to donate both time and resources to ensure the success of the program. While programs like mentoring can surely be done by dedicated and spiritually motivated volunteers, continuing to shift the burden of state programs to the nonprofit, private, and volunteer sectors can go only so far. In addition, such a shift away from government-funded programs is also a shift away from government-*regulated* programs, which have greater oversight and accountability.

Policy Brokers

When I asked the liaison how he saw his role in this program, he pointed to the need to make new connections and get the message about what the governor wanted to do out to the faith community:

> My role is several-fold. Number one: it is to provide administrative oversight to the office. But more importantly, it is to be an advocate for our governor, and to be an advocate for those who need a voice and who have in the past not had a voice, to be there and advocate on their behalf with the governor and with state officials. Then, of course, to connect the governor around the state with faith communities, so that she will have the opportunity to talk about the things that our administration is doing to improve the quality of life here. (April 30, 2005)

I found that this role of messenger—or, as the literature would describe it, policy broker—was perhaps the most important function of liaison positions. As one state liaison put it, she was concentrating on taking a core message and matching state organizations with faith-based groups, brokering the initiatives between these two groups. "My role is primarily to entice faith-based organizations to partner in various ways with state government . . . What we mean by that is that we want faith-based organizations to look to the state as one of its many resources for collaboration" (April 26, 2005). Regardless of the goals a liaison hoped to be able to accomplish, the role often devolved into praising the initiatives (and, sometimes, the governor) without being able to deliver much on the promises of money that had been made or implied.

Overview of Activities

While some states had specific game plans to guide their work with FBOs and the government sector, most liaisons I spoke with worked to define and fulfill their roles as they saw them, relying on a variety of methods to expand outreach to FBOs and increase their social services participation. Depending on the level of funding and other resources available, the means they used tended to fall into seven categories. These were (in roughly descending order of cost):

TABLE 3.1. Types of FBL and OFBCI Activity and the States Where They Occur

Activity	Description	States
Funds to Contract with FBOs	FBLs/OFBCIs contract directly with FBOs to provide services	CO, DC, MT, NE, NJ, OH, SC
Intermediary Contracting	FBLs/OFBCIs contract with intermediary organizations to engage religious groups in non-governmentally funded services	OH, OK, WY
Faith-Based Advisory Board	States create faith-based advisory boards of members of the faith and social services communities to oversee and help implement the faith-based initiatives	AL, AK, AR, CT, FL, HI, ID, IN, MI, MN, MT, ND, NE, NJ, NY, OH, TX, UT, VA, WY
Conferences	States hold conferences for FBOs that help them with capacity building, grant writing, and information about the initiatives	AL, AK, AR, AZ, CO, CT, DC, FL, HI, IN, MA, MD, MI, MT, NE, NJ, NM, NY, OH, OK, UT, VA, WY
Personal Networking	Network with both FBOs and state agency staffs to engage them with the initiatives and share information	All states with FBLs
Faith-Based Web Site and/ or listserv	States create a Web site[1] and/or a listserv for faith-based and other community organizations to inform them of grant opportunities, conferences, and workshops	AL, AK, AR, AZ, CO, CT, DC, FL, HI, ID, IN, KS, LA, MD, MI, MN, MT, ND, NE, NJ, NM, NY, OH, OK, SC, TX,UT, VA, WI, WY

1. Several Web sites were created after interviews were completed in 2005.

Source: Data were gathered from interviews with faith-based liaisons conducted in 2004 and 2005.

funding FBOs directly; funding FBOs through intermediary organizations; providing conferences for FBOs (see Chapter 5); working with or forming administrative boards; personally networking with FBOs and departments within state government; developing Web sites; and running listservs. States using each method are shown in Table 3.1.

Direct Contracting with Religious Groups

Perhaps no area of the faith-based initiatives is more controversial, or more confusing, than when state offices or liaisons offer public money directly to FBOs. Even though some liaisons desperately wanted more money to help FBOs, other states found this avenue mired in potential problems and not at all the way states should be encouraging greater FBO participation in social services. This was, however, the most concrete way a liaison could engage new FBOs; I found it was only possible for FBLs who worked within an OFBCI and controlled a budget. As one liaison whose office provided such funding told me, "What we want is to do is to get organizations off their knees and onto their feet, and the only way we can do that is by providing the operational expenses that these organizations need" (Aug. 30, 2004).

STATE FUNDS. At the time I conducted the interviews, only six states—Colorado, Montana, Nebraska, New Jersey, Ohio, South Carolina, and Washington, D.C.—offered some sort of funding directly to FBOs. Of these, only New Jersey had given the office a reasonably large budget (about $3 million per year) to provide this direct funding to FBOs providing social services. The Washington, D.C., office had made a series of small ($1,000) capacity-building grants. Other states had used money in other state programs to help FBOs. For example, in one state the liaison was able to obtain some Temporary Assistance for Needy Families (TANF) funds to help FBOs with mini-grants:

> We can use some TANF resources here at the state to support such efforts. For example, in June I authorized a mini-grant with an FBO to help them in a collaborative process with another organization to go after a grant from the federal government, a Compassion Capital grant, but it was my seed money that made it possible for them to apply for it. And then they gained that . . . federal government $50,000 grant. (Oct. 13, 2004)

Similar startup initiatives were also used in another state, where the liaison worked out of the Substance Abuse Mental Health office:

> This project is funded through Block Grant Funds. And, you know, I have this certain amount that I've utilized and that process after this first and second year. . . . We received the state incentive grant, and they looked at creating a model utilizing coalitions and utilizing outcomes, logic model [a way to measure effective treatment] to create the program. So I used some of those principles and some of those ideas, and what we did is all the money rests now for "Faith Works"—oh no, well, not "Faith Works," but all the money from 301 system rests with their local authority in the lower part of the state. The lady out of that grant—she is a faith/community liaison. We took $10,000, and what we do is open it up across the system, and we wanted, I wanted, to see if there was a single state authority that had a working relationship with a faith community . . . either congregation, administrative alliance. . . . And out of that, they would form that partnership; they would grow that partnership to form a coalition that's faith-focused or faith-centered. Each county authority writes a county plan, and what I wanted is . . . if they had a critical issue that they wanted to address, if they could do this critical issue through this partnership, that would be

great. In the first year of this funding they could use it for planning purposes. Now I had to admit it was very successful. (Dec. 14, 2004)

FEDERAL FUNDS. Unlike Colorado, New Jersey, South Carolina, and Washington, D.C., the Montana, Nebraska, and Ohio offices distributed money that did not come from the state. Ohio's OFBCI received a CCF grant from the federal Department of Health and Human Services that allowed it to directly fund FBOs. So although Ohio was providing funds directly, it was federal, not state, money that was involved. Later in this chapter, I highlight some problems that some state liaisons had with the CCF and describe how its resources were distributed to states and used by them.

DRAWBACKS AND COMPLICATIONS. I found that although a few states had increased their funding efforts, most still had problems coming up with money that could be directed from OFBCIs or FBLs to faith-based groups. Frustration over lack of money was repeated in many of the interviews, with liaisons stating that FBOs called them asking for money when they did not have any to give. Instead, they had to direct the organizations to federal efforts and other departments that could help them with grants. Many of the liaisons did not know, when they took their positions, that this was the situation. They found out through trial and error that the amount of money for their offices or for FBOs directly was limited; further, they learned that to access whatever money was available, the group they hoped to fund had to go through all the same channels as any other organization. Instead of being aware of this financial reality at the outset, many had believed in the original rhetoric from President Bush and others that new money to help FBOs would emerge and that, as state liaisons, they would see some of this funding, since they were the ones the FBOs were calling every day. One liaison related a story of how he went to others for help when he first started but found that they were in the same boat:

> As you probably know, we in [this state] have two Republican senators. The fellow who works with them, I had them come over, and we just talked about from their perspective what was happening. I thought if anybody knew where the money was, that he did, and he could give me something that was happening from his perspective. Of course, he was in the same situation as I'm in, in terms of directing people to agencies and state government that may have some federal money and could be used by faith-based groups, and to help them understand even from a local level and state level that if they had some needs, they would contact certain agencies in that community or in the state. . . . The only thing I can do is direct them to agencies in their communities or in the state, and have them digging for the information. (March 7, 2005)

In another state, I saw the liaison a number of times over the years as I was working on the project; each time, she asked the same question: "So where's the money?" (Aug. 17, 2004). Not only did I not have the answer; neither did the people who made the promises about new funding.

It is important to remember that even if these groups were able to get public money, they may not have been able to take advantage of it. For example, one liaison found that some FBOs she worked with were totally unaware of what they would need to do to receive funds and then manage those funds (see Chapter 6). Without new money available to help many small organizations do such preparatory work as capacity assessments, it was unlikely that liaisons or organizations could have discovered, early in the process, how much they could or could not do in the social services arena.

As I noted earlier, the liaisons did not agree on what constituted the best strategy to engage these groups. Although it might seem that most state FBLs would want to be able to fund FBOs directly, some liaisons expressed reservations about taking this step. As one told me, "I mean, if what we're about is really leveling the playing field and bringing [FBOs] to get work done in the state, then it doesn't seem to me that there should be the certain pot of money and then all of a sudden that's what you go for" (Feb. 9, 2005). However, although this liaison specifically mentioned leveling the playing field as the goal, later in the interview she also discussed how it might be appropriate to start an "affirmative action" type program for FBOs. This sort of confusion about what to do—even in an individual liaison—is mirrored in the overall confusion of programs, activities, and goals at the state level. For example, although some states wanted money to do more through their offices, other liaisons were more concerned about the legal repercussions that they could face if one of the groups that got money were to violate regulations regarding church-state separation.

One liaison discussed this fear of legal problems for religious groups she worked with; even though she wanted faith-based groups in her state to get funding this was also a dangerous proposition. One day when she went to work with a group of ministers to help them apply for grants a particular scenario of concern came to mind. "First headline, Congratulations, it's January 1st and you [an FBO] just received a 3 million dollar grant! Second headline, it's June 1st and the headline reads 'The Same Church Misappropriated a Million Dollars'" (April 26, 2005). She went on to point out in her scenario the imagined church did not do this out of maliciousness, but out of ignorance of what was or was not allowed regarding church-state separation and government funding.

Another liaison mentioned this as a concern noting that the organizations had a long way to go to be prepared to receive these grants without landing themselves in legal trouble:

> Then I launch into a discussion about what it means to compete, and
> I tell them . . . this [state], it's a football area, so I explain to

them . . . "I would no sooner send you out onto a football field without a proper uniform and without any understanding of the rules of the game than I would send you up for grants." And you can go out and short-circuit the system and hire a grant writer to get you grants, but if you're not ready and you get that money then you could go to jail, you could have audits. . . . The church books could be audited by the government, then you've got Big Brother coming in and you don't understand why, so you need to structure properly. (Feb. 7, 2005)

So while some states have chosen to provide direct funding, it seems unlikely that all states will pursue this process.

Instead, many state liaisons were beginning to seek relationships that did not rely on directly funding these organizations, but working with them in other ways. As one liaison put it, "We believe there are considerable opportunities for collaboration where there is no taxpayer money exchanged, where both groups work together, on the government side because they have policy mandate and on the faith side because they have a divine mandate, and we just identify specific ways they can work together" (Feb. 8, 2005). This could mean expanding previously existing services, helping various faith-based groups partner with larger social service entities, or helping them build their capacity to begin even a small service program such as a pantry.

Intermediary Contracting

Since direct funding of FBOs can invite a large set of problems, some states have taken other routes to help these organizations engage in social services. Taking a cue from the federal government and the CCF, several states have created their own models of intermediary funding to FBOs. First implemented at the state level in Oklahoma under liaison Brad Yarbrough,[2] the intermediary model relied on the preexisting ties of established nongovernmental organizations to help distribute public money. These nongovernmental organizations reached out to individual churches to engage them in providing social services; the individual churches did not receive money directly from the government for those services. These models of interaction were also used in Montana, Nebraska, Ohio and Wyoming. One liaison that worked with CCF funds and an intermediary model stated "It is genius . . . the intermediary organization [model] sets at a very critical focal point for networking, to then sub-contact and organize and then provide technical assistance to very, very small entities" (October 14, 2004).

Yarbrough noted that intermediaries were important because many groups wanted to help but did not know how to get involved. Oklahoma therefore funded the intermediary organizations to organize the efforts of smaller groups, so that the churches were no longer out there on their own.

This model allowed the liaison to reach out to small religious groups and help them begin to offer the services they were capable of performing. He said that as his work with faith-based groups continued, he found that most of them did not have the time or resources for sustained activity; his goal was thus to seek out the more traditionally congregationally focused (Chaves 2004) and, relatively easily accomplished tasks such as running a food or clothing drive, which research has found most churches were capable of doing.

In Oklahoma, three programs were funded under this model: an adopt-a-social-worker program, county initiatives, and a resource directory. These programs have met with different levels of success. The most extensive and highly developed program at the time of my visit was the adopt-a-social-worker program. It was aimed at creating one-on-one relationships between state social workers and congregations. The state OFBCI contracted with two intermediary organizations that then contacted local congregations and asked whether they would adopt a social worker; in adopting a social worker, the congregation agreed to provide help to that social worker and the various families over whom the social worker had some professional oversight. For example, if the social worker had a family that needed winter clothing, the congregation would provide the social worker with jackets and sweaters. This type of need-based material help is similar to that normally given by congregations; because of its short-term nature, it is well within the capacity of even small congregations (Chaves 2004). Congregations were also asked to give help in the form of services, such as helping a family make a budget or learn how to shop for a nutritious diet. In some cases, congregations were given families to help over longer periods of time. While the short-term material needs were fairly easily met by the congregations, the more extensive activities met with some difficulties because of the time commitment necessary to give substantial help to these families and the cultural differences between the families and the congregations. Yarbrough found that whereas some congregations and their members were able to perform these long-term activities, others found it difficult because they lacked the formal training and support normally available to a social worker. In short, while the adopt-a-social-worker program met with some significant successes, it also encountered some unexpected difficulties.

Another state used a model similar to Oklahoma's. That program also relied on engaging the religious sector through the involvement of an intermediary organization; in this case, the intermediary organization had preexisting ties to the social service and religious communities within the state. Also like Oklahoma, this state's attempts to engage congregations productively for an extended period of time had both successes and challenges. As the liaison from this state commented in the interview, his group had a rocky road in getting funded, but have since expanded programs. The OFBCI at the state worked with an intermediary organization to get CCF money for a specific program:

We [originally] funded some of that through some TANF dollars to send out some subgrants and some grant training across the state and start some projects like "One Church, One Child," which essentially asks congregations to recruit one foster parent for every congregation. The next year, [the intermediary organization] was successful in getting the Compassion Capital [Fund] grant, and they're focusing on at-risk kids, elderly guardianships, marriage initiatives and foster care recruitment. So primarily we are considered an intermediary. (Dec. 3, 2004)

After seeing firsthand the challenges to sustained involvement of the religious sector in the provision of social services, liaisons in these states realized that there would be many challenges in involving the religious community in providing the long-term meaningful activity that the initiatives promised. They also felt, however, that intermediaries could effect a great amount of good with very little money in programs like this. This realization that small churches and religious groups needed financial and institutional support to even begin to perform social services is the same as the conclusion that has been reached by outside research, which has found that most churches and small religious organizations do not have the capacity to receive and administer government grants to carry out social services (Chaves 2004; Green 2007). This is at least in part because the main business of religious congregations is not to provide social services. Their business is to spread the Word, save souls, and minister to their congregation and its needs, not necessarily to fill soup bowls and heal the addicted. Even when congregations would like to perform such activities, most of them simply do not have the resources to do so. Organizationally, many are understaffed and lack the financial backing that would make sustained, nonemergency social service activity tenable. While this has been reported in the social sciences literature for many years, most state liaisons did not know this when they took their jobs; therefore, some liaisons met with significant frustration when trying to get new religious groups into the social services fold.

Liaisons saw first hand how thin many of these groups were stretched and getting them to a position in which they could compete with other more experienced service organizations was just out of their grasp. One liaison's story of attempting to get funding to a faith-based group who truly wanted to serve those in need illustrates this complication.

They [FBOs] have really big hearts and they care a lot and they want to work with really important community problems, they're very sincere, I felt very attracted to them. They were in such great need and I thought strongly that if I held just one or two more meetings we'd get somewhere. But I have to say I was truly amazed at how thin some of these people were stretched.

I'm thinking of one example, the Church of God and Christ-African American that's their general heritage- and I worked with this gentleman [the bishop] and his wife. His wife was named Martha and they wanted to help women coming out of jail and prisons. So they have taken in some of these young women into there homes over there years . . . so we developed this concept of a traditional groups home, you know the two story Victorian house, it was a great idea and everyone just loved it, but what I found is that Bishop Tommy and his wife Linda, you know he's not only running the church of Christ and God in [our state], which is like 7 or 8 different congregations scattered throughout the state, but he was personally preaching in 2 of them every Sunday . . . He had congregational business to attend to, all the funerals and people in the hospital and weddings and all the stuff that pastors do. On top of all this, he was asking for help to start a non profit, and he wanted to go the traditional route.

So we set up a training for him, and some other people to learn about forming a 501c3. He brought his daughter, they were very interested, but there are only so many hours in the day and they couldn't get over the barriers [so] it took 6 months to get this planned. I said if you could just get 2 to 3 people even from your congregation, serve on a board of trustees where I could work with them, we could build a board that could reach into the community, we could find some funding, we could find you property to do this, they just didn't have the energy. Finally he was so concerned about making this work, he tried to have the city approve him starting a group in his own residence. Like he was going to move out and let other people come in and operate this.

But there was a problem, "not in my backyard" . . . so we didn't get the zoning approval and that was it, he gave up. He said 'You know I've tried, I've prayed, I've given my own house'. I mean to go into his congregation and ask for people to come forward and start a new project, it just seemed to be something he just couldn't get to. I wanted to give him the benefit of the doubt. If you and I sit here and talk about it calmly, rationally, it shouldn't be difficult to find 2 or 3 people to volunteer to go to a couple of meetings, it shouldn't be that hard, but it was difficult and I think the man was probably getting 3 or 4 hours of sleep a night anyway. So I think that illustrates the kinds of difficulties that some folks are running into. They've wanted to do more, they love the fact that the government was challenging them and inviting them to do more. (Sept. 15, 2004)

The liaison went on to state that if he could just get six months instead of three with each group or another person in his office he felt he could make a real difference, but without the extra time or assistance all the effort he put in would be futile and groups would only get frustrated. Unfortunately, this was a theme echoed by many of the other liaisons who did not want to see the initiative fail, but felt that the half measures most states were using would in some cases do more harm than good.

Advisory Boards

Whereas some state liaisons act on their own, as autonomous entities, 20 states, from Florida to Montana, have created administrative or advisory boards to oversee the activities of their faith-based efforts. As is true with funding efforts, the breadth and scope of the activities that are taken on by these boards vary greatly; however, they do tend to play an oversight role, answering to the governor and state legislators. One liaison described such a board:

> Within a year of [my] coming on board, there was a committee that was developed called the Strengthening Families Committee, and it was generated out of the Governor's Office, the Region 8 Adult, Children and Families Federal Office with Health and Human Services, and out of this department, via primarily my interaction with it. And then we solicited many other organizations to get involved, and one of the sets of organizations or types of organizations we got involved were faith-based. We put this [the advisory board] within a context of strengthening families, since we know the religious community is very interested in whatever they can do to strengthen individuals and families and marriages. So we've literally had 40 different statewide level organizations involved in this committee. (Oct. 15, 2004)

While the hope is that these boards would be of assistance in creating a comprehensive and successful initiative, for some liaisons the boards became just one more thing they had to manage. "We've met a couple of times... things happen so quickly in the granting world and I barely have time to educate them about what's going on so we're in the process of re-visioning the role of the advisory board" (December 3, 2004). The liaison then went on to state that he was looking for new members that would be more interested in being active and engaged in specific faith-based activities. Similar to the liaison position, without committed members on the advisory board it would just end up as more government bureaucracy.

This emphasis on faith-based representation could also lead to skewed representation. As one liaison noted, "Part of our performance measures in the grant were to increase the percentage of faith-based and grassroots community based representatives on the boards. But because of the reduction in the number of boards [due to budget cuts] the number of representatives decreased statewide. However, the percentage of [faith-based] didn't, that percentage rose. So it seemed evident that the boards in deciding which members to keep... were more likely to keep them [faith-based representatives] on" (April 2005).

Personal Networking

Although some states have advisory boards to help them with their activities, many liaisons did not have this type of advice or assistance, and they had to rely entirely on their own networks and knowledge. Even liaisons that did have advisory boards generally had created their own network of connections, and all the liaisons I spoke with engaged in some form of networking with the two groups they aim to connect: the FBOs that hope to receive government grants and the state bureaucracies that distribute the grants. Virtually all liaisons made personal contact with state actors and faith-based groups.[3] Sometimes this was through a phone call every now and then, as was the case in Kansas or North Carolina. Others hosted a series of formal and regular meetings and conference calls, as was the case with Florida, Arkansas, Alabama, or Indiana. Liaisons in most of the other states fell somewhere in between.

Bridging the gap between state government and FBOs was the focus of all the liaisons. Because most liaisons had little or no budget and worked only part-time in the role of liaison, this was the main—and sometimes only—component of their job. As one told me, "This is all done voluntarily, because we do not have a budget for faith-based. So we encourage the faith community to apply for the federal grant opportunities that are available. I see myself as more of a liaison, a customer service type person, more of a coordinator" (March 27, 2005). Another liaison, who had been in her position longer than most, described how she took a three-pronged approach to connecting faith-based groups and state agencies while also offering an array of assistance to FBOs:

> We are a bridge builder. We put people with people. We help build
> collaboration within the state. It has been phenomenal to me how
> these people don't talk to one another. When I brought these faith-
> based substance abuse treatment providers together, none of them
> knew each other, none of them talked to one another. There was no
> mentoring going on. So when new programs want to start up to
> provide a social service in their area, we are also establishing
> mentoring relationships. (Feb. 7, 2005)

The desire to reach out to faith-based groups was predicated on the belief that in the past, states had not done enough to ensure that these groups were an active part of the social services sector. One liaison spoke about the connections they were trying to make by building networking groups to connect state and faith-based entities:

> We do the networking groups every other month. At those networking
> group meetings, we have local speakers, people who have actually had
> a program that has been successful or are maybe working to find
> funding. Our group is made up of agency directors, and those people

who are interested and may actually run an FBO or some other type of
nonprofit—we can all just learn about what each other is doing and
then if someone has advice or a contact, or something like that, we can
kind of use that to facilitate further networking or further connections.
(Nov. 30, 2004)

Building these types of formal connections between both groups was sometimes done in the hopes of ameliorating bad feelings on both sides. As one
liaison noted, FBOs felt that they were perhaps unwelcome, and the government felt that the FBOs were not eligible for funding:

> There is a stigma attached to these FBOs as far as grants are
> concerned, that FBOs aren't necessarily applying for grants that are
> available to either faith-based or community organizations, but they
> aren't applying for them because they think they aren't eligible. The
> whole separation of church and state issue has essentially put them in
> the mind-set that they are not able to apply on equal footing as a
> community organization for those grants. On the flip side,
> government also has that stigma attached that they can't offer these
> grants to FBOs because they are faith-based. (Feb. 16, 2005)

Bridging these gaps of understanding was done in a variety of ways, with
the structure and formality of such networking varying greatly from state to
state. While all state liaisons networked in some fashion, both the amount of
time they were able to dedicate to creating these networks and the degree to
which the building of these networks was systematic varied by state.

In some cases, time and resource constraints resulted in liaisons networking primarily with groups that they already knew about; these liaisons then
become policy promoters that spoke mainly to certain types of religious
groups. They could create excitement and enthusiasm about this public policy
(and, perhaps, its political supporters), but their ability to get money to the
groups they reached did not match the rhetoric. Therefore, what they symbo-
lized and what they said were likely of more importance than any concrete
actions they were able to take.

NETWORKING WITH FAITH-BASED ORGANIZATIONS. To network with FBOs,
liaisons engaged in a variety of activities, including personal meetings, breakfasts with congregations, and talks with community leaders. Like formal conferences, these informal networking opportunities were usually a way of
spreading information about the initiative. As one liaison told me, the best
way to get information out was to go through the churches: "That's really and
truly the main communication arm, and it has always has been" (Feb. 7, 2005).
To connect with FBOs, liaisons relied on contacts they had already made or on
groups that contacted them.

At least some of these communications the liaisons made were used not so much to promote the initiatives as to clear up the misconceptions that organizations had about the initiatives, namely that it would offer substantial new funding opportunities specifically aimed at FBOs. Because the rhetoric had originally been focused on the money, with little talk about equal access, the liaisons had to mediate this confusion with the FBOs that need funding. One FBL said that a lot of the calls he received were from people expecting "faith-based money"; what they received in return was information on where to go to apply for federal grants and information on all the regulations they had to face. As one liaison said, "We have a lot of fragmented groups out there working, and they are doing some things themselves on their own initiative. Now, my understanding is that this movement is designed to yield equal access to faith-based as other groups have always had, and make them feel comfortable in doing it. Most of my communication from telephone and e-mail have been requests for funds that of course . . . we don't have" (March 7, 2005). At other times liaisons were asked to speak with FBOs and explain the initiatives because there was not a general understanding of the initiatives among various communities. One liaison said, "I am constantly requested to come out and explain what the faith-based initiative is and what it's not and just give kind of a preliminary overview, an understanding of what the initiative is" (Feb. 7, 2005).

It is important to note here that it is not remarkable that FBOs were confused. Further, it is not surprising that, as the 2007 Pew study reported, many are still wary of looking for government funds or becoming involved. When the president of the United States promises FBOs money to help the poor and needy—in the State of the Union Address and in repeated public relations messages—and when it seems as if the people to see for this promised money would be the liaisons, who in fact have no money, no wonder churches become confused, annoyed, and no more willing to partner with the government than before the initiatives. As one liaison noted, while liaisons needed to help FBOs get resources to build their capacity, the connections between FBOs and government officials could be challenging:

> Some of these organizations have a big heart, but they're not very sophisticated. And if they are going to go after some TANF funding or other federally available funding and provide a service to their community, they are going to have to be the caliber that can actually compete. So we will do that kind of resource referral . . . and so I connect people based on what I know. And then we also give some guidance to outside agencies . . . how they can approach their counties, what they need to understand about the county systems so they don't inadvertently step on toes when they are just trying to make contact, you know, with the county department. (Oct. 13, 2004)

Even though liaisons tried to make connections between FBOs and government agencies, they still faced problems in their attempts to get the organizations engaged. Some liaisons noted that organizations in their communities were unwilling to make these types of connections without either a lot of convincing or having some money involved. This is something that the Pew study documented in 2007 but that the liaisons have known for many years. As one put it:

> You know, there is hesitation in working with state entities because of broken promises in the past and past experiences. They do not feel the capacity at this time to deal with it. They don't have the structure for it. They don't particularly want to partner because of some kind of issue with another congregation close to them. So you have those kinds of barriers. And they want seed money. And see my major thing is I don't have a strict pot of money just for the faith initiative for the state. And if I did, we would be even farther along than we are now. . . . I'll get a call, and it will be, "We want to do this ministry. Can you come help us?" And I go, and I talk and say, "Ok, these are some things I think you need to do: one, you need to begin formulating a plan. You need to look at why you want to do this." And so when you start putting down the tasks they need to do sometimes it's like, "OK, we'll call you back." And they never call me back. And some of them are looking for money. They are looking for funding. I don't have that. And then, when they see the RFPs [request for proposal forms from the government], you know it's like . . . and we've simplified them as . . . much as we could. . . . But there has been some resistance. (Dec. 14, 2004)

As this illustrates, in networking with FBOs liaisons encountered daunting barriers, since some FBOs just wanted money—and most did not realize the difficulties they would encounter once money was involved.

NETWORKING WITH STATE AGENCIES. While direct networking with religious groups was important, reaching out to the faith community was only one means that FBLs used to change the interaction between FBOs and the government. Recognizing that changing the attitudes and abilities of FBOs was only part of the process, many FBLs had also begun a process of attempting to change how government officials thought about FBOs. To do this, liaisons networked with various state agencies with the goal of altering the entire government social services culture to encourage contracting with FBOs.

Most FBLs I spoke with had instituted a process of regularly contacting state agencies—sometimes even on a weekly basis—by telephone or in person. As one liaison noted, this process was to both inform the state agencies about Charitable Choice and grant opportunities and to help them understand that there were FBOs capable of partnering with them:

Back to the state level, we are assisting almost every state agency right now, whether it is a particular project they're doing or just in an advisory capacity, advising them on Charitable Choice, working with them on a lot of our state departments to do grants with faith-based groups. . . . And we will work with them if they are reviewing applications sometimes, if there is an RFP that has been issued. . . . Helping these agencies understand what Charitable Choice is, that's been a major role that we're trying to play because I think a lot of them were kind of resisting at first. Some of them were unsure what this was, they were afraid it was an affirmative action. We made it very clear that this is not an affirmative action; it is based on who can produce the best results. And then the other thing that we're tying in with is helping them locate faith-based partners because so many grants are coming down from Washington. (Feb. 7, 2005)

This process of bridging gaps with state agencies and trying to create a culture of understanding between FBOs and state agencies was often a prolonged task. Generally, there was one person at each agency who was appointed to work with the FBL and with FBOs. This point person was then responsible for making the agency's contracting system more manageable for these small religious organizations. For example, in one state the FBL created a system in which weekly conference calls were made between the FBL's office and five to seven state agencies, with the FBL asking for specific details on what groups had been contacted and what types of services those groups were prepared to offer:

On these conferences calls, we usually just discuss, and they give updates on what they are doing. We discuss different policies that are taking place. We're going to discuss today the granting system, about organizations being able to self-identify on applications for the state. We're also going to talk about wanting to get their grant information at least three months prior to its release so we can start announcing those early to all of our organizations. I'm personally the master of this for all FBOs around the state. So I'm usually the gatekeeper when anything is announced. (Feb. 9, 2005)

Again, these efforts have met with mixed results. The FBLs I spoke with reported that some state agency officials were very cooperative and liked the idea of bringing change to social services; other officials, however, while not directly refusing to cooperate, did not appear to see any benefit in cooperating. For example, in one state that was creating networking groups, the state representatives who participated in the groups were not the people tasked with decision making for state agencies. The liaison's frustration is clear, though between the lines:

I feel like we haven't done as much as we could do. We're working on that. Hopefully soon we're going to be really putting emphasis with the state agency directors themselves. Most of the people that come to these networking group meetings are not people who can make decisions for the agency or for the division. They are representatives that have been sent by the division director or someone like that. While they are the people who deal with the groups on a day-to-day basis and have valuable input, they cannot really go back and make the decisions. We're trying to focus our attention and our efforts on the state agency directors of the agencies that would be aligned with the federal agencies that have centers for faith-based and community initiatives. . . . We are planning on having a meeting in December to reenergize the agency directors, and tell them this is going to something that we are really going to want to emphasize. (Nov. 30, 2004)

In another state, even getting state agencies to answer a survey about how they engaged FBOs was difficult, with only 11 percent of agencies responding. An additional state noted that when they went through the same process there was simply no motivation for state offices to comply because the state FBL had little authority. In other states, FBLs told me that state officials were occasionally suspicious of their activities and felt that the liaisons were potentially violating church-state separation.

Thus, some of the liaisons may not have had the success they wished for in changing attitudes among other government bureaucrats; however, whether the bureaucrats in question liked this new emphasis may not matter. Instead, what may matter is that the creation of the liaison positions and the OFBCIs may also be leading the gradual creation of a new government culture in which the funding of faith-based groups as well as secular ones is seen as desirable or even preferable. In fact, the longer the faith-based initiatives continue, the less likely the FBLs are to face resistance and more likely it is that there will be significant changes in both the legal and bureaucratic cultures, changes that support the liaisons and what they are doing.

Web Sites and Listservs: Moving through the Digital Divide

When I began researching this topic, very few states had any sort of electronic or technological capacity. In 2002, only New Jersey and Oklahoma had Web sites and listservs to reach the faith community. At the time of this writing in 2008, this number had increased to 17 states with Web sites,[4] and several additional states were doing some sort of listserv or other electronic outreach. Information available on these Web sites varies greatly: some have an e-mail signup, whereas others just have basic information on contacts and the office in the state. One liaison described the state's site:

We also have a Web site, and I kind of maintain the Web site and post, when applicable, information about where conferences are. One thing that we do have that goes out on a weekly basis is an e-mail from our office in conjunction with [a grant-related site].com. Are you familiar with [that site]? It's a Web site that anyone can get on. There is a membership fee. It's well worth it, it's about a $600 membership fee. For smaller FBOs, that's kind of a large amount to pay. Basically, it's an online, searchable database of private foundations, I think. We work with them. . . . I keep the e-mail database for that. We send that out on a weekly basis. They have [information] on grants, private grants . . . some conferences, and so forth. I'm also looking at working on getting another weekly e-mail, or as needed, on other types of grant funding. I get notices all the time from the federal government about grant . . . availability. I can send that out as well. (Feb. 7, 2005)

Even though Web sites and listservs may require the least in the way of resources of the communication options available to liaisons, they do still take time and effort to establish. One liaison said that the Web site in his state had started off on the right foot but that budget cuts made the maintenance of the Web site impossible: "We just launched the Web site, [but] we haven't been able to update some of it because I lost my resource through budget cuts, the Web update. So we're struggling with that, but it is a way to put the faith-based initiatives within a context of something that people can work together on and give guidance to communities toward strengthening families" (Oct. 13, 2004).

In addition to Web sites, some states also created e-mail listservs. Most of the listserv mailing lists were made up of groups that the state had contracted with before the initiatives, as well as other religious organizations in the state that would come to the liaisons for assistance. One liaison described the state's information-sharing process:

We do this two ways. One, an e-mail distribution list that we have set up, so we have a number of organizations that are a part of our e-mail distribution list. Once our office gets information, we disseminate that information via e-mail for them to access. We are also in the process of designing, putting up a Web site so that folks will be able to go to the Web site to also access this type of information. Then, we do prayer breakfasts and forums and workshops and symposiums to also serve as an avenue to get information out. (April 30, 2005)

Most of these listservs were not comprehensive and contained primarily religious organizations that were known to the FBLs either through personal contact or through their previous work with government. In short, while a variety of attempts were being made to bring in new religious groups, the efforts tended to be neither inclusive nor systematic; this appeared to be mainly ascribable to time or budgetary constraints rather than intentional discrimination. As one liaison noted, they were out there working and providing the best information they could to who they could, but this required time, energy, and money, and without those the information is useless:

> You know we're out there, and our primary role is to provide technical assistance. And if you want to make the playing field equal, what we have to do is say that we have done everything that we can do to make sure that everybody has access and can avail themselves to the information that's out there. The next question falls back on them, "What are you going to do with the information that you have?" . . . We're working our butts off to organize all of this information . . . so when we give you all of this information, what are you going to do with it? That's the key. (Aug. 17, 2004)

While in theory it seems like a good idea to get as much information out there as possible to FBOs, other liaisons were concerned that it was actually counter-productive to simply send out emails without culling the information for what was necessary or unnecessary for particular groups. "I tend not to send things out in bulk to groups because it's just too much for them to digest. . . . I send them really focused things that are kind of pre-qualified, because . . . if I send them a 100 things and they call me about 10 of them . . . and they're only restricted to organizations in California, it makes me look bad" (Feb. 11, 2005). Again careful attention from the liaison is required to ensure a satisfactory relationship between faith-based and government sectors.

Bumps in the Road

While resistant FBOs and state agencies would certainly be enough to make one pause when considering the tough road many liaisons faced in creating faith-based initiatives, other factors also impeded their work. The intense efforts made by liaisons to do their jobs—and do them well—were nearly universal, with only four of the liaisons with whom I spoke seeming to consider the position a temporary assignment or something in which they were not full vested.

Problems with Resources and Support

As I recounted earlier, most state liaisons I spoke with were left on their own, with few resources and much to do in addition to reaching out to the religious groups that were already in their personal networks or existing state networks. This situation generally stemmed from a lack of several things: personnel; monetary resources; guidance or regulation; and communication infrastructure, both formal and informal. Combined, these difficulties have greatly reduced the ability of liaisons and offices to actually provide concrete help to the poor and needy.

Internal Conflict over the Compassion Capital Fund

The one stream of money earmarked for faith-based purposes, the CCF, was the object of some contention among liaisons. Some felt that the fund's resources were not distributed fairly or with good accountability, whereas others praised the CCF as at least some effort to provide money and modeled their own efforts on the fund. One liaison, from a state that had been doing a great deal of work with very few resources, had tried to get a CCF grant but was denied. This liaison felt that the application process was geared toward beltway insiders rather than toward states that were able to demonstrate their effectiveness. I also found some criticism of the actual performance of the agencies that did receive these grants. The FBLs I interviewed in one state felt that a CCF-funded organization doing work in their state, which they saw as an inside-the-beltway consulting group, was simply wasting resources because it was not familiar with the local scene; no one from outside could know their community better than they did. They noted that when this out-of-state CCF-funded organization came in to run a grant writing workshop, only 20 or 30 people attended; in contrast, the state OFBCI's own workshop efforts regularly attracted two hundred to three hundred participants (Feb. 9, 2005).

Some states also felt that the efforts of the White House OFBCI were not reaching their doors. When I asked one FBL if he had had any luck connecting with federal resources and the White House, he said, "Yeah, I've talked to [the head of state outreach for the White House OFBCI] several times. But again, it's getting the experts out here to assist us, and that's always difficult. You know, the White House goes around the country and does these seminars—well, we've never gotten one here" (Nov. 8, 2005). Although the White House OFBCI did contact states through letters and met liaisons at occasional conferences, the lack of formal mechanisms to connect states with the federal government and with each other on a regular basis left some liaisons feeling uninvolved and excluded.

Again, these sentiments were not universal. Some states found the White House efforts helpful and uplifting; states that did receive CCF grants were grateful for the opportunity to bring new money to their states. Even so, the scarcity of the grants and the fact that they were the only significant stream of money to the states led to an environment in which government funded efforts might be short lived and were not as comprehensive as once hoped.

THE END OF THE MONEY STREAM. Concerns about the future were especially apparent in states that originally relied on CCF grants to create faith-related offices. These states—Nebraska, Montana, Ohio, and Wyoming—struggled when, after three years, the grant money dried up and when unexpected complications arose, including some untoward consequences from mixing federal money with religious activity. During my interview in one of those states, I spoke with three of the people who were working on faith-based efforts at the time. First, they talked about the background and noted the progress they had made:

> Well, I think that we should probably let you know kind of how we're coming at this whole project. We received one of the first 21 CCF awards, and we have focused that on the issue of behavioral health and working with small faith-based and community organizations to develop services in the area of behavioral health. What we've done is essentially had three rounds of awards and have made some awards . . . grants to small groups, small organizations and agencies. We have done a lot of technical assistance with some awardees and have tried to build infrastructure for them. . . . We have not done a lot of work with mainline congregations; we have had a couple of awardees that have been mainline congregations. . . . We have worked more with faith-based groups rather than with congregations. But then I would guess maybe a half-and-half in terms of faith-based and community-based. . . .
>
> It was an RFP process. And, you know, they had to apply, they had to demonstrate in that application what their goal was, what their plan was. . . . The first year, we didn't actually turn anyone down [for some type of assistance, not always fiscal], and we had about 50 [organizations]. . . . We only actually funded about 25, but we worked with a number more than that. The second year we were more discriminating, but we had more applications. We ended up working with about 65 awardees. In the third year now, we have about 15 from the first two years that we have funded for the third year, then we opened it up for an open competition and we funded about 15 of those, I believe. So that we're working with about 30 this year. (Nov. 21, 2004)

Although they had made progress and have created an infrastructure, the CCF money was about to run out, and the effect on faith-based programs in the state was uncertain at best:

> This is the last year. We are planning our exit strategy as we speak. . . . We will continue to look for other funding opportunities. We think we've developed a pretty good infrastructure to get those small faith-based, community-based organizations involved, and so we're looking at how we can [continue] the project. . . . Well, we're hoping there will be some additional resources. If there aren't, then hopefully we have developed kind of a legacy of helping the faith-based [and] community organizations that we have already worked with, and then we'll have technical assistance materials that other faith-based and

community[-based] can use in the future. But as far as our staffing structure, if we don't have new resources, we probably won't exist.

LEGAL PROBLEMS. Montana and Ohio encountered problems with CCF funding different from those described above. Their problems arose from questions about how religious groups and public money should interact. In Montana, the original state liaison was sued by the Freedom from Religion Foundation for engaging in overtly sectarian activities with government money; one of the organizations the liaison had contracted with, the Parish Nursing program, was also named in the lawsuit. In its decision, the court concluded that the liaison "was motivated not by the purpose of enhancing health care, but to advance and endorse religion" (Freedom from Religion Foundation 2004).

Of further interest, when the lawsuit began, the liaison asked the federal government and White House OFBCI for assistance. However, because the money was being given to the organization through an intermediary, the White House office and the Department of Health and Human Services were able to claim that they did not know details of the activities the intermediary was funding and therefore could not be sued as party to the lawsuit (Oct. 15, 2004). They declined to assist the state or the organization or otherwise participate in the case, a strategy since used in all cases against states and other groups funded through CCF grants, essentially hanging states and small FBOs out to dry. The Freedom from Religion Foundation won the lawsuit but was unable to overturn any portion of Charitable Choice because the federal government had protected itself through the use of an intermediary. Because funding to small faith-based social service groups was done through an intermediary organization the federal government could claim they did not have knowledge of what the groups were doing and that they were not responsible for directly funding inherently religious activities. The state of Montana and the groups with which it contracted were then left with the court costs and legal battles.

The controversial situation in Ohio came about with a change of governor. The Ohio OFBCI was originally funded under a Republican, Governor Bob Taft. When he failed to be reelected, the liaison resigned. The new governor accused the Ohio OFBCI of not being fair in its dealings and ordered an audit of the OFBCI and its use of CCF funds. According to reports (Hughes 2007b), there was controversy in the dealings between Ohio's OFBCI and an organization that had close ties to the Bush administration. In the news article that broke the story, Laura Bischoff (2007) found that there were possible abuses of state funds: "A pot of money intended to help the poor was used to buy two giant flat-screen televisions, pay for two $125-a-month parking spots for a state contractor and purchase a $6,000 study that heaped praise on the state government office that made it all possible. On top of that, the contractor hired to administer the money—We Care America—is paid about $3,500 a day, including a 15 percent charge for 'overhead.'" In all, We Care America was set to receive more than $20 million in public money, and Governor Strickland was quoted as likening the Taft administration's faith-based office to "an ATM machine for some of the most politically connected right-wing organizations." The two sides strongly disagreed about the office and the motives for funding the organizations it did; the recently resigned head of the office denied any wrongdoing and stated that We Care America was the best organization for the job (Hughes 2007b). What is perhaps even more intriguing is that the new Democratic governor has been a strong supporter of faith-based groups in the state and has kept its OFBCI in place. He even continued to fund it, including $11 million dollars administered through the states OFBCI to strengthen families, though this was done under what he argues are stricter rules and monitoring (see Chapter 4 for more discussion of new sources of funding).

Lack of Guidance and Regulation

This problem in Ohio highlights another resource that is often missing from the faith-based initiatives: systematic knowledge about regulations, or over-sight to guide implementation. One of the characteristics I found common to all state policies connected to the faith-based initiatives was a lack of systematic regulation or guidance to direct the actions of the liaisons or OFBCIs. While the federal government did outline specific provisions that religious organiza-tions must abide by when receiving government funds, there was no system in place to ensure that these liaisons and offices were knowledgeable about the rules, or—as was highlighted by the examples from Montana and Ohio—that they in turn explained the rules to the organizations with which they worked. Perhaps more important to liaisons on a day-to-day basis, there were no federal rules or guidelines that made clear the objectives of these offices or suggested how the objectives should be met. In short, there was no systematic state or federal monitoring of the activities of the liaisons or offices nor of the activities of the organizations with which they contracted. Even though there are regula-tions in place regarding funding and accounting practices in state sponsored social service programs, there is no systematic government monitoring of the incorporation of religion into these services; without systems in place there is little to ensure that FBOs are following the rules regarding funding religious activities, even if they know what the often confusing rules are.

This lack of systematic regulation and monitoring is one of the biggest objections by those who have long opposed the faith-based initiative. But it is also a potential problem for liaisons and the organizations with which they contract; without sufficient guidance, they may act in good faith but unwitting-ly violate laws about church-state separation and open the door to lawsuits. Without a system in which the guidelines and rules are presented in a concrete manner to liaisons and by liaisons to other organizations, actors who are simply trying to do good works have been left in a very vulnerable position by the federal government. The White House OFBCI, understandably, has not wanted to have anything to do with organizations that are seen as violating the law, but it has not taken the responsibility of ensuring that states and organizations are properly educated about the legal ramifications of taking government money to provide social services.

While most liaisons told me that they saw the initiatives as a bright spot on the horizon and that they felt many benefits would accrue from having more religion in government, some were concerned by the lack of oversight. They cited concerns about the possibility of state liability in lawsuits over the issue of separation of church and state, and some noted issues of fairness as well. Several of the liaisons with whom I spoke were troubled both by the lack of regulation and by other liaisons' lack of understanding of issues surrounding church-state separation, including what such separation entailed and whether it should be enforced. For example, one of the few liaisons who claimed no religious affiliation expressed reservations about the religious motivations of other liaisons and about their lack of belief in the doctrine of church-state separation. On returning from a meeting on the initiatives that was attended by liaisons from across the country, this liaison said, "I was very scared by what I heard" (Dec. 13, 2005). However, this concern was only shared explicitly by four other liaisons.

Several liaisons noted their role in helping religious groups understand the constitutional requirements of their positions. For example, one liaison in the Midwest described his responsibility to engage in this kind of dialogue: "I'm also trying to make sure I provide adequate oversight of civil rights issues so that we have enough understanding and contractual provisions so that our sub-grantees and what-not . . . they have clear guidance on what's reliable to prevent unintentional or intentional religious activities being done on federal dollar" (Dec. 3, 2004). Another liaison said that her concern was not about church-state separation principles per se but about the practical consequences of violating them: "Well, I just don't want to get sued" (March 27, 2005).

This lack of guidance and oversight has had other intriguing consequences. For example, I found no consistency in something as fundamental as the location of these liaisons and offices within state governments. Some have been placed in agencies that deal with social services; some have been established in outside foundations funded primarily through private donors; others have been created in the governor's office; and one state even established its office under the first lady of the state (see Table 3.2 for a summary). In this aspect, as well as in others, the lack of formal structure in the system has forced each state to reinvent the wheel when it wished to create an FBL position or an OFBCI.

Changes in Government and Challenges to Stability

Since faith-based implementation began at the state level, only two states— California and Massachusetts—have had established liaison positions completely

TABLE 3.2. Organizational Location of Faith-Based Liaison Positions in State Government (2004–2005)

Location	Number of States	States
No position had been created at time of interview, or the position existed for a period but change in leadership had left position vacant or unfunded	18	CA,[1] DE, IA, MA,[1] ME, MO,[2] MS,[2] NH,[2] NV, OR, RI, SD, TN, UT,[1] VT, WA,[2] WV, WI[2]
Position established in the office of the governor or a state agency	16	AR, AZ, CO, GA, HI, ID, IL, KS, KY,[2] MT,[3] NC, ND, NE,[3] NY, PA, SC
Office is administratively under the governor, but had been established in a variety of ways including under Lt. Governor, Office of Volunteerism, First Lady's Office, etc.	13	AK, AL, CT, DC, IN, LA, MD, MI, MN, NM, NJ, OH, VA
State office of faith-based and community initiatives is established under a state agency	2	WY, OK
State office of faith-based and community initiatives is funded mainly through private money, but the office is administratively connected to the governor	2	FL, TX

Except as noted, data were collected from interviews conducted with faith-based liaisons in 2004 and 2005. The situations in some states have changed since then.

1. The state once had a liaison, but the position no longer existed, or was not filled at the time of the interviews.
2. The liaison position was created in 2007.
3. The state created the positions after receiving a federal Compassion Capital Fund grant.

vanish;[5] however, other states have faced significant changes caused by the ebb and flow of political life. In particular, when a new governor is elected, a state office is often mired in new challenges and may find itself lacking support from above; under new leadership, the initiatives are sometimes missing completely from the state's new agenda. This has happened in several states, including some of those that were originally among the most successful, like Oklahoma and Texas. All states have endured some setbacks; the details vary, depending in large part on how and where the liaison positions and offices were created.

The story of one northeastern state's problems illustrates the situation faced by many states. In 1999, the state had a governor who strongly believed in faith-based initiatives and wanted to bring them to the state. While this governor was in office, the initiatives flourished. By the summer of 2004, however, the governor was undergoing impeachment processes and left office. The new governor was less committed to the initiatives, but continued some aspects of them and did not let the liaison go that the previous governor had appointed. This liaison did not stay on as part of the new governor's staff, but he remained active in a different part of the government; he later described the ordeal as a "real roller coaster." This liaison noted that when the governor who had believed strongly in the initiatives left office, work related to the initiatives was pushed to the side. For the initiatives to succeed, the liaison said, "it is so important to have a personal belief and association with the efforts—you must have this for success on a large scale" (April 30, 2005). Nonetheless, he continued to work as the state liaison, even though that position no longer formally existed.

Limited Communication Infrastructure

In addition to the lack of regulation guiding these offices, there is also little infrastructure in place that connects state liaisons and OFBCIs to those in other states or to the federal government. While the networks among state offices were certainly growing, when this project started, none of the liaisons with whom I spoke knew all the other liaisons, and most of the liaisons I interviewed had rarely or never discussed their job with other state liaisons. As a result, none of them knew what was really happening in other states. This lack of communication meant that liaisons often operated as dedicated lone wolves, with each state in effect reinventing the wheel. There was very little shared knowledge about what they were supposed to be accomplishing as FBLs or what exactly their jobs should entail. In fact, I unintentionally became part of my own research by becoming a conduit between offices, passing along information on what was happening in other states to the liaisons and OFBCI staffs I interviewed; some of this information was as basic as which other states had offices.

Both the number of liaisons and the ties they have been making with each other have grown over time. Table 3.3 lists all states with liaisons, along with the network connections that each reported. Of the states whose liaisons I spoke with, five reported no connections to other liaisons. In addition, although there were 30 state offices at the time, on average each reported fewer than four connections with others. A few states were substantial outliers; these included Oklahoma and Texas, two of the earliest adopters, with the most institutionalized initiatives. What is important to note is the difference between states with significant longevity and institutionalization and those in which the position was more recent and thus potentially more ephemeral.

Communication with established liaisons was important for liaisons in other states, because it showed them what some of the possibilities for the position might be. For example, one liaison noted that her time spent visiting with a liaison that had been around for a longer time was very useful, helping her understand her role. When asked why she had made the visit, she said it was "just to get information, just to get a feel for what he was doing, since he had been on the war path, or had been working with faith-based for such a long

TABLE 3.3. Network Ties among State Liaisons, as Reported by Liaisons in Interviews (2004–2005)

State	Number of States	States to Which Ties Were Reported
TX	17	AL, AR, AZ, CO, CT, FL, GA, HI, ID, KS, MD, MI, NJ, OH, OK, VA, WY
OK	16	AK, AL, AR, FL, GA, HI, IL, IN, KY, MD, MI, NJ, OH, TX, VA, WY
OH	13	AK, AL, AR, CA, FL, GA, IA, IN, MI, NJ, OK, TX, WY
AL	12	AK, AR, FL, ID, IN, MD, NJ, OH, OK, TX, VA, WY
VA	9	AL, AR, CT, DC, MD, NC, NJ, NY, OH, PA, TX
FL	7	AL, GA, MI, NJ, OH, OK, TX
MN	7	AL, FL, IN, NJ, NM, OK, TX
NJ	6	AL, AR, CO, CT, FL, OK
AZ	5	AL, DC, FL, OH, OK
CT	4	FL, NJ, NE, OK
MI	4	NJ, OH, FL, OK
AR	3	AL, NJ, OK
MD	3	AL, NJ, OK
AK	2	OH, VA
GA	2	OK, WI
ID	2	AK, MI
IN	2	AL, OH
NM	2	FL, TX
CO	1	OK
NY	1	NJ
UT[1]	1	IN
WY	1	OK
CA	0	–
DC	0	–
HI	0	–
KS	0	–
LA	0	–
MA	0	–
NC	0	–
ND	0	–
SC	0	–

This table displays the number of ties to other state liaisons each liaison reported during the interviews I conducted. Liaisons reported an average of 3.87 ties to other state liaisons.

Note that there is a lack of symmetry in the data: for example, while the liaison in Texas reported ties with liaisons in 17 other states, liaisons in only 7 states reported having ties with Texas. This could partially result from timing, because ties did become slightly more common over the course of my work. Alternatively (or additionally), the discrepancies may reflect asymmetries in the relationships, with those who found a relationship more useful being more likely to report it. At any rate, I believe the overall patterns are valid: there is great variability in the connectedness of liaisons, and the amount of connectivity is very low.

1. This interview was done before there was a state office, when it was a faith-works operation.

period of time. So, to find out some of the things he was doing, to find out some of the things that were being accomplished" (March 23, 2005). Liaisons also acted as cheerleaders and counselors for each other. One liaison who had been in his position for several years stated that liaisons often needed to see each other to cheer up and regain the momentum they had initially felt about the initiatives (Aug. 20, 2004). As another FBL noted, networking with other liaisons was essential to not only being able to do the job well, but being able to do the job at all. "Because so much of this initiative is pioneering [talking with other FBLs] is sort of like a sanity check... It's comforting knowing we have the same problems" (March 28, 2005). Another liaison echoed his sentiment describing her connections to other FBLs as a "lifeline" (Feb. 7, 2005).

Also of interest is that the states with the most extensive network connections were also, as one liaison put it, "the reddest of the red." In the four most-connected states there was significant religious involvement in politics, with active evangelical communities tied to Republican state governments. While there are certainly several possible explanations for the high level of liaison activity in these states, the data do suggest the likelihood that a link between religion and politics is a key factor (see Chapter 6).

Although most states were out of the communication loop during their first year and before 2006, in the time since, it appears that interstate communication is one of the first aspects of faith-based policy implementation that has changed systematically. In the first years the state director at the White House OFBCI had not done anything to address this issue. However, in 2005 after I spoke with the newly appointed White House OFBCI person in charge of state liaison communication, a network was created that allowed offices to communicate with each other and with the federal government's office; monthly conference calls between the White House OFBCI and the state liaisons and OFBCIs were also instituted Thus there has been growth in both the bureaucratic and administrative implementation at the state level and in the communication and connection among liaisons and between liaisons and the federal government. By the time I completed my research, liaisons were firmly engaged bureaucratic administrators brokering a policy that was growing in its prominence and legitimacy, even if it was not appearing on the front pages of the nation's papers.

Liaisons Leading the Charge

While I found that the duties and powers of FBLs varied by state, in all cases they had the primary responsibility for putting the faith-based initiatives into practice in their respective states. Because of the critical role they played in implementing the initiatives and what they represented, closer investigation of both the nature of the FBL position and the characteristics of those who fill it was warranted. My research strongly suggests that the nature of the liaison positions significantly shaped the implementation of the faith-based initiatives at the state level, as did the backgrounds, identities, and commitments of individuals who became FBLs.

There have been few formal policies guiding the actions of liaisons, and when such policies existed, there was generally little oversight to confirm that tasks had been carried out in accordance with the policies. As with previous policies with amorphous goals and strategies (Fineman 1998; Kaler and Watkins 2001; Lipsky 1971; Maupin 1993; Prottas 1978; Santoro and McGuire 1997; Stearns and Almeida 2004; Wald and Corey 2002; Weatherley and Lipsky 1977; Weissert 1994), current faith-based policy has made liaisons into policy brokers while in their role as government bureaucrats, relying on their experience, networks, and beliefs to carry out whatever actions they deem are appropriate to meet the goals of the policy. In general, policy actors are more able to rely on their knowledge and preexisting values when they are operating under few rules and guidelines. For example, Kahn (2001) found that workers in charge of implementing federal welfare-to-work policies in Michigan often improvised because of the lack of administrative regulation. Similarly, Kaler and Watkins (2001:254) observed that "the implementation of social policy is strongly conditioned by the needs, desires and agendas of those who carry them out." These findings about the importance of the nature of the policy actors who carry out social policy without much guidance and regulation make clear that understanding the activities of FBLs is crucial to understanding what has really been happening with state faith-based policies. Thus, to understand the effect of FBLs on the expression of the faith-based initiatives at the state level, it became clear to me that in addition to investigating what FBLs were doing, it was essential to know who they were and what motivated them in their work. My research identified two significant commonalities among the FBLs: their self-selection into the positions and their preexisting ties to particular religious communities.

Self-Selection

One of the more interesting findings about FBLs was how committed they were to the initiative's success. In general, these were not individuals assigned to the job through the usual bureaucratic measures associated with government jobs. Instead, almost all had asked to take on the position, often adding the responsibility of FBL to their other duties. Of the 30 liaisons I interviewed, 18 were already working for or otherwise involved with state government; they sought out the liaison positions and took them on while keeping many of the duties and responsibilities they already had. As one liaison said, "We didn't get this faith-component by default.... It came to this office because I wanted it" (Nov. 8, 2004). Another liaison stated that he found the "initiative really intriguing. Faith-based organizations care a lot and are very sincere, but they need a lot of help. I was very attracted to the idea, and I felt sure that I could help" (Sept. 15, 2004). An additional eight liaisons had heard that the governor was seeking to create a liaison position and actively petitioned for the job. One such liaison told me that she had heard about the idea of the initiative under President Clinton and then Bush and had wanted for some time to become part of the process in her state.

> When the position came open I thought you know this would be wonderful, but I didn't know how [my state] was responding to the FBCI. The majority of my career I worked in social services, not just social services, but faith inspired social services. I worked for the Salvation Army for six years and for the last 12 years I worked for Catholic Social Services. The missions of those social service programs aligned with my personal mission in life and that is a faith-based one.... [But] I thought long and hard [about becoming the liaison] because I knew it would be challenging [because] I didn't know how to work in a political arena. But I am learning quickly. (February 21, 2005)

When asked why they took the job, all but four of the thirty FBLs I interviewed pointed to their personal commitment to and interest in working with the faith-based community. Some of these liaisons cited a deep and abiding faith as the reason for seeking the job. One liaison said, "I felt the call. I really did.... I felt like this was the opportunity to make a difference" (Feb. 7, 2005). Another said, "I was at a place in my personal journey of faith where I realized that community was important not just to me, but to God.... I felt that it was, you know, indeed a calling to get involved (Feb. 8, 2005). One cited a long-term personal need for such work: "Well you know, I feel personally it was divine appointment because I was working as the PR person for the Governor's Mentoring Initiative and Governor's Family Literacy Initiative, and a year later this initiative comes around, and it's always what I've yearned to do" (Feb. 9, 2005).

Others simply stated that they had always worked with the faith community, believed in the initiatives, and wanted to make sure the faith community was part of government. A former liaison said:

> My education is in the seminary studying for the priesthood for about 11 years, I've [also] done some volunteer work along the way with faith-based and grassroots community organizations. So some of the linkages and relationship that, you know, I was comfortable and familiar with came into play.... I mean one of the things that is very evident if you were to look, for instance, at things such as 12-step programs ... I mean I'm making this percentage up, but I don't think

it would be far from wrong to say that 75 percent of the activities occur in a church basement somewhere. Faith communities are willing to provide those types of available space and time and resources for such efforts. (April 15, 2005)

Another liaison, when asked why she came to the position, also pointed to her desire to work with faith-based communities, although she had not intended to work inside the government:

I guess because I came from a nonprofit background and I realized the needs of that particular community and how important the nonprofit and faith-based community is to the [state], and I enjoy working with them. Because I had not really intended on working for the [state] government but what happened, a person that I had worked with while I was at the nonprofit organization called me and said, "This job is for you." So I said, "Well, OK." And I applied, and that's what happened. (Dec. 19, 2004)

Finally, while one liaison pointed to a passion for working with both the underprivileged and the faith community, declaring, "I feel blessed to be in this role" (March 7, 2005), another offered an even more succinct answer, saying that the liaison position had come through the "hand of God" (Nov. 21, 2004).

These statements reflect a general sentiment that serving as an FBL was not just another job; it was a way to change the social service sector in what the liaisons considered to be a positive and innovative manner because the job emphasized working with religious groups. In fact, the majority reported that while the official time allowed for the job was sometimes only a few hours a week, they worked a great deal more than that. They believed that without the extra time they spent on their role as FBL, vital information would not get to the faith community.

Ties to Religious Communities

Given the process by which FBLs were chosen, it is not surprising that they were a very dedicated and religious group. In fact, many of them had extensive formal and informal ties to their religious communities. Nine of the liaisons— almost a third of those interviewed—were or had been pastors. Four had held some other formal position at their local church, and five reported that they had worked extensively within their religious groups in an informal capacity. In addition, 24 liaisons told me that they had experience working with FBOs in a variety of capacities prior to becoming liaisons. As one liaison related, this job was a way to mix her professional and spiritual sides.

It's a once-in-a-lifetime opportunity. I am active with my church; I've been very active in volunteerism for a number of years, not only in the faith community, but in the community itself, primarily in education. I was born and raised in [the city] and was very much involved with the decentralization of the administration of their schools. . . . I've always been a volunteer in both schools and churches I've been affiliated with. (Dec. 15, 2005)

An important aspect of this is that many of the FBLs had strong ties to their own religious communities; further, they relied on those networks to spread the word about grants, conferences, and other information regarding the possible role of small FBOs in providing government-funded social services. One liaison who was a former pastor explained that his role in the faith community gave him an advantage when dealing with FBOs. "I'm able to talk their language. If they throw out a theological term to me, I'll understand it. I know how churches operate because I've worked in churches" (December 14, 2004). During the interviews, several liaisons described how excited they were to connect with religious groups and how important their connections with people of faith were to them. One said, "Yes, I am very involved. I am a retired Baptist preacher, having pastored for almost 50 years. I've been present at our state conventions—Baptist, that is—and of course I have served as president of our Foreign Missions Commission. I have connections across the state, not only among Baptists, but among other denominations" (March 7, 2005).

Another liaison noted the connection between her religious ties and those of the governor when she made the decision to come on board: "I was retired from politics and doing academic work, but I have known the governor for a long time, and so I said yes. The governor is a strong person of faith himself, we actually belong to the same church and he has been a major player in community outreach of the church" (March 28, 2005). Later in the interview she noted that she had an "appreciation for the faith-based initiatives on a personal level" because she was a former director of management and budget under President Bush, so she knew the importance of the faith-based initiatives and that this was a segment of social services that had been overlooked.

This feeling that faith-based organizations had been overlooked by the government was echoed by another liaison. He described how he had been working with the city to develop housing and noticed that faith-based groups were not being approached or partnered with and so he created a coalition of congregations to work on housing issues. He felt "government would be more effective and people are going to be better served . . . when we don't exclude certain groups" (March 28, 2005). He maintained these strong ties to the faith community and was excited to have an even bigger role in developing connections between these groups and government.

This level of connection to faith-based groups and communities while not surprising is noteworthy when one considers that most of the contact between the liaisons and the faith community was through personal networking. Thus groups outside the preexisting networks of the FBLs may well not have had the same level of access to relevant information as groups within those networks. Many of the FBLs interviewed seemed honestly interested in trying to get a wide array of faiths involved in the government granting process; they often attempted to accomplish this difficult task with extremely limited resources. Nonetheless, people generally tend to network with the groups that they know, the people they work with, the people they go to school with, their neighbors, and the people they go to church with. Although their jobs require them to connect with all types of different religious groups, FBLs cannot escape this homophyly. Regardless of the reasons—limited resources or the personal nature of the networks brought to the job—it is likely that not all groups were equally included in liaisons' information loops, and those that were excluded were probably exposed to fewer funding opportunities.

During one interview, I met with a liaison and his pastor. They talked about how other churches could become involved in providing social services and contracting with the government. During our time together they discussed how they were planning a meeting of churches—all Christian—to discuss the faith-based initiatives. They also noted the changing role of evangelicals in America; they told me that they believed that the previous view of many evangelicals—that the focus of religion should be only on internal salvation—was erroneous and that working with government to change the material well-being of others was crucial to being a Christian. In the interview they discussed how there were virtually no mosques or synagogues in their state and so for them it was a "mostly Christian" initiative (Feb. 8, 2005).

This kind of specific connection between one's role as liaison and one's personal faith was a theme in many discussions; however, others specifically noted that they wanted to be inclusive of many faiths including non-Christian groups. Several liaisons noted that they tried to bring in various religious groups through their advisory boards, contracting processes, or networking. As one FBL stated, "We had an incredible advisory committee that at some point had over 30 people [on it from] different faith based groups, non-profit social service providers, and government people. We had Hindu and Buddhist, Jewish, Muslim . . . and a lot of Christian denominations. So we had made a very big effort for outreach and I provided service to people from all those different organizations" (Sept. 15, 2004).

While some liaisons tried to bridge religious gaps, previous religious backgrounds and connections are important to examine. In the interviews, liaisons were asked about their current religious affiliations. Perhaps unsurprisingly, almost half (13) of all FBLs interviewed claimed a conservative Christian background. Five reported that they were practicing Catholics, and four practiced another mainline or liberal Christian religion. Of the 30 interviewed, only two claimed a non-Christian religious background. Four liaisons declined to answer the question; of these, however, none stated that they were not religious. Instead they said that they did not think that their religious background was important to their job. Since the job of the FBL was to connect religious groups with government, the notion that their own religious background was unimportant seems dubious. On the contrary, it is likely that liaisons at least began to build their networks through their existing ties to faith-based groups; intentionally or not, they were thus more likely to be providing information to some FBOs than to others.

Summary and Conclusion

Taken as a whole, the growth of the faith-based bureaucracy over the last seven years is both staggering and disappointing. States have institutionalized the initiatives through an array of administrative measures, so that the initiatives have grown from five liaisons in 1999 to 39 at the time of this writing in 2008, and from one OFBCI in 1999 to 22 today. This shift in bureaucratization parallels a shift in legitimization of the principles underpinning the initiatives. However, there has also been a significant large-scale failure to fund and help smaller faith-based organizations develop comprehensive social service programs and receive government funding.

Instead of a coherent and systematic response to the faith-based initiative, states created myriad faith-based policies and practices. By far the most common way was to create the position of faith-based liaison. Since there were few guidelines regarding their actions state liaisons became the faith-based initiatives in most states, charged with defining how their state would implement the initiatives. They are often solely responsible for which organizations are contacted about faith-based funding opportunities. They define the content of this information, as well as most content at faith-based conferences. And they influence whom in state government these organizations become connected. Therefore, understanding the initiatives at the state level means understanding the role of FBLs and their on-the-ground activities.

FBLs have had to deal with many challenges in implementing the initiative, including a paucity of resources, misunderstandings about the initiatives from faith-based groups, the misgivings of government officials, and the continuous threat of political change and local extinction. In the face of these challenges, the passionate religious commitment that many FBLs share has helped them survive and persevere. Their personal faith has provided the inspiration they need to work more hours than they are paid to work—and sometimes to continue their tasks for free after their official positions are gone. Because their jobs depend on networking and sharing information, the work of FBLs is intimately linked to who they are and who they know. By bringing their religious commitments to the faith-based initiatives, state liaisons bring not only determination and dedication, but also religious connections to bear on their work. Those connections create not only opportunities, but challenges as well.

One of these challenges is that the personal faith of the FBLs can affect who is brought into the information circle of the social services fold. For example, while their connections to a faith community can bring credibility in religious communities and a strong network of preexisting ties, it may also lead them to focus on certain groups while leaving others out, possibly creating feelings of alienation among those who are left out. And while they rarely hold the purse strings, FBLs are now the main brokers of information between FBOs and government agencies. FBLs have encountered additional problems when attempting to change the prevailing views and attitudes of other government bureaucrats; this may be the result of the strong religious motivations and ties of the liaisons themselves. Others in government may see the liaisons as essentially outsiders—as religious representatives rather than government officials—and may thus be suspicious of their motivations. Although this study did not directly address this issue, it is pertinent that one liaison expressly stated the fear that most of the other liaisons, while passionate and dedicated, were not experienced enough in the government sector to really understand how the faith-based initiatives should or could work. Regardless of these challenges liaisons and OFBCIs are here to stay, representing, in and of themselves, a greater role of religion within the public sphere.

4

Making the Initiatives
the Law of the Land

Any good symbolic device, one that works to capture the imagination also shapes our perceptions and suspends skepticism. . . . Those effects are what make symbols political devices. They are the means of influence and control, even though it is often hard to tell with symbols exactly who is influencing whom.
—Deborah Stone, *The Policy Paradox: The Art of*
Political Decision Making

At the beginning of this project, I spoke with one of the first architects of the initiatives, a former advisor to George W. Bush. During that interview he argued that the "original intention of the faith-based initiatives was not legislation" (March 27, 2005). Instead, he said, the early intent was to carry out the goals of the initiatives through administrative changes, thereby changing government culture from within, without having to get legislators on board. States originally followed this pattern, with little legislative implementation between 1996 and 2000: only 41 laws were enacted during that period, in a total of 10 states. Since then, however, states have steadily increased the amount of legislation specifically focused on the initiatives. After the election of President Bush in 2000, 230 additional laws were enacted, and 31 states were added to the total.

This legislation has largely focused on one area: creating a new legal culture that promotes more openness to FBOs. This has been done through two mechanisms: (1) by laws that symbolize a friendlier atmosphere for faith-based groups, and (2) by laws that create greater access for FBOs to the public sector. While these changes in law and legislative culture may have been slow in coming, the cultural goods—as Lindsay (2008) calls goodwill and other intangibles—of the faith-based movement have been making a statement. As explained in Chapter 1, the cultural goods are both the result of social movement action in the cultural sphere and the mechanism for further change. With these two types of laws, a pattern has emerged which has attempted to increase the inclusion and integration of FBOs at the state level. The first type are those that suggest that states work with FBOs, use language that encourages participation, or create an atmosphere that suggests greater friendliness, without mandating this extra participation. This category also includes laws that set up faith-friendly structures such as FBL positions, state administrative boards to work with FBOs, and state-sponsored grant-writing seminars. These are not laws that direct action, but rather *suggest* action. On the other hand, some laws create greater access for faith-based groups and more faith-based practices by direct-ing specific actions to be taken. While these laws do not necessarily create an advantage for faith-based groups—although some argue that they might—they do target FBOs for special help and explicit inclusion in the public sphere. These laws include creating funding streams geared toward the state OFBCI or other faith-based efforts, laws that faith-based programs be made available (such as faith-based prison wards), and laws that require the appointment of representatives from faith-based groups to state advisory boards. Taken as a whole, state faith-based legislation becomes something more than its individ-ual parts: it creates a cultural shift in government toward creating new avenues of access, inclusion, and perhaps in some instances privilege for faith-based groups. Such legislation is the tangible expression of this largely symbolic cultural shift.

Faith-Based Social Policy as Symbolic Politics

As with all social policies, faith-based legislation signifies something more than the mere words of the policies. Faith-based policies are political symbols, and as such these policies can unite, justify, and create systems of power (Cobb and Elder 1972; Edelman 1964, 1971; Stone 1988). As Stone noted in her work on symbols in political action, policies work as storytelling devices that codify ideals and principles, often in a climate fraught with tension and ambiguity about their true meaning (Wysong, Aniskiewicz, and Wright 1994). The faith-based initiatives are no exception. With the laws passed after original federal legislation in 1996, states have begun to create faith-based policies of their own, branching out in ways that the federal government has not (Farris, Nathan, and Wright 2004; Formicola, Segers, and Weber 2003; Ragan, Montiel, and Wright 2003; Ragan and Wright 2005). For a few states, creating faith-based legislation has become commonplace, with government and move-ment outsiders hardly noticing the changes taking place. This lack of attention to state policies may be ascribable in large part to the often ambiguous nature of the legislation; further, when the laws are less ambiguous, they are usually part of larger bills that may not be directly related to the initiatives. In fact, while the federal government has been almost completely ineffectual in enacting laws in this regard, states had, at my last count, passed 271 pieces of legislation specifically incorporating the principals of the initiative. These symbolic policies are the end result—the cultural goods—of sustained social movement efforts, and they have appeal far beyond their original boundaries.

Faith-based laws enacted at the state level tell a story of the changing role of religion in American politics and social policy. Ambiguous legislation allows politicians to benefit from "faith"—broadly and vaguely defined—without the controversy that would come with greater public funding of religious groups. In this chapter, I examine how state faith-based policies, when looked at from a symbolic perspective, represent what David Domke and Kevin Coe (2007) have termed a "God strategy," one based on using religion and religious language to create state policy. They argue that "to compete successfully, politicians need not always walk the religious walk, but they had better be able to talk the religious talk" (4). Faith-based policy is a way for politicians to use legislation as symbolic "God talk." Viewed through this lens of a politically symbolic God strategy, the faith-based initiatives bring political actors the benefit of incorporating religion into state legislation, without having to create significant infrastructure or additions to the social services sector. Of course, some politicians may have other motives as well, including hoping for greater participation from faith-based groups or believing that they offer better services, but when looked at in total, these policies illustrate how the language of faith, in its most ambiguous form, has come to have a larger and more pronounced place in American social policy through the initiative.

The policies of the initiatives tell a story about how religion needs special incorporation into law and that through new statutes, problems in the social services sector will begin to be remedied. These laws are important because they tell the story of how we want to represent ourselves. What concerns and challenges do we face? What solutions do legislators propose with the intention of resonating with the public? While few people other than social science scholars think of legislation in terms of stories and symbols, it is, in fact, a way that these symbols can diffuse throughout the legislative landscape and become part of the public discourse that is powerful and astounding.

The Laws of the Land: Data Collection Methods

Data on all legislation related to the faith-based initiatives were gathered using the LexisNexis search engine. This is the standard tool used in legal research and contains data on all laws passed in all the states. The data available include the content of each law passed, as well as its author and date of passage. Using search terms related to the faith-based initiatives such as "faith-based" and "Charitable Choice," I was able to compile a reasonably complete record of legislative implementation related to the faith-based initiatives. The majority of legislative changes involved encouraging state agencies to contract with faith-based groups for specific purposes or adding faith-based representatives to various state government advisory boards.

In addition to the LexisNexis searches, I also analyzed data from interviews with liaisons, coding for references to state laws or policies. While most liaisons did not directly reference state legislation, some elaborated on why states had created particular policies through legislation. Using data from the interviews and legislative text, an overall picture of faith-based implementation began to emerge. The picture is one of faith-based policy quietly changing the relationship between the public sector and the faith community. There appears to be a slow and inexorable move toward greater cooperation and integration between church and state, and less separation.

Types of State Legislation

Since the first public discourse about the faith-based initiatives became policy in the welfare reform bill of 1996, 41 states have enacted 271 laws specifically addressing the faith-based initiatives. In this section I outline the types of legislation states have passed. The story often told by these policies mirrors the one found in the rhetoric of most supporters: faith-based groups were discriminated against in the past, and a fundamental change in legislation and informal public policy is required to create a fair system.

While the number of states passing legislation and the number of laws passed each year has been growing, most legislation continues to fall into one of nine categories. These nine categories can be grouped under two larger headings derived from a distinction set out at the beginning of this chapter: laws that ensure a friendly environment for FBOs (symbolic laws), and those that create government access for FBOs (concrete laws). Table 4.1 summarizes the legislation related to the initiatives, with the two main categories, types of laws under each category, and the number of laws of each type passed by the states. Clearly, although the faith-based initiatives have for the most part slipped off the front pages of our newspapers, they are becoming well established in the legal landscape.

Although most laws related to the faith-based initiatives are entirely favorable to FBOs, a few states have incorporated a small amount of regulation or restriction into faith-based legislation. Four states have passed laws primarily intended to regulate FBOs in their provision of social services. In addition, portions of some of the laws included in Category 6 in the table regulate the faith-based programs that they encourage or sponsor. Finally, an additional

TABLE 4.1. Types and Numbers of Laws Benefiting Faith-Based Organizations
(1996–2007)

Type of Law	No. of Laws
Laws aimed at ensuring a friendly environment for FBOs (117 total)	
1. Include language in executive orders or legislation that encourages partnering with faith-based organizations including incorporate "faith-based" language into state laws	107
2. Create an Office of Faith Based Initiatives or FBL position	8
3. Create a faith-based advisory board	2
Laws creating government access for FBOs (143 total)	
4. Include members of the faith community on agency advisory boards	59
5. Make appropriations to faith-based offices/organizations	42
6. Encourage or regulate government agencies to use a faith-based organizations for specific government programs, such as drug rehabilitation, prison programs, or youth activities	37
7. Exempt faith-based organizations from standard regulations or licensing requirements	3
8. Assist with grant writing process (or assign extra points to application)	2

Data were collected from the LexisNexis database. Eleven other laws include Charitable Choice in state constitution, religious pharmacy exemption, general regulations guiding faith-based groups and requirement that faith-based groups have a separate 501(c)3 (see full explanation in text).

three state laws require FBOs to create their own 501(c)3 charitable organizations to provide services. While this regulatory legislation is certainly meaningful, it represents less than 10 percent of the total faith-based legislation at the state level.

Ensuring a Friendly Environment

There are several types of laws that tend to foster an environment that welcomes the inclusion of FBOs in the social services sector. These include laws that contain language to encourage partnering with FBOs, that alter the state legal structure to include Charitable Choice provisions, and that establish state OFBCIs or FBL positions. While none of these guarantee FBOs greater access to public money, they do create an overall legal environment in which faith-based groups are clearly seen as integral to the social service arena.

ENCOURAGEMENT OF CONTRACTING WITH FAITH-BASED ORGANIZATIONS.
Seeking to remedy what supporters have argued is an inherent bias against FBOs, some states have passed laws encouraging contracting, collaboration, or partnership with FBOs. These changes are mainly symbolic; the laws do not call for contracting with any specific organization or make such contracting mandatory. Instead, these laws generally state that faith-based groups should be sought

out as partners or collaborators in the state-funded contracting process. In this way the laws contribute to a policy environment that seeks to create a cultural change within government. At the time of this writing, 107 laws encouraging contracting with FBOs have been passed, making this by far the most common type of legislation. The only law related to the faith-based initiatives passed in the state of Wyoming typifies the rather generic nature of these laws:

> The Department of Family Services shall develop a comprehensive plan to improve the lives and future of all children and families in Wyoming. In developing the plan, the Department shall collaborate with the business councils . . . state and local agencies . . . and private groups, services providers and businesses, including FBOs. (State of Wyoming 2004:§1[a])

What makes this type of legislation so important is not only its prevalence, but also how little is known about what such laws actually mean. Though laws that regulate organizations or appropriate funds are fairly straightforward, ambiguous legislation creates a symbolic attempt to comply with goals that are often vague, without a way to concretely measure or assess the effects—or intended effects—of the legislation. What does it mean to "encourage" or "collaborate" with an FBO? Why is this necessary? Does this mean that more FBOs will actually receive contracts? If so, which FBOs? If not, are states passing bills that have little real meaning? This ambiguity is probably part of the very reason for creating this type of legislation: legislators can *say* they are doing something, without in fact making potentially costly or burdensome changes to the functions of government. Thus, these generic, rather positive bills can be used to build political support and coalitions while avoiding concrete action, the details of which would perhaps be less politically palatable.

Another point of interest about these types of laws is that even before Charitable Choice, states and state bureaucracies were allowed to create partnerships and collaborations with faith-based groups but never felt the need to enact a law. This of course raises the question: Why has the implementation of these new, seemingly unnecessary, laws occurred? As with any legislation, these laws are probably a reflection of the desires of multiple stakeholders with diverse motives, which vary depending on the state in which they serve. However, the stories people told me about these laws and the ideas they codify and legitimize is that FBOs have faced problems and that these laws were a necessary remedy. A liaison whose state has passed six bills to encourage state organizations to work with FBOs told me:

> The state has not worked in the past with a large number of FBOs. Just like nationally, for a number of years, these organizations were just not a part of the general process, unless they were a large faith organization, like Lutheran Social Services or Catholic Social Services.

The smaller and medium-sized organizations really did not have an avenue to have access to the information relative to opportunities. Therefore, without that information, they were not in a position to even apply. (April 30, 2005)

This story is similar to those told by legislators in numerous states: states needed to create access and friendliness to get the most participation from FBOs. Notably, these laws codify part of the larger argument about the faith-based initiatives, that without Charitable Choice, small organizations lacked access to information and funds and only through new action could these problems be remedied. One liaison noted that this change in legislative language was important because it created a new environment of cooperation that signaled—to both government officials and FBOs—a new way of doing business:

I think language was important a lot of the time. It seems that putting [into law that] FBOs, that they are eligible entities (although they were already eligible to apply), putting that language in was important. Most groups think of themselves as ministries, they don't think of themselves as nonprofits, although they are. So that is important that it happens across the board. (March 23, 2005)

While this type of legislation has been passed with the stated goal of solving social services problems by granting access to small FBOs, there are by and large no mechanisms to measure the success at doing so. As a result, state legislators can be seen to encourage, and provide help and information to, faith-based groups without ever being held accountable for the results.

CREATION OF OFBCIs AND FBL POSITIONS. While the vast majority of OFBCIs and FBL positions have been created administratively, some states have taken the next step and given these positions greater permanence by addressing them with legislation. Kentucky (2005), Iowa (2004), Missouri (2007), Virginia (2002), Louisiana (2004), North Dakota (2005), Ohio (2005), Alaska (2007), and Maryland (2008) have created FBL positions or OFBCIs by statute. An example of this type of legislation is the Louisiana law, which established an OFBCI to "coordinate opportunities for the state to access federal programs and to identify areas of potential benefit that result from coordinating efforts among the state and federal government and FBOs. The office of the governor may utilize funding sources which are eligible for federal financial participation programs which serve the public interest" (State of Louisiana 2004). Within this brief statute, two things were established: first, that faith-based groups needed someone to coordinate their efforts with governments, both state and federal, and second, that this coordination should include searching for money. In addition, this text claims that these programs serve the "public interest" and so can be funded by the governor.

The benefit to creating OFBCIs and liaison positions through legislation is clear. Legislation establishes them more permanently than does administrative decree, which can lead to greater stability and legitimacy. These liaisons can be more confident than others that their outreach efforts will continue after they have gone, and they can perform their work knowing that what they do has some force of law behind it. However, even when they have a legislative mandate this does not mean a fully functioning office. In one state the liaison was the governor's chief of staff and was tasked with doing this job on top of his already full workload. "Last session the legislature passed a law naming the governor's office as the point office to handle faith-based initiatives, but without any money . . . so we were asked to coordinate this whole effort, but not given any money to do so" (Dec. 28, 2005). So while the office was in place permanently, there was little the liaison could do beyond some networking to spread the news that there was a faith-based office in the state and therefore gain potentially positive publicity.

States have also signaled a friendlier environment to religious actors by adding Charitable Choice provisions to legislation. Three states have taken this step: Arizona (1999), California (1999), and Mississippi (2004). Texas also added a "nondiscrimination" section in 1997 but did not label it as a Charitable Choice provision. The result of these provisions was not that the array of groups that could or could not participate in social services was changed or that specific access or funding was created; instead, these laws reinforced the notion that government needed to create a friendlier and more welcoming environment for faith-based groups, so that the groups would become part of the social services sector. Such laws, of course, do not guarantee that this will actually happen in a way that is meaningful in changing the lives of the poor and needy.

Finally, two states (Florida and Ohio) have passed legislation that mandates the formation of advisory boards to guide the initiatives. Together, the laws discussed in this section tend to create a welcoming—and fairly permanent—place for faith-based groups to seek resources and information from the government.

Creating an Environment of Access

Several types of state faith-based legislation have created direct access and new opportunities for the faith community. While government agencies have always had the right to contract with FBOs to provide social services, some states have passed laws that make this much easier and in some cases mandatory. Over the past 10 years, state laws directing specific access for faith-based groups—through earmarked funding, by creating positions on advisory boards, or by some means lessening the regulatory burden on them—have created a new legal structure that incorporates FBOs in fundamentally different ways.

INCLUSION OF REPRESENTATIVES OF FAITH-BASED ORGANIZATIONS ON STATE ADVISORY BOARDS. A number of states have attempted to level the playing field for religious organizations by allocating positions on advisory boards—for example, for prisons or foster care agencies—to members of the faith community. The inclusion of FBOs was intended to increase the presence and access of religious organizations in the overall government structure. As one liaison told me, "One of the things we discovered is that as we were going through the grants process, if we say that the faith-based community is critically important and not only do we want them to apply, why don't we have them involved in a review panels for grants. And that's something we have not done in the past" (Oct. 10, 2004). Fifty-nine state laws have been passed that require including members of faith communities on advisory boards. As with many other faith-based measures, there are generally no mechanisms in place to control which groups are invited to join advisory boards; thus, there is the distinct possibility that certain types of faith-based advisors will be selected over others, favoring one brand of religion over others.

An example of this type of bill was passed in New Jersey in 2006, when a task force was established to study and develop recommendations on child abuse and neglect. The legislation outlined the duties of the task force as well as its composition. There were to be 29 members—16 members of state government and 13 members of the public. The latter were to be persons under the age of 21, members of the Association for Children of New Jersey, and representatives of an FBO (New Jersey 2006). Inclusion of advisory board members on the basis of their faith certainly creates access for the portion of the public that they represent, and the faith-based members are undoubtedly valuable and active resources in the community. However, questions about their membership on such boards can be raised when one considers the pluralistic nature of American religion: How are these members chosen? These laws contain no provisions governing which organizations or faiths should be chosen or even how that process of appointment should occur. This leaves open many questions: Is access available only to particular groups? Is the influence from certain segments of the population greater than that of others? How can equal access to all religious groups be ensured? This body of legislation also brings up questions about why these now widespread provisions to include members of the faith community on boards did not occur before 1996.

Such problems with implementation are not new. This is another area in which many people—both those who support and those who oppose the initiative—have noted the initiatives' ambiguity as something that is a

challenge, both as to effectiveness and to a clear understanding of the boundaries regarding religion and government.

FAITH-BASED APPROPRIATIONS. A somewhat less common, but more direct,
way that states have offered improved access to faith-based groups has been by
providing funding to such groups or to the offices that either directly (through
small grants) or indirectly (by means of informational resources) help FBOs
obtain funding. Since 1996, legislative appropriations processes in 16 states
have offered some type of funding to FBOs or OFBCIs. Forty-two separate
appropriation bills have allocated approximately $70 million (Table 4.2). This
effort to reach out to FBOs through direct funding of their work or through
funding to those that help them navigate the granting process has steadily
increased over time (Table 4.3). No faith-based appropriations were passed in
1996 or 1997, for example, but in 2007, a total of 10 laws were passed in
10 states. Along with the increase in number of appropriations bills passed, the
overall dollar amount has also increased. In Chapter 1, I noted how changes in
culture can eventually lead to material changes as well. At least anecdotally and
on a small scale, this does appear to be occurring in the states: increases in
symbolic implementation seem to be leading to increases in appropriations at
the state level. It will be interesting to see what happens with President Obama
in office and how the direction he takes on the initiatives affects state spending.

Meanwhile, the legislatures' appropriations have by and large been different from the ones noted by liaisons in Chapter 3; operating expenses for
liaisons and their offices have usually come from the general funds of the
agency in which the office or liaison is located. While faith-based appropriations have funded offices in some states, such as New Jersey and New Hamp-
shire, other states have funded specific programs. For example, in 2000, 2002,
and again in 2007, Florida passed appropriations bills related to the initiatives;
in the latter case, money was directed to faith-based and community groups for
teenage pregnancy prevention programs. "From the funds in Specific Appropriation 551, $1,500,000 of non-recurring maternal block grant trust funds
shall be used to fund community based and faith based teen pregnancy
prevention programs using medically and technically accurate information"
(Florida 2007). Again, the problem is not that public money has gone to faith-
based groups, which are often doing good work, but how much monitoring
and oversight occurs once the funds are distributed and why—since the playing field for faith-based groups was already open—there needed to be new
measures to seek out faith-based groups as partners.

Although many states have appropriated funds to the faith-based initiatives in a variety of ways and through a variety of types of legislation, only
a few states have had consistent appropriations efforts.[1] These include
Massachusetts, under Governor Mitt Romney (R); New Jersey, under Governors Christy Todd Whitman (R), Jim McGreevy (D), Richard Codey (D), and

TABLE 4.2. Faith-Based Appropriations: Number of Laws and Appropriation Amounts, by State and Year (when two laws are noted these are separate appropriation bills)

State	Year(s)	No. Laws	Appropriations	Amounts	Bill Numbers
AK	2007	1	$1,212,100[1]		ALS28-HB95
AL	2005	2	$150,000	$67,863	ALS173-HB248, ALS315-SB1
AL	2006	2	$83,721	$150,000	ALS335-SB75, ALS282-HB272
AL	2007	2	$150,000	$200,000[2]	ALS361-HB213, ALS282-HB208
CT	2004	1	$150,000		ALS216- HB5692
FL	2000	1	$1,000,000		ALS166-HB2145
FL	2002	1	$50,000		ALS394-HB27
FL	2007	1	$1,500,000		ALS72-SB2800
IN	2005	1	$341,209		ALS246-HEA1001
IN	2007	1	$244,064		ALS234-HEA1001
LA	2001	1	$3,150,000		ALS12-HB1
MA	2000–2004	5	$50,000	per year	ALS159-H5300, ALS177-HB4800 ALS184- HB5300, ALS26-HB4004 ALS149-HB4850
NC	2005	2	$2,000,000	$2,000,000	ALS345-HB320, ALS276-SB622
ND	2007	1	$25,000		ALS28-SB2001
NH	2007	1	$200,000[3]		ALS262-HB1
NJ	1998–2000	3	$5,000,000	per year	ALS45-S.N.2000, ALS138-S.N.3000, ALS53-S.N.2000
NJ	2001	1	$6,000,000		ALS130-S.N.2500
NJ	2002	1	$4,000,000		ALS38-S.N.2003
NJ	2003–2004	2	$3,000,000	per year	ALS122-S.N.3000, ALS71-S.N.2005
NJ	2006	1	$2,555,000		ALS45-S.N.2007
NJ	2007	1	$2,500,000		ALS111-S.N.3000
OH	2001	1	$1,000,000		HB524
OH	2006	1	$11,312,500		HB699
OK	2007	1	$100,000		ALS234-HB1243
SC	2005	1	$200,000		Acts115-HB3716
TN	2007	1	$6,000,000		ALS603-SB2334
VA	2002	1	$100,000		ALS814-HB29
VA	2004	1	$100,000	$100,000 (2005)	ALS943-HB29
VA	2005	1	$300,000,	$500,000 (2006)	ALS951-HB1500
VA	2006	1	$300,000		ALS2-HB5012
VA	2007	1	$500,000		ALS847-HB1650

A total of 42 appropriations bills were passed in 16 states between 1998 and 2007. Data were collected from the LexisNexis database. The dates are the dates of passage, not necessarily the dates of funding.

1. Of this amount, $500,000 in general funds was to be used for no purpose other than grants to areas ineligible for Human Services Grants.
2. According to the legislation, "$200,000 shall be expended in coordination with the Alabama Board of Pardons and Paroles to partner with non-profit organizations to provide a comprehensive reentry and rehabilitation program to include job placement assistance, mentoring, drug counseling and faith-based activities for ex-offenders."
3. These funds were for fiscal year 2008–2009, but were appropriated in 2007 legislation.

TABLE 4.3. Number of Faith-Based Laws Passed, by Year (1996–2007)

Year	States (Number of Laws)	No. Laws	No. States
1996	none	0	0
1997	AZ (2), CA (1), FL (1), MI (1), TX (1)	6	5
1998	FL (2), ID (1), KY(1), NJ (1)	5	4
1999	AZ (2), CA (1), FL (1), LA (1), MI (1), NJ (1), TX (4)	11	7
2000	AZ (3), CA (2), CO (3), FL (7), KY (1), MA (1), MI (1), NJ (1)	19	8
2001	AK (1), AL (2), CA (1), FL (6), GA (1), IA (1), IN (1), LA (2), MA (1), MD (1), MN (1), MT (1), NC (1), NJ (2), NV (2), OH (2), OK (1), OR (2), TX (2), VA (1)	32	20
2002	AZ (1), CO (1), FL (4), LA (1), MA (1), NJ (3), OK (3), PA (1), VA (2)	17	9
2003	AZ (2), CA (1), FL (3), IA (1), IL (1), IN (3), KS (1), LA (1), MA (1), MD (2), MI (2), MN (1), MS (2), NJ (1), NM (3), OH (1), OK (3), OR (2), TX (4), WI (1)	35	19
2004	AK (1), AL (1), AZ (3), CO (1), CT (1), FL (4), IA (1), IN (1), KS (1), LA (2), MA (1), MD (1), MI (1), MO (1), MS (2), NJ (2), OK (1), OR (1), VA (2)	29	20
2005	AL (2), AR (1), AZ (4), CA (1), CO (2), FL (3), IL (1), IN (2), KY (2), MD (1), MN (1), NC (2), ND (3), NJ (2), NM (1), OH (2), SC (2), TN (2), TX (3), VA (2), WV (1)	40	21
2006	AL (2), AZ (3), FL (1), GA (1), IN (1), KS (1), KY (1), LA (3), MA (1), MD (2), MO (1), MS (2), NJ (2), OH (1), SC (1), TN (2), VA (4), WA (3)	32	18
2007	AK (3), AL (2), AR (3), AZ (4), FL (3), HI (1), IL (1), IN (1), MA (1), MD (2), MN (1), MO (1), MS (2), MT (1), ND (1), NH (1), NJ (1), OK (5), SC (1), TN (1), TX (6), VA (2), WA (1)	45	23

Data were collected from the LexisNexis database.

John Corzine (D); Ohio under Governors Taft (R) and Strickland (D); and Alabama, under Governor Bob Riley (R), which appropriated money to both the state OFBCI and faith-based treatment programs over a three-year period. Appropriations are generally fairly modest, with the average state's funding being on the order of a few hundred thousand dollars a year.

New Jersey is an exception to this rule, allocating approximately $3 million a year since 1998. In fact, the vast majority of state legislative funding of FBOs has come from this one state. When I spoke with New Jersey's FBL, he said that these appropriations were well managed and did not go to faith-based groups only on the basis of their faith components. Instead, he stated that this money went to both faith and community groups and that this funding was a necessary part of improving the social services sector by the addition of faith-based work, and that without money, real change could not occur.

The Ohio legislature also passed faith-based appropriations including $11 million to the governor's OFBCI for projects relating to the Ohio Strengthening Families Initiative (State of Ohio 2007b). These funds were intended to help alleviate child poverty and reduce out of wedlock births by giving grants through a competitive process to small faith-based groups and community organizations. This particular funding stream is important to understand because it only offers indirect funding through these small organizations to give volunteers vouchers for their work counseling. This enables Ohio to "not only to include faith-based along with secular mentoring organizations but also to offer, along with secular mentoring, mentoring that includes a spiritual emphasis and religious activities to those who seek such help" (Center for Public Justice 2009). Through using vouchers Ohio can offer religious counseling using state dollars and not be in violation of church-state separation because the funding is done indirectly.

While one might assume that most liaisons would desire this type of funding—and indeed some do—others whom I spoke with felt that funding FBOs through a state office was not the proper way to implement the initiative. One liaison argued that bringing in state money would only add to the controversy and could result in illegal actions:

> Every state is different, and states laws are different, so I really don't
> want to get entangled in being contrary to existing state law by
> being a funding office that causes a lot more issues [that] I think would
> stall this office out from fulfilling its mission, which is to get more
> federal dollars into the state to those nonprofits that provide the
> most needed services. If I try to move this office to a funding office,
> I think the goal would be pushed way back. (Dec. 13, 2005)

Even though there was a lack of consensus among liaisons about the role of their office, most felt—as many original supporters of the initiatives did—that while some states were stepping up to the plate to put their money where their faith-based talk was, there were still many unfulfilled promises about offers of greater resources to FBOs. This has been the main complaint of supporters of legislative appropriations. In a recent interview, Ron Sider, an evangelical activist, argued this point:

> I think that the faith-based initiative has been important, even historic.
> I think it did have the effect of developing a level playing field so that we
> no longer discriminated against FBOs when federal funds were available
> to nonprofits and other parts of the private sector. I think the President
> [Bush] failed in this regard by not providing more money. We needed
> what he did in terms of opening up the federal funding to FBOs. But we
> also needed more money, and he did the one but not the other. . . . I think
> what's happened is really far more important than many people realize,
> but we need more resources. (Quoted in Farris 2008)

Thus, although some supporters felt that a cultural change was in fact taking place because of things like legislation and the formation of faith-based government offices, the role of promised funds was not so apparent. This disagreement about whether state offices should fund FBOs or even whether states should fund the initiatives at all mirrors the larger debate among supporters about what the purpose of the initiatives was in the first place. If the initiatives are about discrimination and removing barriers, then simple changes in laws regarding access to level the playing field are appropriate. But if the initiatives are about changing the social services sector in order to get more help to the poor and needy by better funding a potential pool of providers, then changing culture and access is not even half the battle.

Of course, one facet of faith-based funding is ensuring that church-state boundaries are respected. If the Constitution states that government cannot establish religion, or prefer one religion over another in funding, then state actors must have a means for distributing funds in a way that is equally accessible to all and is not unconstitutional. However, a recent study found that many of the people responsible for implementing the initiatives and responding to Charitable Choice funding requests did not understand regulations regarding the constitutional issues of the establishment clause (Jacobson, Marsh, and Winston 2005). This leads one to ask: If those who are in charge of overseeing the initiatives do not understand the constitutional issues, how can we expect members of a small congregation who simply want to help their community to understand the issues? In fact, Wineburg (2007) has argued that this ambiguity is purposeful in the initiatives. He has proposed that state faith-based practices were specifically created in such an ambiguous and pliable manner so that, while not explicitly allowing FBOs who proselytize to receive government funds, they were implicitly condoning these efforts. Others who have a more favorable perspective on the initiatives may be less concerned about motives but are equally concerned about the consequences of such ambiguity for FBOs. In fact, some FBOs that have received funds have encountered problems because of this lack of clarity, and some have even been sued for their entangling religion with social services (see Chapter 3). So far, the consequences for governments have been minimal;[2] however, the consequences for some small FBOs have been lawsuits, which small organizations may not be able to handle. These complications may explain why this seemingly obvious type of legislation has not been not as common as one might expect. Other types of legislation manage to circumvent some of these complications.

CONTRACTING FOR SPECIFIC SERVICES. There are currently 50 state laws on the books that either itemize specific services to be run by FBOs, suggest that these services be run by FBOs, or regulate these services. Perhaps the most common—and most controversial—legislation of this type has been the creation of faith-based prison wings. One of the first examples of this was passed by the Texas legislature and signed into law by Governor George W. Bush, who had pressed for contracting and working with several organizations to provide faith-based services for the state.

These services included Chuck Colson's Prison Ministry, which became part of the Texas prison system. There are many who consider faith-based prison programs superior to other prison programs. For example, Byron Johnson (2004) found that prisoners from a prison fellowship program were less likely to reenter a life of crime. However, in a recent review of research on such programs, David Mears and his colleagues found little evidence to back up claims that these programs were more successful than others, but also very little evidence to the contrary (Mears et al. 2006). Their findings were described in a Florida State University faculty bulletin:

> Regardless of the definitions and measurements used and the manner in which findings were presented, the review found few studies that had generated data credible enough to justify public support—or outright rejection—of faith-based programming. As an example, Mears cites the Prison Fellowship Ministries, founded by Charles Colson, the former Nixon aide who became a born-again Christian while imprisoned for his part in the Watergate scandal. Colson has touted the success of his ministries based on studies that show lower recidivism rates among participants. However, Mears noted that the studies focused only on inmates who completed the program, while comparing its recidivism rates to those of all participants—including dropouts—of selected secular programs. (Fairhurst 2006: 5)

Some states at least acknowledge the need for documentation of claims of superior service. The State of Louisiana (1999) enacted a law to help develop a faith-based prison program that included such a provision:

> The legislature finds and declares that faith-based programs offered in state and private correctional institutions and facilities have the potential to facilitate inmate institution adjustment, help inmates assume personal responsibility and to reduce recidivism.... Such programs at correctional institutions and facilities of this state shall continuously:
>
> 1. Measure recidivism rates for all inmates participating in faith-based or religious programs.
> 2. Work toward increasing the number of volunteers ministering to inmates from various faith-based institutions in the state.
> 3. Develop community linkages with churches, synagogues, mosques, and other faith-based institutions to assist in the release of participants back into the community.

The State of Ohio (2007b) also used measured language when establishing a task force:

> Study seamless faith-based solutions to problems in the correctional system, focusing on diversion programs, programs and services in the

prison system and for families of incarcerated individuals, and the faith-based and nonprofit organizations that provide the programs and services. The task force shall examine existing faith-based programs in prisons in Ohio and other states and shall consider the feasibility of replicating programs from other states and developing model faith-based penal institutions, faith-based units within penal institutions, and faith-based programs to reduce recidivism of offenders after their release from prison, improve prison management, and deal with juveniles who have been held over to or are in the adult penal system or who have parents who are incarcerated.

The situation in Georgia provides one last, interesting example. The state passed legislation (State of Georgia 2006) stating that faith-based prison programs were the most effective in dealing with prisoners; therefore it created a prison chaplaincy appreciation day, arguing that "studies prove chaplaincy and faith-based programs have the strongest capacity for redeeming, rehabili-tating, and successfully moving inmates back to society." While prison cha-plains are certainly important, putting into statute the claim that faith-based programs are the most effective at dealing with prisoners is clearly a step beyond mere expression of appreciation. Taken together, these laws show how states have often favored a faith-based approach when dealing with prison and prison reform.

In addition to uncertainty about the effectiveness of such programs, however, some have noted that these systems can create unfair conditions. For example in a piece in the *New York Times*, Diana Henriques (2006) found that in Iowa prisons the conditions were much nicer in faith-based programs, but the qualifications for these programs barred access for some:

> The cells in [the faith-based unit] had real wooden doors and doorknobs, with locks. More books and computers were available, and inmates were kept busy with classes, chores, music practice and discussions. There were occasional movies and events with live bands and real-world food, like pizza or sandwiches from Subway. Best of all, there were opportunities to see loved ones in an environment quieter and more intimate than the typical visiting rooms.
>
> But the only way an inmate could qualify for this kinder mutation of prison life was to enter an intensely religious rehabilitation program and satisfy the evangelical Christians running it that he was making acceptable spiritual progress.

Iowa's state-funded faith-based prison wings were found to violate the estab-lishment clause (Hughes 2006). Nonetheless, states continued to offer faith-based prison wings that gave special privileges to inmates who selected this option. Although these special privileges are viewed as a problem by those who see them as an example of coerced conversion, states continued to actively pursue these prison wings under the hope and assumption that they would offer a way out for prisoners who had few other options.

In one state where there was considerable outreach effort directed at creating faith-based dorms in prisons, there was also some effort to create secular options for the inmates. In this case the secular dorms were labeled "life skills building dorms." The liaison told me, "See, here's the interesting thing: we have a waiting list of the faith-based ones, but we don't for the secular right now, so there's a lot more [demand for] faith-based" (Feb. 9, 2005). Nonetheless, the availability of a secular option—unpopular as it might be— is important for those who view state funding of specifically religious programs as unconstitutional, particularly when incentives (such as TV and more recreation time) are offered only to inmates who join religious prison wings. Creating a specifically secular option does mitigate at least some of this concern. Proponents of the faith-based options, however, argue that it is the faith-based community that is most willing to come in to do this kind of work. As the same liaison told me, "We have over a thousand volunteers come into that facility each week. Providing programming, really any kind of public dollars will never be used to promote any kind of faith in those prisons. It's all outside resources from those faith and community volunteers" (Feb. 9, 2005). So while a secular option may be available, the legislation of prison treatment and reentry reinforces reliance on the faith-based community.

While I have focused here on prison programs, states have also funded faith-based programs related to other service needs. As just one example, the State of Louisiana (2001) passed a requirement that any youth placed in a transitional residence program must be given a faith-based option.

OTHER MEASURES. States have passed several other types of legislation to create greater access for faith-based groups. For example, three states altered licensing requirements for FBOs, making it easier for such organizations to participate in social services activity. The most controversial of these laws was passed in Texas in 1997; it exempted faith-based drug treatment programs from regular licensing requirements (see Chapter 2 for a more detailed discussion). This law was eventually overturned by the legislature in 2001 because of the number of complaints and lawsuits filed (Ebaugh 2003). Similar issues of potential privilege have also been found in legislation that creates grant-writing programs specifically for FBOs or in appropriations that single out faith-based groups over other providers. In several recent cases in California, Texas, and Wisconsin, funding by the state for faith-based groups that were singled out as preferred providers, either stopped before the cases went to trial to avoid violating church-state separation, or the court ruled that these funding decisions were unconstitutional and favored religious groups (Freedom From

Religion Foundation 2002). The presence of these policies favoring faith-based groups in decision making about grants and funds does lead to questions about the rather opaque world of grant-making at the state level. With these changes and attempted changes in legislation and in government culture, it appears that an environment in which being faith-based is important may be developing; state government workers and secular nonprofits may feel the need to become more faith-based or to partner with FBOs to increase their chances of getting a grant—which would create yet another indirect route to greater faith-based social services activity.

Restrictive or Regulatory Legislation

Only five states have enacted laws that restrict activities related to the faith-based initiatives: Maryland (2003), Oregon (2003), Texas (2003), Minnesota (2005), and Virginia (2005). For example, the State of Maryland (2003) passed a law that specifically declared that the state could not spend tax money on faith-based efforts: "No funds in this budget may be expended pursuant to, or in furtherance of, any policy or program the purpose of which is exclusively or primarily to promote or facilitate the participation of FBOs in state programs providing health, social, or education services, unless that policy or program is principally authorized by an act of the 2003 general assembly."

An additional three states—California (2003), Colorado (2005), and Mississippi (2006)—have required that FBOs get separate 501(c)3 status for their social services activities. While this was standard practice before Charitable Choice was enacted, since then churches and religious groups without separate 501(c)3 entities have been able to receive government money and run programs directly through their main religious organizations. Some have argued that by thus allowing both religious and secular activities to be run under a single umbrella by a religious group can make it very difficult to determine the sources of money spent on any given program—or exactly where money received from the government is being spent. Having organizations maintain a separate 501(c)3 often clears up much of this confusion.

What is perhaps most remarkable about restrictive and regulatory faith-based legislation is its scarcity, particularly when compared to the number of statutes that grant funding, establish links between FBOs and government, or create a friendlier environment that promises greater participation.

Patterns in Legislation

In addition to the patterns in the types of legislation discussed above, two other patterns regarding statutory changes stand out. These include some patterns in location (which I will briefly outline here and treat in more detail in Chapter 6) and patterns in the timing of implementation.

Patterns in Location

Interestingly, of the 41 states that have enacted laws relevant to this discussion, only seven—Arizona, Florida, Louisiana, New Jersey, Oklahoma, Texas, and Virginia—have enacted more than 10. In fact, three states have been responsible for generating more than half the legislation related to the faith-based initiatives: Arizona, Texas, and Florida have together enacted 79 laws (Table 4.4). Florida alone has passed 35 laws, or 12 percent of all state-level legislation. The two states

TABLE 4.4. Number of Faith-Based Laws Passed, by State (1997–2007)

No. of Laws	State(s)	Year of First Law
35	FL	1997
24	AZ	1997
20	TX	1997
16	NJ	1998
13	OK, VA	2001
10	LA	1999
9	AL, IN, MD	2001
8	MS	2003
7	CA	1997
7	CO, MA	2000
6	MI	1997
6	OH	2001
5	KY	1998
5	AK, OR	2001
5	TN	2005
4	MN	2001
4	NM	2003
4	AR, ND, SC	2005
4	WA	2006
3	IA, NC	2001
3	IL, KS	2003
3	MO	2004
2	GA, MT, NV	2001
1	ID	1998
1	PA	2002
1	CT, WY	2004
1	WV	2005
1	HI, NH	2007

Data were collected from the LexisNexis database. Nine states have passed no laws related to the faith-based initiatives. Perhaps not surprisingly, most of the states that passed no such legislation are in the Northeast, where activity is minimal (DE, ME, NY, RI, VT); the other states that had not passed faith-based laws are NE, SD, UT, and WI.

in which a member of the Bush family has been governor—Florida and Texas—together account for 55 laws, or 20 percent of all state legislation. This preponderance of legislation in Louisiana, Oklahoma, Texas, and Florida suggests that a strong presence of the evangelical movement early was a likely cause of greater implementation, regardless of the party of the governor. While this is only anecdotal evidence, Chapter 6 explores this issue in more depth and finds similar results.

While it may not be surprising that Florida and Texas have passed a great deal of faith-based legislation, Arizona and New Jersey also continue to be leaders in state faith-based policy implementation and administration. One possible part of the explanation for this may be that in both states, the person who brought the initiatives to the state was an active in their states black religious communities, communities that have traditionally been strong supporters of the initiatives. Therefore, the idea of creating more funding that could go to churches and their programs could have been part of the reasons for backing such policies. In addition, Arizona has had a consistently strong conservative evangelical movement presence in state politics since 1994 (Conger 2008a, 2008b), pointing to at least some cohesion of support for the initiatives in states where the conservative evangelical movement first made a strong showing.

Patterns in Time

Most states adopted faith-based practices after the 2000 and 2004 presidential elections, when it became more politically feasible to do so because it was clear that the faith-based initiatives were going to remain on the national landscape. For example, before the 2000 election there were only 2 states with OFBCIs; as I write, there are 22, six of which were established through legislation. This parallels the legislative presence of the initiatives, which has exhibited a similar increase over time. Clearly, states have become increasingly active in incorporating more faith-based groups into the social services sector in a variety of ways.

Table 4.3 clearly shows this dramatic increase, both in both the number of laws passed and in the number of states passing them. As it became clear over time that the faith-based initiatives, in some form, were not going to fall from the federal agenda anytime soon, states took their cue.

The Stories in Faith-Based Policies

Political scholars have argued that in many cases it is far better for legislators political career to do something, even if the gestures are largely symbolic, than appear to be doing nothing (Stone 1988). Through the use of political symbols in legislation, the faith-based initiatives legitimate two arguments of their supporters: first, that faith-based groups have been discriminated against, and new policy must be created to remedy the discrimination; and second, that faith-based policies offer a way to cope with the problems created by welfare reform. This seems to be the strategy one encounters when exploring the types of faith-based policies created at the state level. Clearly, some states have created legislation that has helped fund faith-based groups to provide social services, but by and large the laws related to the initiatives have merely added to the story that says the mere removal of barriers will allow new—and possibly better—groups to begin to take up the social services challenge.

Although the administrative and bureaucratic changes involved with FBLs and OFBCIs have made many inroads, these changes can be fairly easily altered by new governors or agency heads; laws, on the other hand, are comparatively permanent. In one state, the liaison spoke to me about the importance of creating an advisory board by statute rather than by administrative fiat: "I guess we'll be the second state to put this commission into statute so that it doesn't matter who is governor" (April 30, 2005).

Necessary Ambiguity

In analyzing federal faith-based policy, several writers have noted both its tendency to be ambiguous and how this ambiguity is part of its power (Kuo 2006a; Wineburg 2007). The malleability of faith-based policy, its openness to myriad interpretations, is important because ambiguous political symbols allow coalitions to be built up around policies and enable leaders to take actions that assemble broad bases of support (Stone 1988). Where more detail is available and ambiguity is reduced, the base of support may be narrower. In analyzing the data, I found most laws did not require a specific action; instead they suggested partnerships or put a person in office as a symbol of outreach and help to the faith-based community. The result is a tapestry of legislation that illuminates the necessity for state actors to appear as if they are doing something to address the needs of social services sector; in fact, the vast majority of laws enacted in this regard are largely unnecessary and use the symbolism of religion to create an illusion of action.

Culture and Connection

State faith-based policies mirror what is happening at the federal level. Instead of focusing on new funding, the original stated goal of supporters of the initiatives, most states have moved toward goals of changing culture and creating connection. State legislative changes are part of the overall top-down strategy of faith-based policy implementation (Wineburg 2007). State actors get to claim faith-friendliness without having to fund the initiatives in a way that is costly or controversial. An important point is that these policies are generally without mechanisms to measure results, so state policy-makers can reap the benefits of being faith-friendly without having to shift funds, create controversy, or measure results. As Wineburg and other skeptics of faith-based initiatives have argued, the politics behind the initiatives are not really about helping religious groups who provide good social services and create hope in places where there is little to be hopeful about. Rather, it is largely a political tool and, as such, has not achieved the concrete goal that many of its first supporters had so fervently sought—new funding for faith-based groups and the social services arena.

Summary and Conclusion

Implementation of new state policies and practices may be more important because of what the policies and practices represent. Clearly, states have increased their legislative implementation of a variety of faith-based practices over time. With legislation, as with other aspects of the initiatives, the ways in which states were creating new faith-based practices were less about new funding for the social services sector than about creating laws and practices that intertwine religion and government in new ways.

5

Calling All the Faithful

*Faith-Based Conferences and Liaison Choices
as Symbolic Politics*

I was somewhat surprised that at the federal government's expense
there was so much out and out religion being displayed and discussed
at these conferences.

—Faith-based liaison interview, February 8, 2005

What we're working on is to change the culture, to recognize that
there are results, fantastic results being achieved, and that those of
us who are policymakers must welcome those who are achieving the
good results of the work of faith.

—President George Bush, White House Conference
on Faith-Based Initiatives, Los Angeles, California,
March 3, 2004

In chapter 3, I outlined the tasks undertaken by FBLs and looked at
how various states implemented practices to increase linkages
between public agencies and faith-based groups. One way that some
states have chosen to build and strengthen such linkages has been to
hold conferences centered on the faith-based initiatives. State
faith-based conferences are essentially public forums for the
faith-based initiatives, sponsored by state funds. Since 1996, at least
23 states have held some sort of faith-based conference. In this
chapter, I describe how faith-based conferences blur the line between
church and state by incorporating a religious message into a public
policy debate. This chapter also examines how this part of faith-based
implementation has been specifically aimed at reaching out to the
black religious community, through the use of religious symbols that

are often found in black religious ceremonies. By relying on culturally resonant religious political messages, the political backers of faith-based initiatives have mainly, (although not exclusively), attempted to build alliances with black religious groups to create a stronger support network for faith-based practices at the state level (Kuo 2006a). After looking at the conferences in some detail, I close the chapter by revisiting liaisons in the light of symbolic politics and race.

Faith-based conferences tell stories in the public arena with the legitimacy and authority of the government behind them. Although the faith-based initiatives have been presented—by those who first supported them and professed their benefits—as a means of alleviating poverty and removing a burden from government, close examination reveals that there are also political goals. The policies and practices of the faith-based initiatives appeal to a number of religious groups: conservative evangelicals, some in the Catholic Church, and, perhaps most important, many African Americans who are involved in their religious communities. In my study of the initiatives at the state level, I have found that state implementation is being used, in part, to try to create new allies for the conservative evangelical movement's goal of softening the boundary between church and state. The presentation of faith-based conferences, along with the appointment of liaisons from black churches, has been part of a symbolic political strategy used to create just such allies.

Conferences for Faith-Based Organizations

At this writing, 23 states sponsor faith-based conferences (see Table 3.1). The conferences usually consist of a main informational session followed by break-out sessions that focus on various topics, such as the grant-writing process, the capacity that groups need to obtain a federal or state grant, and the available resources that can increase this capacity. The conferences for FBOs serve multiple functions, from bringing awareness about opportunities to partner with government to the faith-based community and clarifying the government granting process for them, to allowing liaisons to learn about the state of the religious sector in their area. In addition to serving these very practical functions, however, the conferences also serve political functions, using religious messages and the legitimacy of the state to bring support from religious groups for the initiatives (Kuo 2006a).

A Forum for Faith-Based Organizations

Through conferences for faith-based organizations, liaisons were able to create a public forum around the initiatives and inspire religious groups to become more involved in the government and social services sector. Conferences allowed churches and government actors to come together to discuss the initiatives. "We had our first statewide conference on FBCI on April 30," one liaison told me in an interview. "It was a good networking opportunity for the different faith-based and community organizations to come together and talk about issues that they are facing" (Feb. 11, 2005).

Other state liaisons partnered with various state organizations to focus more on bringing information to faith-based groups: "One of the other state agencies—actually, it's a division of the Department of Human Services; it's called [the state] Drug Abuse Prevention—they have a conference that is solely focused on the faith-based community.... They brought in a group from St. Louis to put on that conference that was a two-day event. That was solely based on faith-based capacity-building" (Nov. 30, 2004). In some cases, the focus was primarily grant-writing. Speakers at these conferences would give guidelines on how create a separate 501(c)3 arm, or about the CCF, for example. Sometimes the topics covered were more basic:

> In September we had what we call the grant writing triathlon, and we had it at one of the local churches, and we had like 125 people. ... It was an all-day information session, and in the morning we had folks from the district government come and talk about funding opportunities and what they look for in a competitive grant. And then we had somebody from the foundation community, and then in the afternoon we had a federal panel where we had folks from the Justice Department's Faith-Based Office, HUD's Faith-Based Office, and the Department of Education's Faith-Based Office ... to talk about opportunities in their different agencies and what they look for in competitive grants, and it was really eye-opening for a lot of the organizations because they talked about things that they never even considered, like following directions. (Dec. 19, 2004)

Like many liaisons, this one had not realized that there would be so much remedial work needed to get organizations on track for government funding.

This liaison went on to say that these conferences were not limited to faith-based groups, but were often attended by groups that had heard of them by word of mouth from various other community organizations. This brings up an important point: While most of these conferences were open to the public, publicity was often limited, so participation was in turn limited to those organizations that were already in the "faith-based loop." When invitations or e-mail notices were sent, they tended to go to FBOs with which the liaisons had previous contact or to those that had previously contacted the state about the faith-based initiatives. Therefore, information on a conference may not have reached all the religious groups in a community, much less unaffiliated members of the community. For example, another liaison said that although they tried to put out the word about conferences, it was really up to the churches and religious groups to call them or look on their Web site to get information about a conference (Nov. 30, 2004). While this may have worked well for the more experienced social services groups, this method of spreading the word requires technological infrastructure resources that many faith-based groups still do not have, and so they are unlikely to get the information presented at conferences.

A Source of Information for Liaisons

As noted above, perhaps one of the most important aspects of these conferences is that they gave the liaisons a greater understanding of the capacities of the FBOs in attendance. Even though many of the FBOs said they felt ready to receive government funds, liaisons often learned that most small FBOs were completely unprepared to do so. For example, the liaison from one southern state reported that a survey of the participants at the state's first conference revealed that most of the groups did not have access to some very basic technology:

> The first two years, it's really about building capacity and really
> looking at what the needs are in terms of grants. We were going out
> there, and we were finding so many organizations that didn't even
> have an e-mail address or a computer, you know. . . . So we partnered
> with one of our state agencies—the Department of Management
> Services has a subagency, and they have what you call the digital divide
> warehouse. . . . So when an organization would come to me and say,
> "Well I don't have a computer, or I don't have these," I can always send
> them to the digital divide warehouse . . . and then if they don't have an
> e-mail, I ask, "Are you close to a library?" And then we get them an
> e-mail address and get them connected. (Feb. 9, 2005)

This reflects a technological capacity far short of that needed to manage a government account. In another state, 21 participants who attended a series of trainings were eligible to receive a mini-grant; however, much to the surprise of the liaison in charge, only 14 of those FBOs even applied for the grant: "I was like, this was money really given away . . . and [the application] was no more than two pages . . . [so] it was really a test to see if they would do it by a due date. They couldn't even do that" (Dec. 19, 2004).

So while political supporters argue that these faith-based groups are the ones who should take over the provision of social services from the government, the reality that the liaisons face is often very different. Further, the liaisons are not the only ones who meet with a surprising reality at these conferences. Most of the liaisons I spoke with reported that a common misconception among groups that attended the conferences was that the faith-based initiatives meant that "there was some pot of faith-based money out there." In fact, not only do most FBLs not have the authority to distribute such money, there are usually no state funding streams set aside specifically for FBOs at all. This general lack of understanding about the initiatives appears consistently when FBLs discuss their attempts to work with the community. The misconceptions held by FBOs are reasonable given the federal and state governments' initial publicity for the initiatives, which described them as new money for faith-based social services.

Collaboration in Conferences: The Role of the White House

While a few states did not offer their own conferences,[1] most states had been in contact with the White House, and many had received information about the initiatives and ideas for their own conferences from conferences sponsored by the White House. Liaisons consistently mentioned strong ties with key actors in the Bush administration that they had formed during these conferences, especially with Jim Towey, the second head of the White House OFBCI and Bobby Polito, the head of Health and Human Services from 2001 to 2005. These key federal actors were mentioned by almost every liaison as people that had either approached them with ideas for their state to become more active or that they could go to for assistance in creating a more faith friendly environment. In addition, liaisons had also made connections at conferences with Stanley Carlson-Thies at the Center for Public Justice and Amy Sherman at the Hudson Institute, both strong and early supporters of the initiative and the general principles behind limiting church and state separation. These conferences gave the White House an ability to have an exclusive forum to shape the initiative, creating excitement and engagement with state level actors. One state liaison discussed how he got the idea for his own symposium from attending a White House symposium:

> During the first three months, I had an opportunity to visit Washington. I met with staff from the White House OFBCI . . . and for our symposium that we are having on March 14, it's bringing religious leaders from across the state. Our keynote speaker will be the director of the White House OFBCI, Mr. Jim Towey. So we have a good working relationship with Washington. . . . I thought [the symposium] was very helpful, and actually the symposium that we are planning for March 14 really stemmed from my two visits to Chicago and Washington. I felt that we needed to do something like that in [this state]. (April 30, 2005)

Another liaison saw the experience as a welcoming to the faith community from the government, something she felt was much needed. "To me it was . . . like we're here, we want to be friendly, we're trying to make it easier" (Feb. 7, 2005). One liaison that had been the liaison over several years described how he saw the conferences as religious events that only eventually began to focus on limitations and boundaries.

> The conferences during the Clinton administration, which were quite honestly . . . saturated with elements of faith and religiosity, invited speakers from the faith community who were virtually giving sermons to the audience on community involvement and the mandate that people of faith have to get into the community. I think a lot of it was without boundaries which later began to be established . . . but this [establishing of boundaries] did not extinguish the faith components that were being added by special speakers and workshop presenters who came from the faith community. They all clearly articulated that what they were doing in the way of social services was being done from a commitment of faith and as a manifestation of their faith. (Feb. 8, 2005)

Another liaison spoke of how much they enjoyed their work and collaboration with the White House, "They support us in every manner that we ask them to. It's a collaborative relationship and a true partnership" (June 25, 2004).

Liaisons, however, did not agree whether these White House meetings and conferences were helpful. One liaison found the experience not as helpful as he had hoped, stating that the meeting he attended was "not put on very well" (Oct. 13, 2004). Another liaison saw them as "expensive and difficult to track what you get for them" (March 28, 2005). An additional liaison described going to a number of conferences and why he saw them as important:

> I went to a White House conference in Pittsburgh just because I wanted to see what that was like. And then I went to HHS [Health and Human Services] conference in Atlanta. And I went to the White House [for] an event in June, and then, you know the Roundtable for Religion and Social Welfare Policy. . . . I went there in November, right after I was appointed, and when I went to that I stayed an extra day, and I . . . went and saw all those guys. So that was the first time I met most of them. And then I went to the Roundtable again. . . . It seems like pretty frequently, it seems like every two months or so.

This liaison argued that the information provided was not very important, but the networking was:

> The information—I sort of make it my business to know what's going to happen at those before it happens. I don't want to learn about it for the first time at a conference. So from that sense, what's very helpful about them, the reason that you go to conferences, in my opinion, is to network and get inspired. And also to get information, but in this thing I'm paying more attention to structure, about what works and how it might work in our state, and I'm really spending time at

networking. I'm yakking at Brad, and I'm yakking at Terri, and, you know, listening to what they're doing and letting them teach me, and I think that's why you do things like that. I don't want to sound negative: I think they were all very good events, I really do, and I'm pleased that they did them. But I mean, I would feel bad if I went there and was surprised by anything. (March 15, 2005)

It is perhaps not surprising that the main benefit of the national conferences was to create networks among the states, the liaisons, and the White House. But it is important to note that it was through these conferences that states and the White House engaged religious organizations with the promise of giving them better access to money to provide social services. While information on access to funds was provided at these conferences, their other function—that of building up a faith-based network and bureaucracy—was certainly at least as important, and was crucial for its role in helping to create a sustainable faith-based movement:

> The White House put it on, and they invited people. . . . It wasn't like their normal regional White House conference, but they invited people from around the country. To some degree, it was invite-only. . . . President Bush spoke, but the fascinating piece was that there was a track for just state- or city-oriented folks who could sit down and talk with other folks of like minds who are looking from a city standpoint or state standpoint. (Oct. 10, 2004)

Through the conferences the Bush White House was able to build strong connections and support for the initiative within states and local governments, potentially creating even broader political support.

Even some of the original proponents of these conferences now recognize their use as political tools. In his book on the faith-based initiatives, Kuo (2006b: 1) stated that the White House OFBCI would "hold roundtable events for threatened incumbents with faith and community leaders . . . using the aura of our White House power to get a diverse group of faith and community leaders to a 'nonpartisan' event discussing how best to help poor people in their area"—with the clear purpose of getting votes for Republican candidates. Kuo later argued that this strategy had worked, with the Republican candidate having won in 19 of the 20 races associated with faith-based conferences.

The Promise of New Allies

As I noted earlier, policies based on beliefs and ideas shared with other groups can create new allegiances and political allies. While the conservative evangelical movement had already gained much influence in the Republican Party, the faith-based initiatives gave it an opportunity to move beyond its base to gain even broader influence; black churches were excellent candidates to become allies in this. The potential support for the faith-based initiatives from black churches has two sources. First, black churches have been more likely than others to have previously partnered with government (Chaves 1999). Second, blacks are closest to white evangelicals in their beliefs about the role that religion should play in politics and public life, with 59 percent of black Americans believing that religion should play a greater role in American politics (Pew 2000, 2001); in fact, most felt that that religion and government should not be separated but should be close in their relationship. Together, these indicated a potential for an early base of support for faith-based initiatives from black churches; political leaders and policy-makers could use faith-based initiatives as an instrumental political tool to attempt to change the dynamics between religion and politics in black churches (Harris 1999, 2001; Smith and Harris 2005).

The story of Bishop Sedgwick Daniels, a well-known African American pastor, illustrates how the Bush White House went out of its way to use the initiative to build support among those in the black religious community. A longtime Democrat and supporter of Clinton and Gore, Bishop Daniels came to the Republican Party after Bush was elected in 2000. Why? It was largely because President Bush used his influence to persuade Bishop Daniels that not only would he be personally helped through the faith-based initiative, but that the Republican Party stood for ideals that were closest to his own. The *Los Angeles Times* reported that Daniels,

> received $1.5 million in federal funds through Bush's initiative to
> support faith-based social services. Daniels' political conversion, and
> similar transformations by black pastors across the nation, form a little-
> known chapter in the playbook of Bush's 2004 reelection campaign—
> and may mark the beginning of a political realignment long sought by
> senior White House advisor Karl Rove and other GOP strategists.
> Daniels says it was not the federal money that led him to endorse the
> Republican candidate last year, but rather the values of Bush and other
> party leaders who champion church ministries, religious education
> and moral clarity. (Hamburger, Riccardi, and Wallsten 2005)

Daniels's new support for the Republican Party was not without critics, especially from other leaders in the black religious community; however, his defection from Democratic Party politics was one sign that the Republican Party was making some inroads in getting leading black pastors to the GOP through faith-based initiatives and morality politics.

While the election of Barack Obama as president in 2008 signals that this strategy has stopped working, before 2008, the Republican Party had hoped for more stories like Bishop Daniels using faith-based initiatives in two ways to build coalitions with black churches: First, many states have offered government-funded faith-based conferences that rely on cultural cues used in religious ceremonies in some black churches (Pattillo-McCoy 1998), thus creating a cultural blurring of the line separating church and state. Second, nearly half of the states that have created of FBL positions have appointed blacks to fill the positions. I argue that these aspects of the initiatives represent a multilayered attempt to create new political allies for faith-based policies in black religious communities. These liaisons and conferences have, indeed, begun to build a new, top-down political and social movement base for a policy that did not come from within those religious or political circles.

In her work on black church culture and politics, Patricia Pattillo-McCoy (1998) argued that the language and symbols used in black church settings create the necessary tools for social action. She found that the same aspects of religion that were present at black religious events were also used at black political events. These cultural cues, she argued, created an environment in which social action about a particular issue is expected.

A key aspect of faith-based policy implementation has been the sponsorship of faith-based conferences aimed specifically at creating ties within black community, with these conferences actively employing and relying on the same cues to social action. However, instead of social action on social justice or poverty issues, these conferences were aimed at generating support for faith-based initiatives and consequently for their main proponents, the Republican Party and the conservative evangelical movement. While this is perhaps not the first time that political leaders have used conferences to help build coalitions with black religious leaders, these conferences are another facet of faith-based policy and practice that makes calls to action through symbolic politics that have a two-tiered goal: changing the balance of political power within the United States by forming new coalitions with certain segments of the vote—in this case, the black religious vote—and using this increased political power to create a new norm for the relationship between religion and state government.

Race, Politics, and the Faith-Based Initiatives

The church has consistently been a cornerstone of black communities.[2] As the center of the Civil Rights movement and the place where most African American political leaders still get their start, the church is not just the spiritual, but also the political, center of many black communities, often working to create new social policies focused on structural changes to society, such as ending legal segregation and ensuring voting rights.

Race and the Role of Religion in Public Life

In several recent opinion polls (Pew 2000, 2001, 2003), African Americans report seeing religion as crucial to public life. This view of religion as integral to politics and to successful political leadership is very similar to that of white evangelicals. Both groups view religion as necessary to successful political leadership and to the well-being of civil society. In addition, the two groups also score closely on variables related to the role that religion should play in the social services sector, seeing faith as a necessary component to solving social ills such as poverty and addiction. Here the similarities end, however. While white evangelicals tend to see individual salvation as the road to success, happiness, and well-being,[3] blacks tend to believe that there are structural causes of poverty, rather than only individual, personal causes (Harris 2001; Regnerus, Sikkink, and Smith 1999; Smith and Harris 2005). In the past, this difference has led the vast majority of blacks to side with the Democratic Party rather than the Republican Party, citing the Democrats as better able to see that there are structural barriers to full participation in the economy.

While a shift of black churches toward the Republican Party would mark a change of this structural versus individual aspect of their viewpoint on social policy, the faith-based initiatives do align with what recent opinion polls have shown: that blacks tend to be very religious and to believe that religion should play a greater role in social policy and politics. The early supporters of the faith-based initiatives attempted to move toward new alliances with conservative black churches that focused on morality politics, which closely aligned them with the white evangelical movement (Edsall 2006). Such alignments would move members of black churches beyond the traditional alliance between religion and politics in the black community and beyond existing alliances with mainstream and liberal denominations that had previously focused on social services and political activism and on social institutions and structures.

Recent opinion polls have shown that it is not just in conservative black congregations that one finds views similar to those of white evangelicals on issues such as gay marriage and the relationship between religion and politics (Pew 2008). Instead, blacks of various religious backgrounds tend to have conservative views on these issues, thus creating the potential for conservative political and movement leaders to use policies related to these issues to make political allies of black churches and religious actors.[4] This is what Drew Smith (2005: 195) calls the "divide and conquer" strategy of the Republican Party: the strategic use of policies such as the faith-based initiatives can "chip away at certain segments of the black vote"—which has traditionally been Democratic—to gain a majority for the Republican Party. There are sufficient similarities between black religious actors and the white evangelical movement in their views of religion, politics, and morality to lead to an alliance of sorts.

This instrumental political potential of the faith-based initiatives was seen early on by researchers, who found that the actions of advocates indicated that they were using the initiatives for political reasons rather than for their stated reasons of helping the poor and needy (Walsh 2001). For example, in 1996, then-Governor George W. Bush of Texas became the most vocal advocate of the faith-based initiatives, and Texas became the state with the greatest amount of activity surrounding the initiative. One segment of the population from whom Governor Bush hoped to gain support was the black conservative religious community. In his first faith-based meeting, Bush noticeably excluded most black religious leaders in the state, not inviting those from the two largest denominations, in favor of a select group of conservative black religious leaders. This attempt at aligning certain segments of the black religious vote with the faith-based initiatives was met with cries of outrage from the excluded groups, which had traditionally been the most active in providing social services. Learning from this experience, Bush, as president, reached out to a wider array of black religious groups, including those denominations he had originally excluded (Smith and Harris 2005).

Race and Party Politics

Black churchgoers do not constitute a homogeneous religious community, and there has been a shift within the black voting bloc over the last few election cycles that has given the Republican Party hope of gaining a larger segment of the black vote.[5] In the 2000 election, Republican presidential candidate George W. Bush received 8 percent of the black vote; in the 2004 election, this grew to 11 percent. While this difference may seem small, the shift was larger in some swing states, such as Ohio, where Bush got 16 percent of the black vote in 2004. Although it is unlikely that the entire shift was the result of religion, there is reason to suspect that the increasing presence of religion in public policy fostered by the Bush administration, along with the Republican Party's appeals to religion and morality, has had a positive effect on the number of black citizens now voting for the Republican Party. For example, in 2004, John Kerry received 20 percent less support among black conservative evangelicals than Al Gore had in 2000 (Hutchinson 2006). This potential to lure black voters from the Democratic Party has led some to suggest that the Republicans are using morality politics to not only firm their base but also to increase their appeal to blacks, conservative Hispanics, and conservative Jews, all groups that consider the moral compass of the country to be shifting in the wrong direction. I argue that the faith-based initiatives are policies originating from evangelicals within the Republican Party that were being used to appeal to certain segments of the black religious population to make this alliance, which may at first seem to be a strange one.

A policy environment that appeals to the morality politics of black church-goers may also be more likely to create other social policies that favor the intermingling of religion and politics. The faith-based initiatives are not the only policies created by Republicans—particularly the evangelical movement within that party—that try to tap into the conservative black vote. Political analysts have argued that the Republican Party has also hoped that policies directed against gay marriage would appeal not just to conservative black voters but to the large numbers of more politically moderate blacks whose beliefs about homosexuality are similar to those of conservative evangelicals (Pew 2008). The faith-based initiatives and gay marriage policies may be part of an overarching political strategy being used to move religious black voters away from the Democratic Party and toward the Republican Party—while also shifting the focus on solving social problems from the systemic to the individual and to morality politics.[6]

Building Alliances via Faith-Based Liaisons and Conferences

As noted earlier, I found two ways in which African American religious audiences have been engaged by faith-based initiatives at the state level: black religious actors have been appointed to fill many FBL positions and faith-based conferences tailored to black religious communities have been offered. As several liaisons noted, black churches have always been locations for social services and community outreach long before faith-based initiatives. One liaison discussed how their outreach to religious groups found a natural audience with black religious groups. "Some of the people I've met have been doing this for decades, there are a lot of people, especially in the African American community, who've been working as faith-based groups doing literacy and job training and these things for years well before the initiative was formed, it is just what they've been doing in their lives" (Sept. 9, 2004).

Conferences as Black Religious Events

In this section, I focus on the use of conferences, looking at four such events: two in Arizona, one in New Jersey, and one in Washington, D.C. These four conferences offered not only variety in geographical setting but also in the type of sponsorship, intended audiences, and in the level of religious activity present.

EVENTS AND AUDIENCES. Of the two in Arizona, one was a statewide conference aimed largely at the black community and sponsored jointly by the state of Arizona and White House OFBCIs. The other was a local event, sponsored between the Department of Labor, the City of Tucson, and Pima County; it was the only one of the four that attracted a primarily white audience and the only one that had no religious elements present. The conference in New Jersey, like the state conference in Arizona, was sponsored by the state's OFBCI and was aimed at churches in the state of New Jersey. The conference in Washington, D.C., was a national conference and had participants from around the country; it included several speeches and discussions by state FBLs. The three large-scale conferences attracted several hundred to over 1,000 participants each, with the vast majority—70 to 80 percent—of those participants being African American church leaders and activists. The larger events were held at large convention centers; the event in Tucson was conducted at a small municipal building, with the participants arranged around small tables of 8 to 10 people so they could easily interact with one another. Attending these four conferences allowed me to get a good feel for how they actually worked and to observe the group processes that occurred. I took detailed notes at all of these events on the actions and dialogue of both the conference leaders and the conference participants.

In addition to my own participation and research, descriptions and transcripts from proceedings at other state faith-based conferences were made accessible to me. And during my interviews with liaisons, I asked questions about any conferences that they had attended. The conferences I attended and describe here fit the general pattern described by the liaisons as well as information from other conference proceedings; thus, while they may not be an ideal sample, they do represent the general pattern of action at faith-based conferences across the country.

As described earlier in this chapter by one liaison, while the stated intention of these events was to bring information and awareness to faith-based leaders across the country, what actually happened was the generation of religion. These events moved from a strictly informative setting to a religious setting by using specific religious cues to signal to their largely African American audiences that although these were government-sponsored events, religion was not only accepted and welcome as part of the event, it *was* the event.

While most discussion on this subject has focused on how religion blurs either legal or institutional boundaries, there has rarely been discussion of how states can create religion through cultural means. However, once one enters a conference on faith-based initiatives, it is no longer difficult to think of the state as an actor in the cultural formation of religion: states are clearly creating religious events through their sponsorship of these informational conferences aimed at religious leaders.

In her work on black churches and political activities, Pattillo-McCoy (1998: 768) found that at political events in the black community, church leaders relied on cultural cues that were identical to those used in black church ceremonies; she argued that "black church culture constitutes a common language that motivates social action." How do these informational conferences turn into events that look more like church services than policy conferences? There are two ways that they act to generate religion. Religious exhortations are used by the leaders of the conference to engage the audience and inspire religious responses, and religious expression at the conferences is encouraged.

RELIGIOUS EXHORTATIONS BY LEADERS. The religious nature of the conferences was not hidden. "I am so proud to be in a room with so many religious fanatics," said Jim Towey, director of the White House OFBCI, at the White House conference on faith-based initiatives in June 2004. While each conference included a short discussion of the importance of the separation of church and state, and reminders that religious groups could not use public money for religious purposes, the tone of the meetings soon changed from secular or generically religious to a religious script readily found at black congregations across America. This was especially apparent at the conferences held in Washington, D.C., and New Jersey, and to a somewhat lesser degree at the conference in Phoenix, Arizona. Much of this religious fervor was expressed by the leaders of the conferences, with many of them making not only overt references to religion in general, but overt references to churches, Jesus, and being saved. In Washington D.C., at a conference with more than 1,600 religious leaders the cover of the Department of Labor's handbook showed a flaming shrub and stated "Not everyone has a burning bush to tell them their life's calling." After the gospel choir and opening prayer, President Bush continued this religious theme and discussed why he thought it was so important to host conferences like these across the country.

> So we [the federal government] have hosted regional conferences to raise the issue [of faith-based initiatives]. I try to talk about the faith-based initiative a lot. Part of my job is to say to the American people, here is a fantastic opportunity to help America become what we want it to be—a land of hope and promise and love and compassion. And so we're having regional conferences like this. I'm proud to report that we've reached more than 10,000 faith-based and community groups with the message that we want your help, that the federal government now welcomes your work. And do not fear being discriminated against by the government. . . . And we're making progress. We're changing the attitude here in Washington, D.C. . . . Listen, what I'm telling you is, is that I told our government, the people in my government rather than fear faith programs, welcome them. They're changing America. They do a better job than government can do. (Former president George Bush June 1, 2004)

The comments that were made by then-president Bush were enthusiastically welcomed by the audience. Similar religiously laced speeches were repeated in varying ways by different speakers at three of the four conferences I attended. At the conference in New Jersey, there were repeated attempts on the part of the conference organizer to create a sense of religious feeling, and to arouse the fervor of the crowd. However, it was not until the keynote speaker, a black pastor from a local congregation, gave his talk during lunch that the event was transformed. He stared his talk by stating, "People of faith can move mountains," and telling them that "if God hasn't called you to do this, then go home." The pastor soon had most of the people in the room standing on their feet proclaiming their feelings. When he was done, the organizer came back on stage and declared that was what was needed at the conference was to "get some churchin' up in here." Once that happened, the tone of the conference changed from one of passivity to one of active engagement and religious proclamations.

GROUP INVOLVEMENT AND RELIGIOUS GENERATION. While the leaders of the conferences were integral in setting a tone that was welcoming to religious exhortations, the participants were actively involved in maintaining that tone. Once the leaders began, the audience soon realized that not only was audience participation acceptable, it was expected. Using religious cues common in black church celebrations, such as a call-and-response and spontaneous religious proclamations (Patillo-McCoy 1998), the audience was clearly attuned to this style of religious and political participation.

At the three conferences at which the majority of participants were black, the audience members created an atmosphere in which religion was integral to the discussion. For example, while President Bush was speaking at the White House conference, the women at my table began standing up, waving their arms, and proclaiming their agreement with what he was saying. They were clearly participating in the style of religious participation common in most black churches. The incorporation of ritualistic action into the conferences began with one woman standing, but soon the other four women at the table joined her; once standing, the women called out phrases such as "Praise Jesus!" or "Amen!" when the president made a statement that resonated with their religious beliefs. Similar scenes were taking place throughout the ballroom. Instead of being passive recipients of the speakers' messages, the audience members became active participants; cues found in black church ceremonies created an audience-wide activism and enthusiasm for the faith-based initiatives. While most audiences at public policy conferences may have a hard time keeping their attention focused on what is being said, these audience members were excited and integral to the conference, transforming the conference from one that informed the public about a social policy to one that generated religion—while using public money.

Other Audiences

At the Tucson, Arizona, conference, most participants were white, and the conference contained virtually none of the aspects of black religious events that occurred in the other three conferences. This divergence warrants attention: it

appears that in aiming their conferences at particular audiences, the conference organizers are well aware of their potential effect on the religious communities with which they are working. Thus, their use of black religious cues
was specifically aimed at generating new political actions and actors related to
faith-based policy.

Faith-Based Liaisons as State-Sponsored Religious Social Movement Actors

Conferences are not the only way the initiatives are being used to woo black
political allies. While state FBLs are government employees, their work is often
more similar to that of movement actors than of government bureaucrats and
the choice of actors can be illuminating.

An Unrepresentative Sample

Of the 34 states that had created FBL positions during my data collection, 15
had appointed African Americans to the positions; nine of these liaisons were
pastors of various denominations. In other words, a quarter of all state liaisons
had extensive professional connections to black churches in their states, and of
the remaining six black liaisons, four had other informal church leadership
affiliations. Therefore, 13 liaisons—more than a third of the total—were strongly connected to black churches. This proportion was far greater than the
proportion of blacks in the country—about 13 percent nationwide, with no
state exceeding 37 percent (Census Bureau 2006)—which strongly suggests a
motive other than fair representation in the selection of liaisons. The appointment of leaders of the black religious community to liaison positions may be
seen as a both a symbolic gesture of unity, as well as a means of placing
someone with similar beliefs into the position. Of course, these liaisons
brought with them the connections to make the initiatives—and perhaps
their supporters—known and accepted in their communities.

Frustration and Tension

Although many of these liaisons had actively sought their positions, some were
clearly aware that their appointments were not just about their own desire to do
good. The liaisons themselves were dedicated to improving the state's social
services system, and they were doing the best they could with few resources.
Liaisons in these circumstances sometimes found themselves becoming cheerleaders for initiatives with little substance behind them, creating waves of
excitement in their communities that often turned to disappointment. The
lack of financial and institutional support has meant that while there had often

been early support for the initiatives from many black churches, there has since been frustration among those who saw the potential of the initiatives being lost to politics while community members in need received no new assistance.

Summary and Conclusion

Researchers in public policy have long found that policy creates new politics and new political activists. The integration of religious culture into state-sponsored events finds its perfect fit in the faith-based initiatives and clearly reaches out to the black community in attempts to create new politics and new political allies. This use of cultural mechanisms to bring in black religious leaders and the community to support the initiatives is especially important because, as Omar McRoberts argues, this mechanism is about "altering the cultural and political milieu upon which religions operate" (McRoberts 2006: 6). The use of religious-cultural cues in the faith-based conferences creates a new type of event that can be construed as blurring the line between church and state.

The activism of the black church in social issues is well known, so it is not surprising that the faith-based initiatives have a great deal of support and appeal in black communities. Both the cultural cues used in the conferences and the political appointees made seem clearly intended to attract segments of the black community as new political allies for supporters of the initiative. One intended—though unstated—consequence may be a shift in voting patterns toward the Republican Party.

Conferences embody state sponsorship of the cultural construction of religion. These political events use the trappings of black church services to create a friendly environment in an attempt to gain new supporters for the initiatives within the black community, appealing to the belief among most religious blacks that religion should have a larger role in state politics. However, since the faith-based initiatives focus on making changes in the individual, rather than in the social structure, they are inherently at odds with the black church's traditional view of political and social services action. It seems clear that conference organizers had been using religious elements found in black churches to create a new constituency for the faith-based initiatives—as well as a new constituency for the political party that created the initiatives.

6

Here, There, but Not Quite Everywhere

Why Are There Faith-Based Initiatives?

It is so important to have a personal belief associated with the faith-based effort, you must have this for success on a large scale.
—Faith-based liaison, interview with the author,
May 5, 2005

I think there needs to be a lot more clarification on the relationship between church and state . . . I think there are a lot of unanswered questions concerning the appropriateness of using taxpayer generated funds through basically religious organizations to deliver human services.
—Faith-based liaison, interview with the author,
October 15, 2004

Policies and practices are important because of the stories and norms they represent. They are both part of the process of change and a result of this change (Lindsay 2008). In earlier chapters, I examined the personal stories of faith that moved liaisons to act, the norms produced and changed by faith-based laws, and the stories of conferences aimed at reaching new audiences. In this chapter, I move on to examine the possible underlying reasons for the creation of these policies.

The Roles of Religion and Government

In the United States, one of the longest lasting and most fervent cultural battles has been about the respective roles of religion and government. Stories about the importance of religion in solving social ills are a metanarrative of the larger disputes about secularization and the declining authority of religion in the public square. This dialogue and the attendant shifts in political and social norms regarding the church-state relationship have been part of the nation's cultural landscape and have occupied the public's social conscience for much of American history. Some social scientists and political commentators argue that the present is no different, and they propose that we are living in an era in which religion is becoming increasingly important for understanding government policies and politics (Dionne 2008; Wallis 2008).

Understanding faith-based initiatives is part of this process. To understand why states have implemented these policies, we must of course take into account the specific factors that have led states to be more or less likely to create these policies. But we must also understand the policies as part of a larger story, and as part of the personal stories of many of their advocates. The reasons behind faith-based policy implementation illustrate how the role of religion in public life can change and how the activities of a social movement, occurring at the right time and right place, can result in attainment of at least some of the movement's goals. The success of a social movement often relies not only on dedicated members and organizational resources, but also on political opportunities that allow the movement to achieve its goals by appealing to other groups.

Since the implementation of the 1996 welfare reform bill, states have had to find new ways to make social services available to those in need. The faith-based initiatives offered one attractive solution to this problem, and, as an apparent result, more of these initiatives were established over the subsequent 10 years. Whether it has been by enacting laws, creating Offices of Faith-Based and Community Initiatives, or appropriating money to FBLs and groups, state policies and practices enhancing the role of religion in government have consistently grown. Why have states done this? I have found two main reasons for state implementation of the faith-based initiatives: (1) religiously based belief among supporters of faith-based initiatives coupled with political access, and (2) fiscal necessity. While the descriptions found in the data may not present a full picture of why implementation has occurred in various states, they do point to systematic similarities across states.

Shifting the Focus from "What?" to "Why?"

In the last three chapters, I outlined state activity surrounding the faith-based initiatives; in this chapter, I move away from describing *what* happened to examining *why* it happened. I argue that to understand why these policies were instituted, one has to look at the larger cultural processes of devolution and desecularization to see how the faith-based initiatives meet the affective and instrumental needs of various state actors. The initiatives have promised to serve the instrumental needs of politicians who need new fiscal resources for their states in the wake of welfare reform, and they also connect to larger meaning systems of those who believe there should be a new relationship between religion and government and that the best way to help the poor is through faith.

Why Have States Created Faith-Based Policies?

This new institutionalization of religion through the faith-based initiatives has occurred at least in part because of the multiple stakeholders who have acted within state governments to support the initiatives. One great appeal of the initiatives has been their malleability—they could (and do) appeal to a large number of people because of the vagueness of their promises of bringing a new wealth of resources from and to religious groups in service of the greater good. While the initiatives began with support from evangelical movement actors in Texas and in the federal government, their appeal soon spread to other groups, creating cohesion around their principles and ideals while simultaneously purporting to meet the instrumental needs of states in fiscal crisis. They promised state actors new political support and federal funding at the cost of little, if any, new state money.

In the following sections, I outline how the initiatives appealed to the emotions of one set of stakeholders and the instrumental motivations of other groups. While I did not directly ask liaisons why they thought the initiatives had come to be, many offered reasons to explain why their states became active when they did. Many echoed the sentiments of the first liaison from Texas, whom I quoted extensively in Chapter 2: state faith-based policies appealed to the deep desire of many to help the poor, coupled with the belief that the best way to do this is through religious groups (which the government should fund but otherwise leave alone). Politicians could easily benefit from this ideology even if they did not share it. This view of the proper role of religious groups in the social services sector and their potential for good works was not always reflected in interviews with liaisons, however. Some liaisons were far more pragmatic, viewing implementation of faith-based policies as smart politics, necessary to get essential fiscal resources to states that were in dire financial straits as a result of welfare reform.

Using information from interviews with liaisons and quantitative data I collected on states, state practices, and potentially significant variables measuring the political, social, and economic environment, I have found a complex interplay among religion, politics, and money underlying implementation of the faith-based initiatives. Below, I examine both the liaisons' understandings of implementation and the political, demographic, and socioeconomic factors that appear to have affected states' decisions on adopting faith-based practices.

Religious Sources of Faith-Based Policy Creation

According to Cobb and Elder (1972), symbolic policies that appeal to people's emotions are effective because they summon core values and political communi-ty. The initiatives draw on a deeply held underlying belief that religion has a special place in American society, and they have the potential to have widespread emotional appeal. Many, especially conservative religious groups, see religious organizations as representing values that have been displaced in the modern world; further, they believe that by bringing such organizations to the fore, our society may encourage the rebuilding of a community in danger of being lost.

Creating Cohesion: The Appeal to Religious Actors

The use of this symbolic policy can come in various forms. It may be an appeal to religious ideology, opposing church-state separation, or an emotional appeal, in which the initiatives promise to render the best possible help to the poor. In whatever form, the initiatives have offered a set of cultural goods that has appealed to various state actors.

In the early days of the faith-based initiatives, the most important supporters and networks involved were evangelical movement activists who were in very powerful positions in state and federal government (Black, Koopman, and Ryden 2006; Formicola, Segers, and Weber 2003). Texas governor George W. Bush and Missouri senator John Ashcroft brought national attention and the power of the government, both federal and state, to the initiatives. They did not need to get government behind their movement because they were the government. This type of access—inside of politics—is something that social movement research-ers have argued is key to success. When examining the faith-based initiative and the ties between liaisons this is evident in the centrality of faith-based liaisons in the highly conservative states of Alabama, Florida, South Carolina, Oklahoma, and Texas; each of these states are the most actively engaged in spreading the word about the initiative and each is in a state with very strong ties to the evangelical movement within the state Republican Party. This access of the evangelical movement to state governments is key to shaping debates about faith-based initiatives. Social movements, in the case of faith-based initiatives, are able to effect change in social policy by gaining access to political institutions and organizations, and then using these positions to reframe debates and shape perceptions (Andrews 2001; Gamson 1975; Giugini, McAdam, and Tilly 1999; Jenkins and Eckert 1986; McAdam and Su 2002; McCammon et al. 2001; Piven and Cloward 1977; Soule 2004; Soule and Olzak 2004; Tarrow 1998).

The influence of the evangelical movement has lately been seen at all levels of government, with movement actors enthusiastically pursuing the inclusion of religion as an integral part of public policy and political life (Bartkowski and

Regis 2003; Conger and Green 2002). In particular, the evangelical movement has grown in power and prominence by increasing its influence within the Republican Party and by supporting a variety of public policy issues that further its goal of making a permanent place for religion within government (Conger and Green 2002; Green, Guth, and Wilcox 1998; Green, Rozell, and Wilcox 2003; Kniss and Burns 2004). In many states, the resurgent evangelical movement has been able to gain insider status, becoming strongly identified with the Republican Party, and gaining an institutional hold on some state governments (Conger and Green 2002; Green, Guth, and Wilcox 1998; Green, Rozell, and Wilcox 2003). In a recent manuscript, Conger (2008a:18) argued that the greatest potential of the Christian Right lies in its influence in the states. Movement leaders had the "right idea when they urged supporters to look to state level policies over a decade ago," Conger writes. "They have found a venue that suits the movement's unique strengths and have mobilized and assimilated a whole generation of supporters and activists into the intricacies of state level political action." By means of a complex array of alliances, Protestant religious conservatives have achieved increasing success and acceptance in the Republican Party, bringing certain ideas about the role of religion in public life to the forefront of policy and politics.[1]

This influence of political elites has the potential to lead to greater implementation of faith-based policies and practices because of the movement's influence inside state political environments (Conger and Green 2002; Lindsay 2008). This influence in state politics, by way of the Republican Party, may lead to increased support for these policies and practices; in addition, previous movement success in other policy areas may lead to a friendlier policy environment, by showing politicians that there is a base of support (Green, Guth, and Wilcox 1998; Green, Rozell, and Wilcox 2003).

In addition, the initiatives appeal to others, outside the evangelical movement, who have similar affective interests in creating social policies that enhance the role of religion in helping the poor and needy. Democratic supporters of the initiatives have long praised the faith-based community as being central to efforts to help the most vulnerable in society. Former vice president Al Gore embraced aspects of the initiatives during his presidential campaign. His support had been conditioned on not allowing discrimination in hiring practices, but included providing fiscal support to faith-based groups. In essence, this is the opposite of the situation under the Bush administration.

President Obama has also pledged support for the initiative while changing some aspects of the Bush administration policy. The newly formed Office of Faith and Neighborhood Partnerships has a 25-member advisory council in charge of creating a new direction for the initiative. However, he has failed to live up to a campaign promise to overturn the Bush administration executive order that allowed discrimination in hiring practices. Thus it appears that even Democratic Party politicians are not immune to the cultural changes established under President Bush and at the state level. So while there may be some policy differences among those who feel the initiatives are the right thing to do, ties of affective support create a degree of cohesion around the initiatives. It is not that state actors conspire to create these policies across states, but rather that these symbolic efforts appeal to multiple constituencies of actors because of the meaning systems to which they were attracted.

Social Movement Theory: Religious Social Movement Change

Study of the faith-based initiatives offers two important advances in the examination of the role of social movements in creating social policy. First, while during much of the twentieth century researchers pointed to the declining social significance of religion (Weber 1922), recent experiences in the United States, the Middle East, and Eastern bloc countries have taught us otherwise (Casanova 1994; Chaves 1994; Parsa 1989; Riesbrodt 1993). Successes by religious social movements in each of these countries have led researchers to reconsider religion as a vital source of social change and an important influence in social and political decision-making (Chaves 1994). This institutional influence of religious groups is a particularly underdeveloped area in research on social movements. Researchers often focused on the role of secular organizations in gaining institutional influence (Skocpol and Amenta 1986), neglecting the role that religion and religious movements may be able to play in achieving access to government institutions. By examining the effect of previous success of the evangelical movement in state political institutions on the success of the faith-based initiatives in a state, the question of whether such access by a religious movement helps advance further access and success can be explored.

Second, while some social movement theorists have argued that by gaining access to the political system, social movements begin to implement their goals through policy changes (Zald 2000), most research has been focused on how social movements succeed through outsider movement activity such as lobbying or protests (Gamson 1975; Giugini, McAdam, and Tilly 1999; Jenkins and Eckert 1986; Jenkins and Perrow 1977; McAdam 1982; McCammon et al. 2001; Piven and Cloward 1977; Tarrow 1998). Contrary to this, I focus on how partial movement success at penetrating government can be strategically parlayed into permanent and wider movement access. Instead of success being measured by passage of an entirely new and complete policy or by attainment of major influence in government structures, we can begin to theorize movement success as steps in a larger process. By looking at movements in this way, we can see how social movements influence policy through a cycle of access and success within government institutions and social policy structures; previous government institutional access and success can create new access and new success through social policy. I offer two hypotheses to test the effect of social movement action relating to the faith-based initiatives, based on two measures of social movement presence and strength.

Hypotheses

In the next sections, I lay out hypotheses regarding variation among states in implementation of the faith-based initiatives, and the data I used to test them.

STRENGTH OF THE EVANGELICAL MOVEMENT. The movement literature suggests that the greater the influence of a social movement in state politics, the more likely a state will be to enact laws in its favor (Burstein 1998; Burstein and Linton 2002; Haider-Markel 1998; Nice 1994; Soule 2004; Soule and Earl 2001; Soule and Olzak 2004; Soule and Zylan 1997). In many states, resurgent evangelism has been able to gain political status by becoming strongly identified with the Republican Party and having a strong institutional hold on state government (Conger and Green 2002; Green, Guth, and Wilcox 1998; Green, Rozell, and Wilcox 2003). The status of this religious constituency as an influential political movement within a state's political structure may have important influence on whether the state establishes a FBL position or enacts laws creating special status for religious groups; both are acts that can create an institutionalized link between religious organizations and state government. In this case, the faith-based initiatives, by advancing the role of the evangelical movement in state political structures (Wineburg 2001; Bartkowski and Regis 2003), would be the second step (after becoming part of the Republican Party) in a process that is creating a permanent place for religion in government. In short, then, my first social movement hypothesis was that the more influential the evangelical movement was in state politics, the more likely a state would be to appoint an FBL and to create faith-based legislative changes.

PREVIOUS SUCCESS OF A MOVEMENT. As I said above, research shows that states with greater social movement strength in state politics should be more likely to implement policies that favor that movement, especially in the beginning stages of policy creation. Thus I hypothesized that when there were more strong connections to the evangelical movement within a state's political system, it was more likely that the state would embrace a variety of faith-based policies. In the data I collected on implementation as related to various state characteristics, I found this was the case.

For example, in all but two states, the liaisons had personal contact with the White House and faith-based leaders in various federal sectors who were tasked with helping to ensure that states were creating faith-based policies. Some of these states had liaisons whose connection to the faith-based movement went back many years. For example, in one southern state the liaison had an early relationship with the people supporting the initiatives:

> I worked there [in Washington, D.C.] for about three years. . . . Part of their mission was to look at faith-based opportunities. So, I was familiar with a lot of the people who were in the faith-based arena, like Amy Sherman and Mr. Lazarus with the Center for Public Justice, and some other different types of organizations . . . [that] do a lot of work on the faith-based initiatives, so I was familiar a lot of the people and a lot of the players. I had also interned here at the governor's office when I was in college, so I still knew a lot of the people. (Nov. 30, 2004)

Another liaison had even stronger ties to those at the federal level starting out at the George W. Bush White House and then moving to Capitol Hill. On Capitol Hill she worked with a variety of key federal politicians, including former congressman J. C. Watts from Oklahoma (R), Congressman Mark Souder (R-IN), and Congressman Aderholt (R-AL), all of whom were trying to get Charitable Choice language attached to all appropriations bills. She also had extensive contact with other top supporters including Stanley Carlson-Thies and David Caprara. She felt that her experience in Washington, D.C., would be an asset to her state; therefore, when she returned home and had the opportunity to work on the initiative she pursued it enthusiastically. "It has been neat because so many of the resources and the things that I learned about in Washington I felt like I'm now going to be able to use that and bring what I learned back to my home state" (Feb. 7, 2005). This type of personal connection, dating from before the initiatives began to appear in the state, helped to create an environment in which the natural move would be for that state to pursue the activity. Once a liaison was in place, the White House OFBCI could engage in outreach and partnerships with the state; the degree to which this happened varied by state.

The faith-based initiatives are but one of several sets of U.S. policy initiatives with religious connections. Another well-defined set of social policies strongly influenced by the resurgent evangelical movement concerns family life in general and gay marriage in particular. While many states have enacted defense of marriage acts, several states have gone much further, creating extremely strict policies regarding gay marriage and related family matters. The presence of these laws and policies can be taken as a measure of a state's vulnerability to conservative evangelical influence on public policy. Building on the idea that a state's experience in a policy area will influence its action on a new policy initiative in a related area (Soule and Zylan 1997; Zylan and Soule 2000), it seems that states that have implemented other religiously based social policies will be more likely to implement this one. Specifically, I hypothesized that states with laws restricting gay marriage and related family matters would be more likely to appoint an FBL and make faith-based legislative changes. Table 6.1 summarizes the variables I used, and their sources.

TABLE 6.1. Factors Potentially Affecting State Implementation of Faith-Based Initiatives

Factor	Measures	Data Sources
Intrastate Factors		
Political Characteristics		
Social Movement Activity	Evangelical presence in Republican Party	Conger and Green (2002); Green et al. (1998)
	Strong anti-gay-marriage/family laws	National Gay and Lesbian Rights Task Force (2006)
Previous Policy Environment	Republican vote percent in last presidential election; # Democrats/Republicans in state	U.S. Census Bureau
Political Environment*	legislature; political affiliation of governor Conservative/liberal makeup Berry et al. (1998, 2005) of voters and state government	
Social Welfare Need	Poverty rate	U.S. Census Bureau
Social Welfare "Problem"	Generosity of state welfare Program	U.S. Census Bureau, National Center for Children in Poverty
Demographic Characteristics		
Religion	Congregational affiliation	Glenmary (2000)
Immigration	% pop. legal immigrants*	U.S. Census Bureau
Other Demographics	% population over 65*; % population African-American	
Socioeconomic Characteristics		
General Economic Indicators	Unemployment rate*; Gross State Product per capita	U.S. Census Bureau
Interstate/Diffusion Factors		
Mechanisms of Diffusion Time	Region Effect over time*	U.S. Census Bureau

*Data collected on variables and analyzed, but not found to be significant in any models.

TABLE 6.2. Event History Regression for Probability of State Creating a
Faith-Based Liaison Position and/or Office of Faith-Based Community Initiatives

Variables	Model 1	Model 2	Model 3	Model 4	Model 5	Model 6
Constant	-3.10^{***}	-3.14^{***}	.43	-7.30^{***}	$-.07$	1.88
	(.67)	(.60)	(.66)	(1.45)	(2.48)	(6.33)
Evangelical Social Movement Presence						
Strong	1.33^{*}	–	–	–	1.35^{*}	2.40^{**}
	(.65)				(.66)	(.96)
Midlevel	$.69^{*}$	–	–	–	.36	.12
	(.35)				(.47)	(.80)
Previous Policy Success						
Gay Rights Measures	–	$.54^{*}$	–	–	$.39+$	.13
		(.23)			(.24)	(.33)
Model of Welfare State						
TANF Coverage[1]	–	–	$-.64^{***}$	–	$-.60^{***}$	$-.70^{*}$
			(.11)		(.15)	(3.26)
Political Variables						
Republican Voting Rates	–	–	–	$.09^{***}$	.02	$-.05$
Control Variables				(.02)	(.03)	(.05)
Gross State Product	$.03^{*}$	$.03^{*}$	$.05^{*}$	$.04^{*}$	$.06^{***}$	.04
	(.01)	(.01)	(.02)	(.02)	(.02)	(.07)
Poverty Rate	$-.06$	$-.04$	$-.10^{**}$	$-.02$	$-.20^{**}$	$-.21^{*}$
	(.06)	(.05)	(.05)	(.05)	(.08)	(.10)
Time (2005/pre-2005)	2.23^{***}	2.11^{***}	1.58^{***}	1.68^{***}	1.90^{***}	2.34^{**}
	(.50)	(.54)	(.54)	(.52)	(.60)	(.63)
% African American	.01	.02	.02	.02	$-.02$	$-.04$
	(.02)	(.02)	(.02)	(.02)	(.03)	(.06)
Pseudo R^2	.10	.10	.20	.14	.24	.25

This table shows event history regressions for the probability of a state appointing a faith-based liaison for all years (1996–2005), including direct-effects models and a full model. Standard errors are in parentheses below. Each model shown tests a different combination of factors.

Significance: $^{*}p<0.05$; $^{**}p<0.01$; $^{***}p<0.001$
1. The percentage of the eligible population covered by TANF.

The Results of Movement Influence

The data for the hypotheses outlined above were analyzed using STATA; see Appendix A for details. The results are summarized in Tables 6.2 and 6.3. Looking at variables that measured the evangelical movement's influence on the state Republican Party, I found that when the evangelical movement's influence was either moderate or strong, the effect on enacting laws, appointing liaisons, and creating offices was significant. States in which the evangelical movement had made the greatest inroads into state politics were the most likely to exhibit the various faith-based practices. In fact, the odds of a state's creating a liaison position were more than double when there was a strong evangelical movement presence in the state Republican Party, when

TABLE 6.3. Negative Binomial Regression: Total Number of Faith-Based Laws

Variables	No. of Laws	(Std. Error)
Constant	.57	(.3.19)
Conservative Social Movement Presence		
Strong Christian Right Presence in State	1.08[*]	(.52)
Medium Christian Right Presence in State	.59 ^	(.37)
Previous Policy Success		
Anti-Gay Marriage and Family Policies	−.05	(.08)
Political Variable		
Republican Voter Rates	.01	(.04)
Welfare Burden		
% of Eligible Population Covered by TANF	−1.02	(1.72)
Control Variables		
Gross State Product	.02	(.05)
Poverty Rate	.04	(.10)
% African American	2.50	(.05)
Pseudo R^2	.04	

This table displays the results of negative binomial regression of the log number of laws implemented in a state and overall implementation of the initiative through FBLs and laws.

Significance: [*]$p<0.05$; ^approaches significance at the .10 level

compared to weak or no influence (Table 6.2, model 1). The same was true for faith-based legislation: states that enacted the most faith-based laws were those with the greatest influence of the conservative evangelical movement within the Republican Party (Table 6.3).

In addition, states that had already accepted religiously tinged social policies were more likely to appoint an FBL. For example, if a state had extremely conservative anti–gay-marriage policies in place, it increased the odds of the state's appointing a liaison by a factor of two and a half. It is important to note that variables measuring overall levels of conservatism, political power by party, and evangelical denominational membership were not significant; only the variables measuring insider political power by the evangelical movement or previous susceptibility to religious influences were good predictors of state implementation. As Conger (2008a:18) pointed out in her new examination of the influence of these groups, "The Christian Right blooms where it is planted. . . . In many states the movement is able to be very successful in influencing politicians and policies." In short, it was not just the presence of evangelicals or conservative political actors that made adoption of faith-based policies possible; rather, it was the presence of a desecularized political environment and politically active evangelicals working inside the established political realm that predicted the implementation of these policies.

EFFECTS ON OFFICES OF FAITH-BASED AND COMMUNITY INITIATIVES. I also examined the factors that affected the creation of OFBCIs (see Table 6.2, model 6).

The direct-effects models used were the same as those described above for FBL appointment, and so are not presented in detail here; results were positive and significant as for the FBL models. The results for the full model were also similar to those for liaisons: States with a high evangelical movement presence in the Republican Party were the most likely to create state OFBCIs. In fact, states with a strong evangelical movement were even more likely to create OFBCIs than to create FBL positions. That means that the states most likely to have created OFBCIs—which have greater institutional structure, more employees, and possibly a longer longevity than liaison positions—were those in which the evangelical movement had also made the greatest inroads into state party politics. In fact, the odds of a state with the highest rating on the conservative evangelical movement presence within state Republican Parties scale creating an OFBCI between 1996 and 2005 were 11 times greater than in states with middle or low rating on the scale. Therefore, this is at least initial evidence of some success of a social movement within political institutions creating further success and access. Increasing institutionalization was most likely in states where evangelical political power was already the norm. This is important when considering the future of the initiatives, suggesting that they could move from policies that are largely cultural and symbolic in nature, toward policies that alter the material rewards available to religious organizations.

EFFECTS ON NUMBER OF LEGISLATIVE CHANGES. To examine whether legislative implementation of the initiatives by states was susceptible to the same factors as were appointment of liaisons and OFBCIs, I tested the effect of the same independent variables on the number of legislative changes made. The results, shown in Table 6.3, were remarkably similar to those for liaisons and OFBCIs. Again, implementation of the faith-based initiatives was more likely in states that had greater evangelical movement strength within state government and a weaker welfare system. On the other hand, the previous policy environment in a state was not a significant predictor of overall legislative implementation; this points to the real importance of social movement action as having previous personal access to government institutions. However, these laws are also congruent with the overall emphasis on changing culture or rerouting money rather than on allocating new money to provide social services.

Overall pattern of state implementation illustrates something more complex and far-reaching: a cultural change in the understanding of church-state relations from one of separation to one of cooperation between religious groups and government agencies, which appeals to many people's sense of fairness and faith.

The Place of Faith in Public Life

In my interviews with liaisons, all but six specifically mentioned that the initiatives were beneficial because they created a new understanding of the relationship between religion and government. In one of the first interviews I conducted, the liaison spoke to me at great length about his own understanding of what was happening with the faith-based initiatives and about why it was so important in changing our conceptions of the role of religion in the public square. This liaison's reflections on the initiatives mirrored the arguments made in the original rhetoric surrounding the initiative, stressing that there was a need to change church-state relationships, because the current view of a wall separating church and state was fundamentally flawed:

> I think there is a growing debate about whether this separation of church and state was in fact being articulated by the press and by national organizations correctly. So I think there were many in the church community who were already sensing that they were being displaced from the public square and were looking for reason to reclaim their presence in the public square. To some degree I think our coming along and affirming the role of the faith community and being from the government, the faith community saw it as being affirmed by the government. I think that, indeed, there were a lot of ministers, clergy, and pastors who, you know, sincerely wanted to know how they could positively work with the government. (Feb. 8, 2005)

It is crucial to note that this liaison was an evangelical Christian and was one of the first to create faith-based policy at the state level. This supports what I found in the quantitative data: that the early implementation of the initiatives was more likely in states with strong evangelical elite actors. Again, this is not about collusion among these actors, but about shared mutual understandings of church-state separation, confirming the original vision through specific movement actors within government. For example, in another state, where the liaisons were not evangelicals, the liaisons also expressed support for the initiatives because of the decrease in church-state barriers they represent:

> Well, [the other liaison] talked about [how] from a historical perspective we've always funded FBOs. However, your smaller FBOs often encounter barriers to contract development. . . . They may get the prize but not the pay . . . so you can become this funded agency, and that's where sometimes we encountered the hurdles . . . particularly before Charitable Choice. I worked with one organization where we had to work with them to practically rewrite the proposal, you know, because of crosses on the wall. . . . It was the perception . . . things that appear overly sectarian. And hostility towards the efforts . . . it was difficult. (Aug. 17, 2004)

When I asked whether those barriers or hostility had changed, the liaison replied, "Well there's still a hard choice, but it's easier."

Liaisons felt that the initiatives would make creating partnerships easier; further, most of them thought that faith-based groups would be able to come in and do something different and perhaps better. Even in one of the few states where I heard ensuring church-state constitutionality mentioned, the liaison still felt that the initiatives were necessary to find a new way for the state and religious groups to work together:

> Well, I'm trying to do it because it's the right thing to do. The church has no business using federal dollars to proselytize, and I want to make sure that doesn't happen on my watch because it's not right, and it's also unconstitutional. So that's a real important part of the job. At the same time, I want to acknowledge that faith is tremendously important to most folks, and . . . faith organizations should have the right to participate as partners in solving these problems, and really they're not going to make significant progress unless we all find a common ground that we have and can work together. (Dec. 3, 2004)

SUPPORT FROM ABOVE. In discussing their own understanding of how and why implementation occurred, some liaisons offered reasons that were not only about their feelings of faith and how that spurred implementation in their state, but also about how the importance of faith was understood by those in charge of their offices. One liaison related a story about how this happened in his state:

> I began attending federal conferences in 1999 and 2000, addressing the then-President Clinton faith-based initiatives. I found myself very intrigued by the collection of ministers and government officials talking about how they could work together to provide social programs. And I was further impressed that these conferences, hosted by the federal government, seemed fairly saturated with the talk of faith. So I reported that to some of our local state officials, and I increasingly felt that it would be a good idea, so we tried to capture some of the good and some of the benefits of this federal movement to the state level and began to articulate these thoughts in a strategic document that I prepared [for the state] in April 2000. And I gave a copy to [the governor], cabinet secretary of HHS, and to the Department of Human Services, and it was the cabinet secretary who jumped on it, felt that it was a significant issue and that the plan that was presented was good and well-thought-out, and began to, as cabinet secretary, to try to implement the proposed plan. (Feb. 8, 2005)

Through his own work, belief, and perseverance, this liaison brought the faith-based initiatives to his state and realized his vision for a period of time. However, since his departure, bureaucratic pressures and inertia have taken their toll, and the state's OFBCI has struggled to maintain its level of activity and attention from other government actors.

The sense that the time was right for these changes came not just from the liaisons themselves but also from those higher up in state government; this theme was repeated in several interviews. In an interview in another state, the liaison, who was in charge of a very active office, argued that the role of the governor was key to creating the office and keeping it going in such a strong and active manner:

> I think one of the things you'll want to know is that the office considers itself a leader and a role model for other states to emulate . . . being an example of what can really be done in a state, if a state gets the commitment or has the commitment of the governor and/or state commissioner. . . . It started in [a previous] administration, when the new governor brought in Madam Secretary who has a passion for the faith-based community, and so that passion allowed the office to grow in the direction that it is now. It's really the commitment and the resources that the state provides for the offices of faith-based initiatives. (Aug. 20, 2004)

This sense that it was necessary to have someone at the top supporting the goals of the initiatives was echoed by the liaison in another state, whose office was active mainly in outreach to the community:

> The governor strongly believes that the faith community is an important partner in helping to move [the state] forward. We look to the faith community because the values that these individuals have that are aligned with the values of our governor. She likes to say to reach out and touch the least of these. So that is what we are looking to do, to provide to uplift and provide direction for those that need the most help. We want to rely on the faith community to work with us and to partner with us to allow us to do that. There is an old African proverb that says, "No matter how high a house is built, it must stand on something." It must have a strong foundation. We believe that the faith community can be a strong foundation to help us provide many of the services that citizens need, and to address many of the critical issues that are facing citizens here. (April 30, 2005)

While religion is certainly not the only reason for states to implement faith-based practices—as I will discuss later in this chapter—understanding the religious commitments of those inside government can shed light on implementation. A relatively new liaison described how important it was to him to see President Bush openly advocating a larger role for faith-based groups in the public sector:

When the president came out talking about social policy and the faith-based initiatives, initially in the 2000 campaign—and to be fair, other people were talking about it too, Vice President Gore, and President Clinton has always been a big supporter, as has Senator Clinton. But you know, it resonated, and I think it resonated with a lot of us, because we saw it working on the ground and that there could be a more fruitful collaboration between government and faith groups, in particular, that could maintain the integrity of those groups and maintain integrity to our Constitution and the establishment clause, and that it was just the way government was behind the times. Behind the times in a lot of different ways. Behind the times when it comes to Supreme Court case law. They were being overrestrictive, and those who were hurting from it were the people on the ground. I saw this, and it really resonated with me, about a closer partnership. I saw that it really worked and got really, really excited about needs that could be met, people that could be empowered, lives that could be transformed. (March 27, 2005)

This feeling that good things could come out of the initiatives because of the special relationships that faith-based groups could cultivate was discussed by other liaisons who believed that this was an opportunity to do more than was traditionally allowed in government work. "Well, for me, it's a very well-rounded piece. It's the piece that touches not only the hearts but in this case the soul of the people around the state and gives them the opportunity to interact with state government and do really awesome things" (Feb. 9, 2005). As another liaison stated, "I think anyone who looks at this will [see] the FBCI is an awesome opportunity . . . Churches have for so long been providing services to the community. Before there were government agencies there were churches. . . . I believe that there is a this wonderful opportunity where you can bring government agencies, non-profits and faith-based groups together to provide efficient, effective services to those in need" (Feb. 21, 2005).

A CLOSER RELATIONSHIP. This desire for a closer partnership between church and state came through in my discussions with other liaisons as well. The overall sense was that faith groups had been kept out of the public square, and it was now time to welcome them back. One liaison, a former minister, said of working on the initiatives, "First off, I agreed with the federal legislation, and I also realized that I could maybe help effect a change in the state. I was qualified in the sense that I understand the government side and their concerns about working with FBOs, but I could also understand the faith-based side and their concerns working with government." Later in the interview he described how these concerns really came down to "a philosophical difference. Some people believe that the of separation church and state is that the government shouldn't have much to do at all with religious groups . . . but there is less concern as the years go on" (Oct. 13, 2004).

Another liaison used language similar to President Bush's to describe her feelings about changing ideas regarding church and state. "I just think there is such a misconception with the meaning of the separation of church and state...[it is] just that the constitution says that a church should not be established by the government, it does not say that because you're a faith-based organization and you provide social services you cannot compete for a grant...in fact that's discriminatory" (Feb. 16, 2005). She explained how she shared these feelings with the groups that came to her for help and that this was one of her favorite aspects of the job to "educate people about what it [separation of church and state] truly means."

So even though there is little evidence that the majority of FBOs had been clamoring for something like the faith-based initiatives to occur, liaisons still saw the initiatives as necessary to show these groups that have access to government funding: "So when you say, Does the state have any funds for those organizations? Well, yes they do, obviously because of the very reason the president set up the initiative. They're entitled to...I don't want to say entitled to, but they're entitled to requests or to put in petitions just like any other organization is" (Nov. 8, 2004). So these extra efforts to increase access are being made—even when many recent studies and the liaisons themselves have found that a significant proportion of religious organizations either could not, or would not, take advantage of government funding when offered (Green 2007). Regardless of the implications of this finding, this sense that religion should have a new—or renewed—place in the public square was coupled with a deep and abiding conviction that this was the right thing to do for the greater good of all involved. When asked what the liaison's role was and how the faith-base policies came about in her state, one liaison replied, "There is not a good government solution to [these social problems]. We can do things better, but what we've got to do is create an opportunity of loving people who are called into this work to come into the lives of these children and love them. Government doesn't do that" (March 15, 2005). A few sentences later, the same liaison described a group she had been working with that was willing to do this kind of service:

> There is, probably two miles from here, an elementary school, 410
> children, in a really tough neighborhood, and a very affluent suburban
> church four miles from there. [The church] prayed for years about an
> urban mission, and they picked that neighborhood. They have 40 to 60
> volunteers in that school every week. They are not evangelizing; they
> are getting kids off the bus, and they are in the lunchroom, they are in
> the office, they're just about everywhere. That church a year ago bought
> a church in that neighborhood. The volunteers and the principal from
> that school are going to that church. Guess where the kids are going?
> [That church.] Guess how many have been saved, born again, this year?
> Twenty-one. They're bringing their parents with them.

When asked what her office's role was, she said that it was to "promot[e] these types of relationships. Working where you have partners that are interested in trying to put these things together. How do we get people who really are called to serve engaged in some of the work that we're doing?" Clearly this liaison was excited about the new help—and new hope—that was going to the poor and needy because of the new relationship she was helping to create between the government and religious groups; however, her statements also point to another tension in implementation of the initiatives. While the federal supporters of the initiatives argue that they promote a clear understanding of church-state separation, the implementation of these principles is often much more difficult in practice. Creating a stronger relationship between churches and state government offices necessarily creates a more complex relationship between these two groups, one that requires systematic regulation that is not present at this time. Even though this liaison knew that churches and faith-based groups could not proselytize while on school campuses, the line between helping children and converting the children they helped often seemed blurry.

Feelings of hope and a belief in the initiatives were reinforced by other people, especially those in leadership positions. In some cases, the liaisons felt their beliefs were renewed and inspired by what was happening at the federal level. The use of affective symbols by the president resonated with the beliefs of some liaisons. In her description of a trip to a White House conference, a liaison from a southern state described how the president, with whom she disagreed on some policy particulars, nonetheless echoed some of her deeply held sentiments:

> Just listening to the way that the president spoke with so much
> passion when he talked about the service to those that were in need
> and his desire to have them have choices, which sort of really helped
> me to see a different view of how important this is to him. . . . We like
> having choices, and some people would say that the people in need
> don't know how to make decisions for themselves, but he would
> disagree with that, and I would disagree, and I respect that. . . . So, I
> sensed and felt a lot of that same passion coming from the president
> when he made reference to that. (March 23, 2005)

In short, the conversations I had with liaisons about their offices pointed to a systematic implementation of the initiatives as a political and cultural symbol emphasizing a greater role and need for religion in social services. The effect is greatest on creating a new dynamic between church and state; such an effect is no less important than a financial one—but is likely to create disappointment on the part of those who saw its appeal as an agent of tangible change in the social services sector.

The discourse surrounding the faith-based initiatives mirrors a much longer and deeper battle in the United States over the relationship between church and state. As the words of the state liaisons illustrate, creating the appropriate relationship between church and state is not static; however, while many discussions about church-state separation are in the theoretical realm, the changes created by the faith-based initiatives are very real.

This blurring of lines and boundaries was discussed by a member of one state's advisory board. During our interview, he said that there needed to be more education about church-state separation, given that the federal government and initiatives had left a lot of unanswered questions. The rules for FBOs need clarification, he said, and the FBOs' role in delivering social services must be one that respects the Constitution. He noted the need for caution, saying, "There has been an overextension of religion, and we are struggling with this, and it can lead to awkward situations where you have to tell an organization 'You can't start with a prayer.' But [one of the groups getting funds], they start with a prayer and some inherently religious activity was funded, and I object to that" (Oct. 15, 2004). The case the board member was discussing did prompt investigations in his state, but these have not led to greater clarity on where the lines between church and state are drawn. Thus, while the hard work and good intentions of many supporters of the initiatives to expand faith-based social services certainly cannot be ignored, neither can the reality that state faith-based practices have institutionalized religion in a fundamentally new way within the public sphere.

Instrumental Symbolic Policy: The Fiscal Opportunity for Success

Although faith-based initiatives have been discussed in mostly religious terms, it is easy to see that there are strictly pragmatic and fiscal reasons why politicians might have wanted to bring more religious and volunteer groups into the social services sector to relieve some of a state's fiscal burden. In addition, by creating faith-based practices, state actors could signal to the president that they supported his initiatives and that he should send grants their way. If successful, such a program would fulfill every politician's dream of being responsible for providing better public services without raising taxes or making cuts elsewhere.

Where the Need Is Greatest?

Policy implementation theory suggests that a state will be more likely to innovate or implement new policies if it feels greater pressure from a problem (Evans 1996; Grogan 1994; Haider-Markel 1998; Lin 2000; Nice 1994; Raeburn 2004; Zylan and Soule 2000). Since the faith-based initiatives are touted as a way to solve problems of poverty, it would follow that if pragmatic concerns are paramount, these policies should be more likely to be adopted where the problem of poverty is greater[2] or where the welfare system is less developed. For example, states that are more generous in their TANF coverage should be less likely to need faith-based initiatives because they already have programs and policies to help the poor and needy. States with less well developed programs, on the other hand, should be looking for opportunities to find new ways to improve services.

PROBLEM-DRIVEN POLICY IMPLEMENTATION. Based on the above previous research, I tested the hypothesis that states with higher poverty rates would be more likely to create an FBL position or enact faith-based policies than those with lower poverty rates and proportions. Poverty rates, measured as percentage of population living below the federal poverty level, were taken from the U.S. Census Bureau (1996–2005). Welfare burden was defined as the proportion of children eligible (by federal standards) that actually received money from the state's TANF fund. Since passage of the 1996 welfare reform bill, states have been able to make their own policies regarding welfare coverage within the context of federal guidelines; this measure was therefore a good way to tap into the overall state coverage. Data for this variable also came from the U.S. Census Bureau (1996–2005) and the National Center for Children in Poverty.[3] States that provided TANF benefits to a higher proportion of eligible children would be less likely to create these policies because they already had adequate state welfare coverage and thus would not need to use faith-based policies to cover gaps in their system. Simply put, states with good TANF coverage would not need to rely on the faith-based sector and would not be expected to create policies they did not need, and so would be less likely to create or implement faith-based practices.

POLITICS-DRIVEN POLICY IMPLEMENTATION. The social policy literature also looks to politics for reasons that states implement policies (Burstein and Linton 2002; Evans 1996; Grogan 1994; Lin 2000; Nice, 1994; Zylan and Soule 2000). Research has shown that policies favoring religion and free-market outcomes are more likely to be present in states with a majority of Republican voters (Nice 1994; Zylan and Soule 2000). In this case, it is the conservative political environment—rather than social movements—that favors these outcomes. The faith-based initiatives can be construed as being both religious and free-market in nature, so their implementation may be affected by the strength of Republican presence in a state. Therefore, I tested the hypothesis that states in which the majority of votes cast in the previous presidential election were for the Republican candidate would be more likely to appoint an FBL or enact faith-based policies. This correlation was not significant in any of the models—it appears that politics per se has not driven implementation of the initiatives.

Do States Need Faith-Based Help to Solve Welfare Coverage Problems?

Other variables related to policy hypotheses were significant, however. I looked at the relationship between the state poverty rate and welfare coverage. Results for poverty rates were significant in none of the models except the final ones (see Table 6.2, models 5 and 6), when poverty was significant—but in a direction *opposite* to that predicted. However, as predicted, states with more comprehensive welfare coverage were less likely to appoint FBLs or create faith-based legislation (see Tables 6.2 and 6.3). In other words, the likelihood of implementation was greatest not necessarily in the states where poverty was the greatest, but in those states that lacked a strong social safety net.

STRETCHING STATE DOLLARS. When a state's needs are greater, actors within that state will be more likely to create new policies and practices. In my interviews with state liaisons, almost all brought up the perceived fiscal benefits of creating faith-based practices—such policies could attract new federal money and allow religious groups to create a safety net to replace the one that the government was no longer providing. While liaisons often argued that fiscal necessity was of paramount concern, they were not ideologically concerned with the initiatives' move toward devolution and noted the continuing need for resources to help people in their states. One liaison acknowledged that the state office was created in a particular way, and in a particular branch of state government, to ensure receipt of federal money that would have been cut off had the office not been there (Feb. 7, 2005). In another state, the liaison described how the initiatives were a way to bring new resources in while leaving state coffers largely untouched:

> When I started at that time, faith-based wasn't a key component of what we
> were doing. It was a conversation, but it wasn't anything formal. That was
> one of the first things I did, I wrote like a brief outline of where were are
> now and this is what we could do if we wanted to create an office. It was
> like an options menu: Do we want to create an office? Do we want to have
> liaison relationship? Or do we not want to be involved at this time? So then
> we chose the liaison route for now because it required the least amount of
> staff, plus we hadn't identified a funding stream to help support that work
> [in state government] which is one of the issues that we looked at.
> Federally, there are faith-based offices in seven different agencies, and they
> can appropriate dollars to [state faith-based offices]. (Oct. 10, 2004)

The potential for state actions following from the faith-based initiatives to allow states to secure outside dollars while spending relatively little of their own money was a consistent theme throughout the interviews. While discussing faith-based efforts and why the state had an OFBCI to work with FBOs to provide services, one liaison said, "It leverages the dollars and makes great use of volunteers. It also has strengthened the relationship of the faith groups around the state" (Nov. 8, 2004). This liaison went on to argue that getting faith-based legislation passed at the state level would be easy because "it has no fiscal impact." He went on to state that the initiative was really about assisting government to do its job in a politically expedient manner. "I think it is our job to help those who can't help themselves and the faith-based and community-based organizations are just the perfect fit to help government do its job. And so I'm interested in that because number one, there's money available on the federal level and when the president says go left, you go left because that's where the money is going to be." In fact, in another state the liaison noted that they worked with each branch of state government to specifically create a faith-based piece that reflected the president's goals and platform:

> Every one of our state agencies has liaisons working on a specific piece that deals with this area. For example, the first lady Laura Bush in the president's State of the Union Address will focus on at-risk youth.... So our faith-based and community liaison at the Department of Juvenile Justice is really working on ways we can promote values within our juvenile justice system.... Department of Health is working in abstinence education, HIV/AIDS, and nutrition. (Feb. 9, 2005)

This instrumental appeal of the faith-based initiatives was succinctly summarized by yet another liaison: "I am a firm believer in resources, in resources" (March 23, 2005). Or, as another liaison said when discussing why his state pursued the initiatives (though in a very small way), "So how can we bring in extra dollars into the state? Whether we're spending it directly in the office or the communities get it . . . it really doesn't matter as long as we're able to increase the percentage that's coming into the state to create more programs or to continue the existing programs or enhance them" (Oct. 10, 2004). Later he discussed meeting with federal officials to find out whether there were "ways that our state can strengthen what it's doing to receive additional funds. How do we heighten our position to be considered a great location for faith-based funding?" Thus, states were sending out the signals to federal officials that they were in on the faith-based game. Even though the new funding did not materialize at the level promised, states responded to what they saw coming from the White House. Clearly, they hoped to get in on the action. Said one FBL:

> We are thinking about working very closely with various state departments and look[ing] at ways in which we can apply for federal grants through our different state departments that would be used to help us support activities with that particular grant, in that particular department, with the support of the office of community and faith-based initiatives. So it would be a partnership between our office and

several of the different departments that actually have a relationship, in terms of securing federal grants with the federal government. At the same time, focusing more on many of the grant opportunities that are coming out of the seven agency centers for faith-based and community initiatives that are tied to the White House OFBCI. We are also looking at ways in which we can approach the foundation community, people that support various aspects of projects or initiatives coming out of this office. So, we are looking at some creative ways to support the needs of the office. (April 30, 2005)

MAKING BETTER USE OF EXISTING RESOURCES. These instrumental concerns about new money were often coupled with the belief that while faith-based groups were often already providing some level of service, government could increase those services by providing some much-needed assistance: "I believe that a lot of individuals survive by turning to the community FBOs and grass roots before coming to us. . . . We need to strengthen the existing pools of providers and broaden capacity" (Dec. 13, 2004). This feeling that the faith-based groups were important because they were on the front lines was echoed by others. The sense was that if these groups were doing the good work first, they should be encouraged:

Basically we felt that those were the people on the front lines who had day-to-day contact with populations that we may not have been able to reach. . . . We also had a sense that it was important to bring their voices to the tables where decisions around employment and training were made. A lot of times, particularly in urban areas, barriers that residents face are multiple and complicated. . . . So we encouraged them at every opportunity that we had, the leaders of faith-based and grass-roots community organization to step forward to attend meetings, to hopefully offer themselves as possible members of boards. (April 15, 2005)

Or, as another liaison put it, "Our focus is on strengthening families, and one set of organizations that are . . . involved in trying to help that happen in partnership . . . with governmental and nonprofits and for-profits is the faith-based community" (Oct. 13, 2004). All of these statements suggest that religious groups need the initiatives to do more good works than they could before; whether or not this is true, it has resulted in substantial new efforts by state actors to create faith-based policies intended to increase these contributions to the social services sector.

NEGOTIATING THE TERMS OF THE RELATIONSHIP. Although the initiatives have great emotional appeal and value for many people, it is important to note that for some—especially many of the early supporters of the initiatives—there has been tension caused by the gap between the fiscal support they felt they had been promised and the actual implementation of the initiatives. Though the initiatives appealed to states in fiscal need because they offered the promise of more money and better services, this is not what they delivered. One former liaison was particularly distressed about the direction in which he saw his state going, commenting that the governor's office would not "pay for things like going to White House conferences; we are not allowed to get travel assistance. I think they don't want to be successful, and it was adopted as symbolic" (Dec. 10, 2004). He went on to describe his overall disappointment with the initiatives and their original political roots:

> I think the White House vision was not broad enough. . . . There has been a lack of leadership from the top. . . . There have been coalitions made, but the governor has no tight relationships, so the faith-based community is waiting till he's out. The way this is being implemented, it can't impact the faith community. It can't make an impact because it's not about money.

This liaison's statements are typical of a concern on the part of several liaisons: that there was a lack of political will to do much besides create the offices. Once that was done, these liaisons felt they had been left to do what they could with what few resources were provided, allowing those who created the offices to gain political benefit without having had to put up the money needed to make real changes.

In another instance, I asked a liaison if he thought the governor might be willing to create an office. His response was telling about the political will, and perhaps ideology, necessary to create a more substantial faith-based program:

> Nope. He's had plenty of chances to do it. There have been very general purposes associated with TANF, essentially towards resource development, but nothing ongoing, or permanent. In the year 2000 he did an executive order, ordering a number of departments to review their contracting restrictions, their language, and identify where there were any encumbrances for FBOs to contract for government services, but it was never followed through with by the governor's staff. So what I say is there's been some interest, but it hasn't been deep or consistent. (Oct. 13, 2004)

Interestingly, this lack of "deep or consistent" interest was highlighted in answers to questions I asked about whether states had received any objections to these practices. With the exceptions of the liaisons that found themselves under legal fire in Montana and Ohio, the other liaisons reported inquirers and occasional skepticism, but nothing that was lasting or consequential. For example, when I asked the liaison from another state whether she had experienced any opposition to what she was doing, she said, "Well, there is nothing to oppose. My position in everything is nonspecific, as far as the service with the faith community ... because my whole focus is on identifying resources, ensuring that we maximize the use of existing resources. . . . I think that has kept it from being real oppositional in any of the work that I am doing, because I am a real neutral person in the job that I have to do" (March 23, 2005). Even when objections were reported the liaisons did not feel they represented what people in the state really wanted and were merely a "very vocal minority" (Feb. 8, 2005).

But Are the Faith-Based Organizations Ready?

While bringing new religious groups into the social services sector to help make up the difference between a state's needs and the available federal resources may have been useful in some cases, states have generally found this transition much more difficult than originally expected (Chaves and Wineburg 2008, Green 2007). In fact, many of the initial efforts by liaisons to get grants to these organizations did not meet with success; instead there was skepticism on both sides:

> You know we've had little bits of disagreement. I think initially there were some people that were disappointed that our grant focused on behavioral health because they wanted to do something different. And then there's always some skepticism by the provider community. . . . The faith-based groups are coming in, and they will lower standards. Then I think we've had some hesitancy from FBOs, too. . . . They see this as [a] shifting of responsibility to them and not a great deal of funding. (Nov. 21, 2004)

Another liaison commented on some of the distinctive problems inherent in small FBOs, noting that the "smaller faith-based nonprofit organizations, they don't have the capacity to do the research to find funding, so basically we do it for them. . . . We let them know that it's really important to have this Internet access ... and then if they tell us that they don't have a computer, we try to get them information on organizations that will give them free computers" (Dec. 19, 2004). Or, as another liaison noted:

> You have everybody from the startup who has no understanding of federal grants and, "Yeah, I've got a bookkeeper; my wife keeps the books. She keeps them in a notebook that we keep under the mattress." Well, you can't do that when you get a federal grant! To, "Yes, I've already got half a million dollars in federal funds but I want to know how to leverage this to do more." So meeting people where they're at and trying to adapt to that has been a challenge. (Oct. 13, 2004)

Finally, a liaison in a state with a fairly well developed office found that even with all the help faith-based groups were being given through technical assistance and capacity building efforts, many FBOs were just not ready:

> And most of our calls are really remedial, I mean, I have never had a call from someone who said, "Okay, I have a 501(c)3, I've been doing this counseling program for ten years, here's my success rate." And just when you start with a basic checklist, it's "Do you have this?" "No." It's very remedial, and then we just put them, refer them to some of these people, put them in the faith-based information loop. (Feb. 10, 2005)

The amount of technical assistance and support needed by small faith-based groups raises questions about how many resources state offices should invest in trying to make these groups viable social service providers; it seems unlikely that supplying them with new computers and new networks will be enough.

Finally, in one state another problem arose when faith-based groups appeared to just be "going after the money" and not doing the real partnership work necessary to create sustainable activity:

> Let me tell you something . . . we had a proposal come in, they got top grade . . . we were going to fund them until we went . . . it was a nonexistent building. Well, it was a building, but there wasn't a program or anything, and they came in and got top grade until we did the research and found out that we didn't know these people. (Aug. 17, 2004)

Although this liaison was able to find out about the faith-based group that had not done the work necessary, not all states are going to be able to investigate potential cases of misrepresentation. Potentially if there is a perception that faith-based groups are what government is seeking out as partners, it may be more likely that some groups will make the appearance of being faith-based, even if they are not.

A Complicated Mixture

In some states, of course, the descriptions given by liaisons illuminated a process of implementation that was not as purposeful as those described above, but implementation still went forward because the rhetoric and politics surrounding the initiatives.

> Well, obviously because of the [2004] re-election, the faith-based initiative is still one of the governor's top priorities. . . . We've only been at this for one year, and so now that we have another four years of President Bush, and we know the faith-based initiatives will be highlighted for another four years, we will take more of an aggressive role. We should, and could, and will take a more aggressive role. (Nov. 8, 2004)

Table 6.4 shows the various combinations of reasons for state implementation, based on the liaisons' stated degrees of fiscal need and religious appeal. Using data from the interviews with liaisons, I divided the states based on whether there was a stated faith focus in the state's faith-based practices. Eighteen states had an explicitly faith-focused agenda, with the affective concerns of the policy clearly being both felt and practiced by liaisons. Liaisons who expressed a faith focus were more likely to be in states where there had been a strong evangelical movement presence within the Republican Party since 1994 (Alabama, Arkansas, Florida, Georgia, Louisiana, South Carolina, Ohio, Oklahoma, Texas) and in states that were early adopters of these policies. Of course there are exceptions to this, with New Jersey and New York clearly not having had a strong evangelical movement presence in state politics but still having strong faith-based movements; but it appears that in the early stages of faith-based policy implementation, the religious values of the liaison, as well as the evangelical movement power in the state, were important to state faith-based practices.

One interesting tension in all of this can be seen in how these offices may be changing over time. Many of the liaisons that were the most faith-focused when I interviewed them are now no longer in the liaison positions. Also, liaisons in states that had implemented the policies later did not have the same

TABLE 6.4. Patterns in Instrumental vs. Affective Reasons for Policy Implementation

Focus	Description	States
Faith-Focused: High Affective and High Instrumental	States whose actors expressed both of these concerns implemented policies for both fiscal and faith-based reasons. They showed fiscal need after PWROA,[1] as well as a faith focus.[2] These states were likely to be early adopters (2004 or before).	AL, AZ, AK, CO, FL GA, HI, IN, MD, MI MT, NE, NJ, NY, OH, OK, SC, TX
Fiscally Focused: Low Affective and High Instrumental	Religious concerns were not paramount in these states; instead fiscal needs were most likely to be cited. These states were more likely to be late adopters (after 2004).	AR, CT, DC, MN, NM, UT, VA, WY
Other	State liaisons in this category were either very new to the initiatives in their state, or were in the position temporarily. Neither fiscal nor religious concerns were dominant; instead, actors were performing tasks they had been assigned.	ID, KS, NC, ND

1. Personal Work and Responsibility Act, enacted in 1996.
2. This does not mean these states were necessarily discriminatory, but actors were more likely to be focused on creating greater involvement from the faith-based sector than were state actors who were less acquainted with the initiative or were more focused on the potential fiscal benefits rather than on the faith-based elements.

clear faith focus as the early liaisons; thus it could be that over time the faith focus, especially the evangelical movement faith focus, could be waning, and a more professionalized and bureaucratic set of faith-based initiatives may be emerging. While it is too early to tell if this will be a continuing pattern, it is interesting to note that as these offices and positions continue over time, the actors most concerned with the faith-based aspects of the initiatives were eventually replaced or quit because they felt the focus had shifted away from religion and toward a symbolic political platform. Even if the liaisons or government officials are not ideologically tied to implementing faith-based initiatives, these changes still represent a cultural shift toward cooperation and collaboration between church and state.

The Affective and the Instrumental: Religion and Fiscally Conservative Politics

Although federal and state governments have not lived up to many of their early promises about the initiatives—most notably, in the lack of significant financial resources for the poor and otherwise needy—the initiatives have had an impact. There has been a new integration of religion into government, in a way that appears to make government less necessary and religion more impor-tant. This perfect storm of religion meeting devolution of social services to the private sector has created a new set of institutions that make religion more prominent while seeking to take government at least partially out of the picture. As one liaison put it, "Social problems are not completely solvable by government.... So [the faith-based initiative] is part of a larger vision of engaging communities and religious organizations and business in the busi-ness of taking care of each other" (Dec. 3, 2004).

In some ways, this new version of the hollow state, as described in Chapter 1, is nothing new at all. For many years, government social services have been chipped away in favor of a larger role for private organizations and nonprofit agencies (Milward and Provan 2002), and in some ways the initiatives' goal of increasing religious group involvement is just another example of this. But in another respect there is something fundamentally new and different about the faith-based initiatives and about how they are being enacted that bears exami-nation. While this confluence of religious and fiscal policy is evident at the federal level, one interview with a state liaison yielded a good illustration of how faith-based policy captures this relationship between religion and devolu-tion. The liaison articulated how the initiatives could enhance fiscal responsi-bility, because they used resources in a better manner:

> Of course, in my eyes that's a big piece of what the faith-based initiatives
> are, and Jim Towey says that when he gets up to speak that FBOs are

often overlooked even though they are the most effective and efficient providers of such services. So I just think that is very important, and because I am a bottom-line kind of person . . . I would like to see all tax dollars, especially mine, being utilized efficiently. (Feb. 7, 2005)

Summary and Conclusion

State liaison positions, OFBCIs, and legislation related to the faith-based initiatives have come about as a result of a complex mix of instrumental and affective reasons. Regardless of the reasons for implementation, however, once created, these liaison positions, offices, and laws become part of the structure of state politics and in effect institutionalize religion in state government (Bartkowski and Regis 2003). The information collected from those intimately and passionately involved with the initiatives together with the quantitative data gathered point to a system of faith-based practices that is more about hoping for change than about tangible change being realized. This is not to deny the efforts made by individuals working in the system who have attempted to create new networks, change attitudes of government officials, and bring new services to those in need through their individual, and often valiant, efforts. Rather, it is to point out that they have done this with very little financial or institutional help or support. As one liaison said, "I had been working with the governor, and I thought the campaign had made a commitment to empower faith-based groups; this is not what has happened" (Dec. 10, 2004).

What these liaisons and policies *have* created is something new in state government: a permanent institutionalization of religion. In fact, some of the liaisons noticed the seeming practical redundancy of their positions, noting that "we have always worked with FBOs" (Aug. 20, 2004). This, of course, raises a question: If this activity has really been going on all along, why the need for liaisons, offices, and legislation?

The variety of reasons for implementing faith-based policies has resulted in a peculiar tension within the coalition of supporters of the faith-based initiatives. Many of the supporters from religious circles hoped to see more public money go to religious organizations, as promised by President Bush in 2001. Fiscally conservative supporters, on the other hand, wished for devolution of government services to religious organizations without giving them more money. These conflicting reasons for supporting the initiatives are being played out on the ground, with those on the fiscal conservative side clearly winning. In a 2008 op-ed piece, David Kuo and John Dilulio, two of the earliest supporters of federal faith-based policy, wrote:

> The initiative prescribed $8 billion in tax credits and new spending, including at least $700 million in a "compassion fund" to benefit

exemplary programs. It was designed so that small congregations and ministries that had long served needy neighbors on shoestring budgets—and not just large, national religious charities—could get their fair share of government aid. It did not happen. . . . Every nonpartisan study has concluded that the initiative has not delivered the grants, vouchers, tax incentives and other support for FBOs that the president originally promised.

Instead of gaining a flood of new fiscal support, the initiatives have largely relied on bureaucratic and institutional changes that appeal to a wide base of supporters, without any large-scale change in how social services function in the United States.

One of the last interviews I conducted was with a liaison who had been a long-term government employee; she was one of the few liaisons who had been appointed to the position without actively seeking it. This lack of ideological investment in the initiatives may have given her a view of them that was inherently different from that of many other liaisons. She said that although she saw the potential of the initiatives, she had concerns both about other liaisons' general lack of understanding of how government works and about whether the other liaisons would be able to effectively communicate rules regarding government grants and church-state separation to the new faith-based groups they were contacting. "The other liaisons are not at the same level of knowledge about government. How does government do this correctly, rather than primarily focusing on the initiative? The initiative is misunderstood," she said. "No one wants to talk about certain aspects of it" (Dec. 13, 2004). Later in the interview, she added that it was

extremely important for states to know each other, because we need to do this in a way that is legal, and coming together as a group is how you go about that. I have been surprised by hearing about programs getting money that have religion at the same time. Public funds should not have a religious component. If you can't remove the religious dimension, you should not get money. We need to monitor these groups like any grant recipient. Monitoring schools with a faith-based component should be the same as the secular.

Her concern about liaisons' lack of knowledge about church-state separation is particularly important in light of the recently increased state appropriations for funding for FBOs (see Chapter 4). A recent study showed that the share of grants awarded to faith-based groups increased in six federal agencies between 2002 and 2004 (Montiel and Ragan 2006). In addition, the number of states setting aside faith-based appropriations increased from none in 1997 to 10 in 2007.

Whether such funding increases occur or not, symbolic politics argues that the importance of state policy resides in what it represents. By creating policies and practices that present religion as a legitimate and necessary partner of government, the faith-based initiatives are meeting the goal of those who support the initiatives because they appeal to their desire to bring religion more prominently into the public sphere. Therefore, perhaps the most important consequence of these new positions, offices, and laws is the cultural change they represent: a move towards acknowledging and supporting a greater role for religion in the political sphere. This effect may, indeed, increase: social movements that gain political access and otherwise meet with success can create space for further movement access and success.

Whether the faith-based initiatives came about because of increased fiscal pressure, the political savvy of those who saw its ability to resonate with so many, or the increasing presence of conservative evangelicals within the Republican Party—or some combination of all of the above—the result is the same: faith-based initiatives have blossomed at the state level. The legal, legislative, and administrative changes created surrounding the initiatives are creating a new norm, a norm that represents integration of religion, rather than separation.

7

Religion, Policy, and Politics

Institutionalizing Religion within State Government

Symbols are the currency of politics—ideology, discourse, and political mobilization would be impossible without them.

> —Rhys Williams and Jeffrey Blackburn, "Many Are
> Called, but Few Obey"

What does faith-based mean these days? Does that mean we are really religious and it is a protestant view of the world? I think there's a lot of concern about the definition these days.... Everybody is trying to figure out how to make the thing work, or what it is even supposed to mean in the first place.

> —Faith-based liaison, interview with the author,
> Dec. 13, 2005

The Expansion of the Faith-Based Front

Moving away from the Jeffersonian idea of separation of church and government, through faith-based initiatives states have by and large embraced a strategy of cooperation and institutionalization. Whether by design or coincidence, these changes have fundamentally altered the nature of the relationship between church and state in the Untied States. At the state level, these changes have occurred mainly through the three mechanisms that I outlined in Chapters 4 through 6: bureaucratic implementation, legislation, and public rhetoric. Whether these changes came from the desire to have a more faith-focused agenda, through a pragmatic strategy of pursuing aid from either FBOs or from grants from the federal government, or through a politically-motivated "God strategy," the initiatives have altered the discourse surrounding religion and government from one of separation to a culture of cooperation. A new norm based on the belief of the inseparable nature of religion and social services is creating a new role for religion in the public sphere. The positions of the candidates in the most recent (2008) presidential election would seem to indicate that these changes will be long term, rather than merely the interesting historical footnote some had predicted.

The ambiguous nature of the faith-based initiatives has meant policies and practices created in their name can appeal to a variety of constituencies because they offer seemingly simple solutions to many complex social problems. As Edelman (1971: 83) argued, social myths generated at least in part by our political leaders and their social policies "permit men to live in a world in which the causes are simple and neat and the remedies are apparent." The myth created by the faith-based initiatives was that the simple addition of a dose of religion could solve the social problems of poverty and addiction. Whether this was true did not matter; the empirical reality on which the policies were based need not be verifiable. It was the stories on which they were based that were important. Using the power of political symbolism to create faith-based policies, new political myths were created and new political realities generated.

No Simple Solution

Promises, Promises

When President Bush began promoting his faith-based initiatives, there were promises made—promises of money, promises of hope, and promises of help, all to those who needed it most. Most of those promises made early on have not come true. Instead of rallying the "armies of compassion," the president's faith-based initiatives have become what critics are calling a "faith-based photo-op" (Burke 2008). What researchers have consistently pointed out is that, by and large, faith-based groups could not take over many aspects of the social services sector (Green 2007, Wineburg and Chaves 2008) even if they desired to do so—which many simply do not.[1] Furthermore, while some groups may have been eager to receive government grants, the promised money never materialized. Instead of providing more material resources, the initiatives had the ironic and unintended consequence of sending more people out for the same pot of money that had always been available. The initiatives were not the simple solution that so many had hoped they would be. Although they had originally been discussed as being about fiscal assistance to organizations doing work at the grassroots level, they became something else entirely.

A REVISED VERSION. This first version of the faith-based initiatives gave way to another version, one that was focused on creating cultural rather than material changes in government and in the social services sector. Instead of outreach with the backing of fiscal support, the initiatives became a series of symbolic gestures to faith-based groups and to the public at large. Like President Bush's politics at the federal level, this God strategy appealed to many constituencies and was still wrapped in the vague promise that state governments would receive some relief from the financial burden of caring for the poor and needy.

Thus the overall impact of the faith-based initiatives may best be measured not in dollars and cents, but in the effects of this new role for religion inside government institutions and of cultural understandings that are being trans-mitted by these policies. Social policy theorists have long argued that policy creates new politics and new political allies (Edelman 1964, 1971; Lowi 1969). Support for a social policy is not necessarily due to the material resources generated, but by what the policy represents. What makes the faith-based initiatives so appealing to so many politicians—and to their constituencies— is that so little input is required to derive the potential benefits of putting churches at the forefront of social services delivery. This was, and is, appealing to many politicians who, to put it bluntly, could get all of the faith-based bang without spending the buck.

SYMBOLS AND CULTURAL GOODS. State faith-based practices have served two functions. First, as political symbols they appealed to both the instrumental and affective concerns of those creating the policies, as well as those living in the states where policies are created. Second, these policies simultaneously represented the cultural goods of the faith-based initiatives; they represented social movement success for those who initially created the initiatives, because their hopes included a new norm of religion and politics. Thus they have been a success in and of themselves, and they are a potential path for creating further institutionalization of religion within the state.

These faith-based practices have, in effect, created multiple initiatives, with different and often disparate goals: one that says the initiatives are about funding and one that says the initiatives are about access and cultural change. The consequence has been the creation of a new legal and bureaucratic culture that views religion as integral to government—and not the creation of more and better help for the needy. This lack of great success in actually improving social services is largely due to the lack of commitment from those at the top, not from those at the bottom. While some states have clearly made progress in creating better networks, helping groups assess their capacity, and attempting to over-haul government culture, most states have had problems and lack the fiscal backing to carry out deep and meaningful actions that move beyond creating an office or liaison position and leaving the rest up to them.

As I said in the last chapter, liaisons have found that even with this effort, most religious groups are still not able to apply for or carry out extensive social services, a point borne out in recent research (Green 2007). This may be in large part because of the lack of significant and consistent fiscal commitment to these efforts from the states. Of the 39 states with liaisons, 29 do not have any specific appropriations to support the liaisons' actions. Even so, the commitment of those at the bottom—the liaisons in their offices, the FBOs out in the field—did not wane over time, despite the fact that they got mixed signals and varying stories about what their role could and should be in state government and social services.

Two Views

These two faces of faith became clear in the interviews I conducted. Some liaisons, as I have shown in earlier chapters, clearly felt cheated and perhaps misled when there was little or no money to help them help the poor. Others, however, stated that they thought all along that the initiatives were not about new money but about access to existing government funds that faith-based groups had felt excluded from applying for. And here one might ask: if the initiatives were only about ensuring access, and these groups already had access, then why the need for new policies? Why have Charitable Choice or other faith-based initiatives? Were creating these policies and fostering greater access the means to a different end?

Institutionalization of Religion in State Level Government

Church-state relations in the United States have never been without controversy. Whether secularists feel the influence of religion is too great, or religious activists believe their voices are ignored, a variety of groups have sought to create a norm and interpretation that best suits their view of an appropriate relationship. Too much religion—or religion of the wrong kind—is not acceptable, but no religion of any kind is often just as unacceptable. In a nation that embraces religious pluralism, any dramatic shift in the fluid mixture of religion, politics, and money in public life creates the potential for new problems, new cries of outrage, and new sources of mistrust among religious groups. Why would a state adopt a policy that has the potential to stir up these problems? The answer lies in the complex interplay of religion, politics, and money.

Church-state relationships in many ways changed dramatically over the eight years of the Bush administration. Legal changes in understandings of the funding of religious organizations, shifts in the composition of the Supreme Court and other judiciary offices, and the overall legislative influence of the administration on issues such as stem cell research, abstinence education, gay marriage, and intelligent design have created what may be one of this country's largest cultural and legal shifts in the understanding of the role of religion in the public square (Henriques 2006). This combination of religiously based law and social policy is creating a new dynamic, and the faith-based initiatives are at the center of the debate.

Faith-Based Liaisons

As I discussed earlier, the creation of the position of FBL is the most common, and probably most important, way that states have implemented the faith-based initiatives. Government infrastructure has been altered by these positions, which have created new roles for religion; this has had policy and political ramifications. The changes have the potential to alter not only the political climate within government, but also that of other social institutions that come into contact with state politics and government. State liaisons act as conduits between religious groups and government agencies; and whether liaisons see their positions as the result of underlying political motivations or not, they bring with them their own religious beliefs and connections. Intentionally or not, liaisons can alter the political landscape by controlling who gets information and assistance in gaining access to government funding.

Regardless of what they are actively doing to change the social services climate, what they represent is important. Until the creation of these positions, there were no bureaucratic positions inside state government whose specific functions were to reach out to the religious community and engage them to be part of government-sponsored social services. The fact that they explicitly represent faith-based groups and that they work to increase the presence of such groups in government affairs demonstrates a new way in which religion is becoming part of politics.[2] This is the case regardless of the particular faith of the liaisons. Their very existence is enough: they are the embodiment of what President Bush saw as the new direction for church-state relations—one in which cooperation and integration, rather than separation, are the norm.

Legislation

Many of the legislative changes that have taken place at the state level are also a significant departure from the traditional model of church/state separation. Various legislative changes have encouraged faith-based groups to provide social services, and they have tended to create an environment that may give these groups a privileged position by placing their members on advisory boards, funding OFBCIs, and changing the legal environment to encourage state partnerships with FBOs. Such legislative changes codify the story behind the faith-based initiatives, and the story is that FBOs are a crucial part of the social services system and that new legislation is needed to ensure their active participation. What is perhaps most striking about these changes is the quantity and quality of the legislation over time. While the story of the initiatives has largely disappeared from the front pages of newspapers, lawmakers continue to add policy changes to the books. These permanent changes to state law create another level of integration between religion and government. They set a new place at the government table for FBOs—one that is largely unnoticed and is not clearly necessary.

Conferences

Finally, while liaisons and legislative changes have altered the administrative and policy landscapes in the states that have adopted them, many of the conferences held as part of the faith-based initiatives have also altered church-state relations by using state dollars to fund conferences that integrate religion into the policy discussion. Many of these conferences have been modeled on black church culture and embody state sponsorship of the cultural construction of religion. Using the trappings of black church services to create a friendly environment, they have been used in an attempt to gain new supporters for the initiatives from within the black religious community, appealing to the belief among many religious blacks that religion should have a larger role in politics. It seems clear that conference organizers have been using religious elements found in black churches in the hopes of creating a new constituency for the faith-based initiatives—as well as a new constituency for the political party that created the initiatives. Of course the election of Barack Obama as president illustrates the failure of these politically charged events to help the Republican Party gain much permanent legitimacy within the vast majority of the African American community.

Combined, the liaisons, legislation, and conferences have created an environment that places religion at the forefront of state policy. By beginning to change how religion is viewed in the United States, the rhetoric and implementation of the initiatives have created a larger space for faith-based groups in the public sphere, largely refocusing the relationship from separation to cooperation and institutionalization. Religious groups have historically played a crucial role in the delivery of social services in America; however, this new alliance is likely to change the dynamics between church and state in significant and lasting ways.

Symbolic Politics, the Evangelical Movement, and the Politics of Welfare

I began looking at this issue with one central question in mind: Why have states implemented practices related to the faith-based initiatives? The federal government encouraged, but did not require, states to make these changes.

However, state actors did make significant changes, which have lead to an integration of religion into government at a level that has not been seen before in America. Why did states embrace these policy changes? If, as I have found, there was little in the way of new funding to help those in need of social services, what was the purpose?

The Strength of the Evangelical Movement

As discussed in Chapter 6, the first set of variables I found that affected the likelihood of a state's adopting faith-based policies and practices was the previous effect of the evangelical movement in the state. Two variables related to this movement strength significantly increased a state's willingness to appoint FBLs, create relevant laws, and generally emphasize the faith-based initiatives at the state level. States in which the evangelical movement had greater influence within the Republican Party were more likely to create liaison positions and pass faith-based laws. Previous success of the evangelical movement in the policy arena was also a significant predictor of future success of the faith-based movement. Together, these factors suggest a situation in which faith-based policy implementation was intimately linked with the strength and power of the conservative evangelical movement within state governments. This is perhaps not surprising, since the faith-based movement got its start when the evangelical movement's elite had inside access to politics through George W. Bush and John Ashcroft, among others.

The reality of faith-based policy implementation leaves many questions about the intent of many of its supporters. The lack of substantial new funding streams to social service organizations renders dubious President Bush's argument that the initiatives were about help to the needy, an example of compassionate conservatism. Meanwhile, the underlying goals of many within the conservative evangelical movement are being met: for those who want a closer connection between religion and government, there has been at least partial success, as the initiatives have done their job of creating a new norm of legislation and bureaucratization of faith.

Fiscal Necessity

As established earlier, fiscal necessity was a major influence on a state's response to the faith-based initiatives. The allure of the faith-based initiatives as a fiscal solution to social services needs was based on political symbolism that was powerful and deeply rooted in American culture: personal faith (or the lack thereof) was not only the cause of poverty and addiction but was also proposed as the best (or only) solution.

Two things contributed to the success of the initiatives after the 1996 welfare reform bill was passed. First, states were facing a crisis as a result of the welfare reform. They desperately needed to find ways to plug the many fiscal holes that the reforms had left, and state officials were searching for any help they could find; sometimes just the attempt or the appearance of helping was enough. In this climate, the faith-based initiatives were offered not only as a better solution, but as a cheaper one, too. Religious groups made up of volunteers were expected to take on the roles previously taken by trained professionals in government-funded social services organizations. Thus, the burden of the welfare state would at least be partially pushed into the private sector.

Unfortunately, my conversations with liaisons showed that most states have found that FBOs cannot take over for shortcomings in government-funded social services: they are simply unequipped to carry out high-quality social services on a sustained basis. Although many organizations are doing wonderful things in their communities, the solution to the drastic cuts resulting from welfare reform cannot come mainly from the faith community, especially if it is not given significant new funds to carry out new projects and services. This reality has, of course, not stopped politicians from creating polices and practices that rely on the perpetuation of this myth. The power of the political symbolism created by the initiatives has proved to be something that legislators and government actors are not willing to give up; on the contrary, it is becoming ever more popular, in ever more states.

A second factor contributing to the success of the initiatives is part of the long history of welfare and social services in the United States: groups that are in need are seen by some as morally deficient and often undeserving of social services unless they are willing to make a personal change. While this view is certainly not universal, and there is a renewed progressive religious movement in the United States with younger evangelicals who see the need for a broader agenda (Slater 2007), there are still some religious and secular actors who blame the poor for their own situation. This is not new. Welfare reform movements at the turn of the previous century were similar both in their outlook on the causes of poverty and in their proposed solutions. While many people have certainly found solace in religious groups and in the help they offer, blaming the growing rates of poverty, the decreasing social safety net, and the stagnation in wages over the last 20 years on a lack of religious belief lacks empirical support. It is only through comprehensive social policies that address both the individual and structural roots of poverty, addiction, and homelessness in America—with faith-based groups as part of the process—that we can begin to find real remedies for the increasing tide of social despair facing many communities in this country. Recent work from religious groups shows that there is great concern among the religious community, a desire to make these changes, and belief that action by both religious organizations and the government is necessary to create the comprehensive help that those in need require (Leland 2005).

Policy Suggestions: Manageable but Meaningful

Motivations behind the faith-based initiatives are numerous; so too are opinions regarding what to do next. The question of whether the initiatives should be pursued at all and whether they are good for the country may reasonably be debated. I will assume for now, however, that the initiatives have worked their way into our collective political life—and that they may be expected to remain for some time. Given that the initiatives appear here to stay, what can—or should—be done next? As one liaison stated, "let's not throw the baby out with the baptismal water" (April 30, 2005).

Perhaps not surprisingly, FBLs are a rich source of possible answers to these questions. In fact, many FBLs offered suggestions not because I asked them to, but because they felt strongly that there are better ways to go about creating a stable and useful relationship between government and the faith-based sector. Notably, some clearly realized that the goal of the vast majority of congregations and religious groups is first and foremost to minister to their flock (Chaves 2004). Although many groups wanted to become part of the social services sector, they often had to do this under the constraints of limited resources, limited workers, and limited professional experience. In spite of these limitations, the liaisons also knew that these FBOs wanted to take a bigger role, and it was their job to help them do so in a way that was successful for the groups and useful for the individuals they were trying to help.

Assessing the Playing Field

States are very different, so it should be no surprise that FBOs vary considerably among states, both in size and in their willingness to engage with the government to provide social services. States also vary in the number of faith-based groups that are already involved in providing social services. One of the first and best tasks for states starting to create faith-based initiatives was to survey the lay of their land. Some states were able to do this, surveying both FBOs and state agencies. However, with little authority or funding backing them up, most states met with frustration when trying to complete this task—if they were able to start it in the first place. Some liaisons, for example those in New Mexico and Michigan, were able to survey FBOs to get an accurate picture of their involvement in order to move on in a balanced and orderly fashion. However, most states were not able to complete good surveys; without an understanding of what was already in place, the players who were or were not working together, and what organizational capacity was available, states were flying blind and creating policies and outreach methods that may have been totally inappropriate for the groups with which they were working.

One liaison described a process by which she gathered information about the FBOs she was working with, about the private organizations in her state that could help them, and about the state agencies she could then connect these groups with. After successfully amassing that information, her hope was to increase the numbers of FBOs receiving outside federal grants in her state:

> In early January, I'd like to do a mailing to [the database of FBOs in the state], and direct them back to a Web site that I've established for the faith-based initiatives, to have them update their contact information and also fill out a survey that is going to ask the organization questions about what their capacity-building needs are. What I have found in my state, in 2004, we only had 10 nonprofits in our state apply directly for discretionary grants. Those 10 I want to build upon, so we have 15 or 20 more in the class of 2006 applying for federal grants. Many of them have never gone through the process, and need some help to do that. Another goal of mine is, I have come from the private sector, so I have had a lot of private companies and executives in those companies step forward and say, "If you need our skill set, match them to the nonprofits that need capacity building, whether it's board training or RFP training or writing or CPA help." I am going to match those people who have stepped forward on a volunteer basis to the nonprofits, and have a mentoring program. So, I am going to basically handpick, with advice from other folks in our state, the next class, the class of 2006—I've already been meeting with those nonprofits and getting their agreement that they will apply for federal grants, and try to match them with the correct federal grants, and getting their needs met in terms what they need from us to be able to do that. (Dec. 13, 2005)

This process required not only time and money, but also careful insight and planning based on the particular needs of the state. There are many things states can learn from each other, but in most cases, a one-size faith-based initiative does not fit all.

Funding the Initiatives

To do an adequate initial assessment of its faith-based landscape, a state must be willing to invest some money, and ideally the assessment should be reviewed over time. But the reality, of course, is that most states lack the money, personnel, and other resources required to sustain even minimal networks and outreach to faith-based groups. Many states that adopt the initiatives do not have full-time staff or funding beyond basic office space and overhead. In one liaison's succinct description, "We have what's called a 'zero' budget" (Dec. 28, 2005). Needless to say, this limits the work such liaisons can do. One liaison told me that he was becoming the person that other government agencies came to, looking for money—he was the state liaison, after all. But money is one of many things he did not have:

> A person from our Department of Social Services came over and was talking to me . . . she has been designated the responsibility of working with groups and of course, she is employed not from faith-based money . . . and she is looking for the funds also. She came over and we talked. She was hopeful that I would be able to direct her in a way that she could get some funds, and of course I was directing her back to where she came from. (March 7, 2005)

Many liaisons were left in this position of not being able to do much more than tell people where to look elsewhere for money. They often felt that the government had been spending time and government funds to build FBO's capacity, but no money was delivered to help these organizations use that capacity (Dec. 14, 2004).

But such liaisons do need to be careful what they wish for. As I discussed in Chapters 4 and 5, once states and religious organizations become either funders or funded institutions, the watchful eyes of many groups turn toward them. Before funding FBOs, states need to consider very carefully how they are going to explain, and then enforce, guidelines regarding constitutional issues to religious organizations. As the liaison from one state described, while the state recognized that more religious groups were going to be receiving money, it had yet to figure out how to ensure that the recipients would not break any constitutional boundaries:

> Our standards are such [that] where all of our authorities are licensed by our Department of Health and Environmental Control, all of our treatment folks are credentialed nationally and by the state. They don't have to be both, but at a certain level in terms of supervision, they have to be nationally. Technically, any faith-based entity who wants to provide treatment inside of our state under our funding, they have to meet those standards. We haven't begun to broach that yet. . . . That's something we'll have to deal with. (Dec. 14, 2004)

Unfortunately, most states have not created a systematic way to deal with constitutional issues and federal guidelines surrounding the use of public money; as I noted in Chapter 3, the consequences can be harsh for both the state and the FBOs with whom they are contracting.

Creating Consistency in Monitoring and Understanding of Regulations

In Montana and Ohio, state liaisons and offices rapidly found that distributing money through their OFBCIs to various faith-based groups fell under the scrutiny of groups outside and inside government. One strategy to avoid violating the law would be to pay more attention to developing regulations and monitoring programs before funds are distributed. State and federal agencies could take the time to create consistency in these efforts and educate not only the groups that will receive public money but also the liaisons who counsel the FBOs about government contracting. For example, requiring that churches create a separate 501(c)3 to fund their social services activities would limit the chances of problems. As is the case in most endeavors, prevention of problems is much less expensive than intervention after a mistake has been made.

One liaison found this out the hard way and helped a group get government funds and then had those taken away after they had begun work. "We had to stop funding the Prisoner Reentry Program, which I feel terrible about because it's a great program but it was inherently religious and we couldn't segregate the money clearly enough. Nor was Johnny, the guy who runs it, willing to really change his program and I certainly respect that" (Oct. 15, 2004). Until the lines are clarified and a continuity of regulations in place in all states, groups such as the one above are in danger of starting a well intentioned program and then finding themselves either without the funding required or even in legal trouble, creating bad feelings on all sides.

The question of what aspects of religion are permissible during provision of services is one of the larger problems that have been created because of the ambiguity of the faith-based initiatives. While the liaisons I spoke with understood that proselytizing was not allowed, for some this appeared to be the limit to their level of understanding, probably because the rules about what types of activities are not allowed are very complex. And in some cases, state rules may be stricter than federal government regulations. In one state they found a way to deal with these complications by having the faith-based advisory board keep up with state and federal church-state regulations in order to reduce the likelihood of legal problems (Feb. 21, 2005). If states can work with legal experts to create consistent education around these issues, then problems with funding FBOs could largely be averted. For the most part, the rules about what is acceptable are already out there;[3] it is consistency in enforcement and understanding that is lacking.

Building Bridges with the Government

When the faith-based initiatives were first introduced, it was not always made clear that to receive government grants, FBOs would have to work with and partner with government agencies and other social services groups. In Chapter 3, I discussed how liaisons have networked with government agencies. This kind of networking is a critical step because, more often than not, state agencies are the ones who control the money. However, liaisons and FBOs also need to work with secular agencies in a way that is respectful of the knowledge and expertise of all parties.

In an example of good practice, one state liaison did a careful assessment of where the state stood in its work with FBOs:

> The first thing, when I came in, was wrestling with the question of what these state offices are supposed to be doing, or strategic planning, and can we best position ourselves . . . to move forward, better engaging . . . the small grassroots . . . serving people. The first question I had is: How far had this philosophy gotten down in state agencies? Charitable Choice requirements? Equal treatment requirements? All these things. How far down was it? Also, where were our agencies in their current work with faith- and community-based groups? What were they doing? What was their interface? [So] we asked three major questions: What is the current work going on with faith- and community-based groups? What are barriers to greater partnerships? What are the opportunities? Really trying to spark innovation, getting people to think that it's not just about financial partnership, it's about information sharing, it's about communication in general. It's about access, it's about all these issues. . . . There were liaisons appointed specifically for this task from 10 state agencies, and we begin to have these discussions and to go through and see how far are we in answering these questions. I think it is a very important step for us, priming the pump, getting the internal house in order and making sure the infrastructure is there on the state government's side. (March 27, 2005)

Such partnerships require work and understanding from both sides. This can happen only when a liaison makes the effort to build bridges among the various kinds of groups, showing each that there is something to be gained by working in partnership. For example, one liaison brought in representatives from federal and state agencies to help local FBOs understand the requirements of church-state separation and the government granting process:

> We even had a workshop when the whole [CCF] initiative came out, and there was talk about churches separating their social service programs from the churches and [how] they should start 501(c)3s. We had someone who really had the expertise in working with the faith-based community and doing that come and give a session on how to apply for your 501(c)3. (Dec. 19, 2004)

Only by working with one another and talking about the problems—and the potential solutions to those problems—can the crucial bridges be built.

Building Bridges with Communities

While working with government agencies is certainly one aspect of increasing the social service activity of FBOs, providing government-funded services is only one way that FBOs can help their communities. Many can seek less formal collaborations within their communities. This is similar to the approach proposed by the liaisons in Oklahoma and Wyoming. Although in those cases, some money was given directly to service-providing organizations, the greater portion went to organizations that were the most likely to reach out to the community and create lasting relationships, as, for example, in Wyoming's "One Church, One Child" program, which asked every congregation to recruit one foster parent for an existing foster-parent program. This type of informal partnership provides not only a great entry-level opportunity for FBOs that would like to engage in social services but also offers something to the community that is not available elsewhere. Educating liaisons about informal opportunities such as these is likely to lead them to a better understanding of their communities and may eventually create an environment in which more organizations provide help on a regular basis. Having a church adopt a foster parent is, of course, a far cry from having them run extensive programs, but it could be a first step in the right direction.

Again, these unfunded collaborations can highlight and use the capacity of religious groups for the benefit of the population. They can build on existing resources and prepare faith-based groups for taking on greater responsibility in the future. So while small religious groups are often at the forefront of their communities, there is a limit to the amount of the work of meeting social service needs that they can take on. With expert help from intermediaries that have reliable information and a working knowledge of the granting process the two groups can potentially find a way to make the best use of their skills and resources. However, if FBOs are asked to find and administer government grants without the proper training and financial support, the result may well be frustration, disappointment, and a resistance to future involvement.

One aspect of building bridges is making sure that the FBOs know each other. In many states, the liaisons were surprised by how little contact there was among faith-based groups; one said that "the whole movement seems to be disorganized, certainly in this state. . . . We have a lot of fragmented groups out there working, and they are doing some things themselves on their own initiative" (March 7, 2005). In another case, the liaison speculated on how much good could be accomplished if groups would pool their resources; maybe one small group could not do much, but five, ten, fifteen or twenty could do a lot:

> Because if we could get all those groups to come together then we
> could do some really, good work, we could do more, even better work
> than we're doing now. Because we were at another thing and the
> pastor tells us, he says, "We have 22 ministers who have come
> together, brought their churches together for Bible study." And I think
> that's fantastic. But you know the next question I asked? I say, "Now,

are all 22 of them part of your consortium to bid on grants and do—?"
Oh!... If you can come together to do this, why can't you come
together and apply for funds and establish an organization where the
funds would be allocated equally based on the service that you
provided and the whole bit? (Aug. 17, 2004)

Another liaison echoed similar sentiments:

I think it's a lot of real grassroots efforts. And the ones that really have
been successful... one of things that we're trying to do in addition to
the technical assistance and the cash is to link them up to other groups
within their communities whether that's funders or other kinds of
agencies that they could band together with. We're really doing that
networking whether it's in a rural area or inner cities. It's been real
valuable to them.... One of the things we did is we went out and did
community forums around the state. I think we had 18 or 19 different
forums, and it kind of surprised me that oftentimes these people
hadn't worked together before. In the behavioral health area, it seemed
like I'd go out to communities and it was those same providers that
were at every meeting but the faith-based and the community
providers oftentimes hadn't been involved. But getting them to know
each other and to know the formal delivery system I think has been
really good. (Nov. 21, 2004)

It is crucial to note, however, that when liaisons do bring groups together,
there is the potential for tense situations and rather difficult contacts. However,
if liaisons are effective in their intermediary roles, when they do their homework
on differences among faiths and bring groups together with sensitivity and
understanding, then potential problems can be averted. As one liaison noted:

The fourth day in office I met with a senator from [my state] who is a
very religious person. He indicated to me that the religious
community is a very opinionated community, and that it's probably
the most difficult one to work with. I hadn't thought about that, and I
am still choosing to overlook some of those biases and things until
someone really confronts me with it; I am just going to talk to anybody
that will listen to me, and try to get everyone focused on what the
ultimate goal is for our state, which is to help those most in need, and
everything else stops at the door. (Dec. 13, 2005)

Later in the interview, the liaison noted that there was tension not just among
religious groups, but also within the larger social services community:

I think there is skepticism in both. I've modified my presentation such
that I state pretty close up front in my presentation that we are taking
the inclusive approach on this, and faith-based and community is the

whole program, and so, we're looking at all nonprofits that provide much-needed health and human services in our state. In the first two weeks, I didn't realize I was going to get that kind of reception. The secular nonprofits were very skeptical of the faith-based. Once I explained to them that we are inclusive in this office, then that seems to make people much more comfortable.

By educating herself and reassuring groups about her role, this liaison was able to persuade groups of the potential benefit of working together.

Helping FBOs Become Prepared

As I detailed in Chapters 3 and 6, in interviews many liaisons expressed surprise at the inability of FBOs to live up to what the liaisons felt were rather minimal requirements for partnering with the state or receiving funding, such as attending a series of workshops or being able to send and receive e-mail. Liaisons sometimes found that expectations regarding even the most basic tasks had to be adjusted. As one liaison told me:

We did a four session series [of workshops], and the reason we did it in four sessions is because [the agency head] wanted to do "all days" and I was telling her it's kind of hard to get them to commit all day, because a lot of them are the only person to do whatever it is their ministry needs. So we did a series of half-day workshops.... The first session was on finding funding.... The second session was on writing competitive grants and then a workshop on grants.gov with Dun and Bradstreet, because its going to be a requirement of the feds that they have a Dun and Bradstreet number, and then we had a final workshop on best practices. (Dec. 19, 2004)

As this example shows, recognizing limitations does not mean that these groups are unable to help or to successfully receive training or provide services. It does mean that liaisons and others in their offices need to educate—and be educated—about the ways they need to work with FBOs to enable the groups to receive grants and become integrated into the social services sector.

Many FBOs want to participate and do something to help, but they are often limited by staff, size, and budget. By realizing that FBOs work under these constraints, liaisons can better work with these groups and create sustainable partnerships. Most FBOs are never going to have the capacity to apply for, receive, and carry out work under a government grant; however, most are able to contribute somehow to their communities. Some FBOs can start with small-scale projects and then work up to writing grants and developing larger programs. In one state, the liaison worked with the preexisting Division of Volunteer Recruitment to help FBOs learn about their own capacity.

They have several different areas that offer, free of charge to any type of nonprofit, organization training. They have volunteer training. They have capacity-building training. They actually came up with a capacity assessment that they don't actually do for the organization. They give it to the organization so that the organization can do their own capacity assessment and see, "Okay, this is what we need to work on. This may be our strength, but this is our weakness," and that way it is not the government telling them "You're just not ready" or "You need to work on this." It's something that they see for themselves. (Nov. 30, 2004)

Another liaison (Dec. 13, 2004) described a two-step process developed to work with religious groups to ensure that they knew what was required of them—and that they understood that the initiatives were not going to result in money just being handed over. She described two-day trainings with individuals from the FBOs in which they talked about infrastructure, vision, and mission—not just chasing money. The FBOs would then be given homework based on the training. After four weeks they would meet again to discuss funding and program implementation in depth. This liaison had many creative approaches to bringing knowledge to FBOs and to preparing them for the experience of applying for a government grant. By creating ways to educate and empower the FBOs, this liaison created new avenues that could lead to increased help for the needy.

Creating Buy-In

Finally, and perhaps most important to the success of the initiatives, faith-based groups and government agencies have to be on board. FBOs have to want to provide social services, and government groups have to want to work with them. They both need to buy into the idea that both are needed and that they are capable of working together. If faith-based groups feel that the initiatives are just a political scheme or just a way for certain groups to get money, they may not be willing to work with government agencies or with the liaisons. FBOs also need to be committed to providing services and to providing them on a long-term basis. Once faith-based groups do have the necessary buy-in, the FBL still has a multifaceted task, which goes beyond merely pointing FBOs in the direction of funding. The FBL needs to continue to assist FBOs after they receive funds, to continue to guide them in a direction that is beneficial to all involved.

Some liaisons have made progress in creating and sustaining buy-in. One liaison offered workshops and services such as grant-writing assistance for a small fee. She argued that this would help ensure that only those who really wanted to contribute and participate would come to the workshops. "We really talked about this [and] set a nominal fee to get a commitment, but didn't want to undervalue the training. We looked around to see what might be available from other agencies. One person said they couldn't pay the $10 to $20 registration fee—if they can't pay, then that's not a place that can benefit from the training" (Dec. 13, 2004). In another state, the liaison noted that even before she could start networking and building bridges, she needed to create buy-in, not just from the FBOs, but from state agencies. She outlined her planned networking strategy to me but had put off implementing it because state offices had not yet bought into the idea of a FBL or state faith-based initiatives:

> We were looking to do a road show where myself and several other
> different agency representatives will go around the state and hold
> town hall—type forums or just meetings. Right now we are looking at
> using junior colleges and other local universities in different regions,
> kind of as the location, and have forums where groups come in and
> meet one-on-one with agency representatives that might be of
> particular interest to their program. So if it's someone who wants to
> start a prison reentry program for someone who is leaving
> incarceration, they can meet with someone from the Department of
> Corrections who is actually handling the faith-based community
> initiatives for that agency. We had originally had planned to start that
> much earlier, but we had realized that we needed to get the buy-in and
> needed to get the focus back in with the agency directors. (Nov. 30,
> 2004)

Gaining legitimacy in the faith-based community is another problem that FBLs encountered. In one state where there had been several federally funded grant writing workshops run by outside groups, the FBL found that faith-based groups were not attending these programs (Feb. 9, 2005). She felt this was mainly ascribable to a lack of communication between the federally funded organization and the local community. She argued that the outside group, which had received a CCF grant to do a nationwide series of workshops, did not have any connections with the local communities and was therefore seen as useless by the local FBOs; the local groups felt that the outside group had no idea of the problems and needs facing them on the ground. The FBL believed that such outside groups actually made her job more difficult not only because they took a share of the much-needed money but also because they essentially wasted the money because there was no buy-in or trust from local organizations.

To create successful buy-in from both agencies and FBOs, states need to take action in several areas. First, they need to have good knowledge of their own territory, of the FBOs within the state, the legal requirements in the state, and the relationships that are already in place between government and faith-based groups. Second, states need to refrain from creating faith-based rhetoric and promises they cannot meet; broken promises will only make FBOs less likely to trust and want to work with government. Third, state agencies and actors need to offer real help; this does not necessarily have to come in the form of new grants, but may be in the form of helping FBOs with capacity assessments, grant writing, or networking. Finally, states need to ensure that whatever is offered is equally available to everyone. In a country that is built on religious pluralism and the assurance that one faith will not be favored over another, states must make concerted efforts to ensure that favoritism does not occur. States have to move away from faith-based politics and promises, and move toward truly equal assistance if they wish to engage the faith-based sector in new ways.

Bringing It All Together

The best of the larger-scale programs will, of course, take into consideration all of these factors, creating government and community partnerships and educating liaisons about the legal limitations, while also creating buy-in from the local community. This will probably be a long and complex process, and one that does not result in social service programs being taken over by faith-based groups. Instead, it will create interplay and discussion among all those involved. One liaison I spoke with found that when she began working to create ties within the community to build a new program with the help of a local religious groups there was a great deal of excitement and desire to partner to do services. Rather than reaching out to specific FBOs to run particular programs, she noted that it was best to build on resources already available and to help the groups that were providing those resources further their own goals by working with state agencies, while making sure they met the necessary requirements:

> One [faith-based social service] that we do have here is a Presbyterian group that was developing a resource of volunteer visitation centers across the state. I was contacted to ask about how to make sure that the requirements of the division were going to be met to develop this volunteer resource. . . . A [volunteer visitation center] is where children that are in foster care have a place where they can visit their biological parents in a nonagency-type environment. What the churches have pretty much said is that [they] will make our churches available and have people that will supervise those visits, trained to be able to do that, so that it would not take away time for the case worker. . . .
>
> There is no [government] money necessary. [The centers] are just completely staffed and trained through the church. They are not asking for, and we are not pursuing, federal grants to do this. They see it as a mission, one of their approved missions. (March 23, 2005)

This example shows how a liaison achieved success by helping a religious group to meet a need and to navigate government bureaucracy. It was an unfunded collaboration that helped the community without unduly burdening the volunteering group or risking violations of church-state constitutional issues.

These unfunded collaborations seem to work best when liaisons are proactive in creating ties and connections with religious groups in the community. One described how it was a process that had to be cultivated over time and then would begin to reap rewards.

> The coalition building process is ongoing in the community. . . . One of the things we kicked it off with 2 years ago was a community marriage and family agreement. The idea was to develop a community policy for churches where the faith leaders would agree not to marry couples without solid premarital instructions. So we went out and we had a committee made up of faith leaders in the community, we developed policies and we put an agreement together, then went out and promoted that to all of the churches. As a result we had over 50 churches, parishes and wards signed on to support the original community marriage and family agreement, so that was kind of the ice breaker, it got everybody on the same page. And then using that list of 50 something faith groups, that was kind of our prospective list. We went from there to those people, pastors, and leaders to get then more actively involved. Right now we have about, just under 20, I think about 17 churches and state leaders involved in actually providing direct services in counseling and so forth. (Feb. 23, 2005)

In another state, the liaison described something very close to this process that occurred when he began his tenure as liaison (Dec. 10, 2004). His primary function was to help create a threefold transformation in the state: changing the way state government dealt with nonprofits, changing the state government culture to better meet citizens' needs, and transforming FBOs to improve their business models. In particular, he was tasked with developing and empowering organizations within the state—rather than bringing outsiders in—and with creating development through bricks-and-mortar projects and encouraging partnerships with for-profit sister corporations to develop sustainable funding. The liaison I spoke with began this process, but was soon replaced—largely for political reasons, he believed—by a new liaison who was not as closely connected to the religious community but was more of a government bureaucrat. The liaison argued that while he had helped get the community engaged during the campaign process, he was replaced after the election and after his usefulness to the governor was over. The first liaison expressed disappointment about this change and about what he saw as the resulting lack of will to do much beyond creating the office.

In the end, what all the liaisons wanted was to help the groups they worked with to create and develop sustainable programs. As one liaison said:

> I believe . . . in knowing what you do and doing what you do well. What I mean by that is—and we said it earlier—is maybe I can't be a primary [social services provider] . . . maybe all I want to do is run the best darn day-care on this side of town. Well then, I have to partner with somebody who is a primary [service provider] who is going to list me as their primary day-care. . . . They're going to take care of the administrative stuff, and they're going do all that, but my costs are going to be taken care of in that contract. . . . Just like we have the big guys that know how to write the grants and all of that, I think they need to move people, but what we find about the little grassroots organizations is that they don't want to be the little grassroots organizations. . . . They want to be the Catholic charity. And I'm telling you, that Catholic Charities didn't get there overnight, and they're not going to go away overnight. So what I say is you have to figure out what you do best and do that. (Aug. 17, 2004)

The Future of Faith-Based Initiatives

While I have discussed state implementation between 1996 and 2007, there are still many questions left unanswered, including perhaps the most important one: What happens now, under a new president? The success of the faith-based initiatives depends both on whether President Obama supports them and on how entrenched and durable the changes that have already been made prove to be.

A New Administration

In a campaign speech, Obama outlined his vision for the initiatives if he were to be elected. His vision appeared to be a combination of what the liaisons who came on in the beginning had hoped for and what people who are concerned about constitutional issues were worried was not happening. He proposed a faith-based effort that actually does what was promised to help the poor and needy, rather than merely being a symbol that serves to gain votes, appeal for money from the federal government, or alter culture so that integration rather than separation becomes the norm. His vision for the initiatives combined oversight with funding—new funding that would in fact go to faith and community organizations:

> President Bush came into office with a promise to "rally the armies of compassion," establishing a new OFBCI. But what we saw instead was

that the Office never fulfilled its promise. Support for social services to the poor and the needy have been consistently underfunded. Rather than promoting the cause of all FBOs, former officials in the Office have described how it was used to promote partisan interests. As a result, the smaller congregations and community groups that were supposed to be empowered ended up getting short-changed. (Obama, quoted in Burke 2008)

Promising to ameliorate the disappointment many liaisons and other supporters felt after the White House made clear that the initiatives under Bush were going to be more about politics and perceptions than about money, Obama laid out a plan to create a new faith-based office. This faith-based office would be different from the ideologically linked office that came about under President Bush. The initiatives would continue, but there would be a different direction, a different flavor to what was offered to and asked of the states.

Since taking office, Obama has made good on some of his promises. He created the White House Office of Faith-Based and Neighborhood Partnerships which consists of an advisory council made up of leaders from diverse religious groups. However, he did not eliminate the hiring provision that was established by president Bush that allowed faith-based groups to hire only co-religionists even while receiving government funds. This was a great disappointment to many who see this hiring provision as an egregious breach of the separation of church and state and who felt he backtracked on a campaign promise because of political pressure from evangelicals and other religious actors within his own party (Mooney 2007). Additionally, many of the members on Obama's faith advisory council are from conservative evangelical groups. This has led some to argue that Obama's faith-based initiative is just as political as Bush's; however, instead of trying to court black voters to build a coalition around these initiatives, Obama is courting moderate and conservative religious voters (Zeleny and Knowlton 2009). Both of these steps signal continued use of the initiative as a symbolic political tool. Whether Obama can move past this and create real faith-based policy that helps alleviate burdens on those in need remains to be seen.

Change Already in Progress

There is some evidence that a change is already happening at the state level, with more secularized versions of the initiatives popping up in some states. Preliminary research by Pamela Winston, Ann Person, and Elizabeth Clary (2008) indicates that while state offices are continuing to reach out to FBOs, they are reaching out to secular community-based groups as well. However, their research focused on the eight most established state liaisons and offices, and further study on the other thirty-one states needs to be conducted. Even so, this finding highlights again how secularizing forces are often part of interrelated processes. In *The Secular Revolution*, Christian Smith (2003) described a secularization of many aspects of American life but found that it was part of the continuous ebb and flow of the relationship between religion and the public square. In some states, we may one day find a secularized "faith-based" initiative, but in other states we may still see faith-focused offices and politics. It is entirely possible to have both occurring in different states at the same time. States that have a culture committed to keeping a brighter line of separation between church and state will not be likely to embrace the initiatives, or they will implement them in forms with more connections to secular groups. On the other hand, states that have entrenched conservative religious actors and politics will be more likely to implement policies that focus on the faith aspects of the initiatives and to maintain initiatives that are about creating cooperation and accommodation between church and state. In short, the point is this: the twin processes of secularization and desecularization can cut both ways, and future research on how the faith-based initiatives change over time should yield interesting results on the growing complexities of their implementation.

8

Conclusion

What Is Success?

Early supporters of faith-based initiatives touted them as a new hope—for government and for the poor and needy. Religious groups were going to come out of the woodwork, bringing a new brand of social services into the public fight against poverty and addiction. This prediction has for the most part not been borne out. Faith-based groups may have shown some new interest in becoming a part of the process, but they were soon told that there was no new money to be had. Further, obtaining funding requires navigating the bureaucratic requirements of government, an arduous process that is simply beyond the capacity of many FBOs. Without the means to properly audit money if they were to receive it, many groups find themselves unable to compete with established programs that have qualified staffs with experience in these practices. And while some new groups are participating in the social services system, they are far from being able to take over the responsibility from the government. In the end, small churches and religious groups are primarily in the business of ministering to their flock—not of running day-care centers, drug rehabilitation programs, and prisoner reentry offices. The help they can offer is generally limited in scope but can be incorporated into the existing system—to the benefit of the system—if the time and understanding to do this is taken by state actors.

None of this was obvious when states began implementing the faith-based initiatives. States were apparently not aware that many of the groups they wanted to bring into the social services fold were simply unprepared to deal with the intricacies of government funding. So the states sought out the groups in good faith, using information campaigns—conferences, new offices, and new positions—and tried to incorporate the FBOs into the social services network. However, not much else was provided; instead there was little additional funding, support, or regulation of groups that did get contracts with state government. Consequently, the initiatives have not been successful in their initial, purported goal of having religion take over a significant portion of social services provision from secular nonprofits and government agencies—or in the goal of helping the needy.

In the beginning, there were many who believed in these faith-based policies—not as symbolic actions to alter the norm of church-state separation, but as serious social policy offering help to the poor. Since this help has not materialized, some of the most vocal supporters of the initiatives have become its most vocal critics. Insider frustration with the lack of real funding behind the initiatives started with John Dilulio, the first White House OFBCI director. In a letter he wrote after leaving office, Dilulio voiced his frustration that the faith-based initiatives, along with many other policy issues, were essentially a political ploy with no real teeth (Susskind 2003). More recently, David Kuo (2006a), who originally worked at the White House OFBCI and had been a strong supporter, stated that the faith-based initiatives were used as a political vote-getting tool intended to bring in new political allies and support from the evangelical movement. These original supporters are people who, like many liaisons, believed the president's speeches and thought that money would be provided to help the poor. They did not want the initiatives to become what they have become: a symbolic policy that is really about creating political allies and support while simultaneously giving religion an institutionalized voice in government. And some, including Kuo, continue to hope that the initiatives will be implemented in a way that fulfills their promise of helping the poor and needy (Kuo 2006b)

Faith-based policies have flourished at the state level because of the confluence of fiscal need, social need, and religious belief—and the political rhetoric surrounding them. These have created a phenomenon that is beneficial for many politicians and political leaders, who can say they have helped and show off their new offices and policies, without having to come up with new money or prompting a controversy over spending government money on religious programs. Faith-based initiatives seem to have been used by many politicians for just such self-serving political purposes; it has been easy to tell a good story with and about the initiatives, because neither major party has been required to back the talk with money. Their symbolic value alone is so great that the faith-based initiatives have flourished without the nourishment of funding.

In a recent interview, Jim Towey, a former director of the White House OFBCI, said that the prime achievement of the faith-based initiatives was how they have "changed the culture of how religious groups are treated in the public square" (Gross 2006). The policies and practices that make up the faith-based initiatives at the state level do not do what their supporters originally promised; rather, they have created a new relationship between church and state. If this is the measure of success, then the initiatives have indeed succeeded.

Appendix A: Data and Methods

In this appendix, I outline the variables considered, data sources, and methods of analysis used to examine three variations of the dependent variable (different measures of implementation of the faith-based initiatives) and several key independent variables.

Dependent Variables: Measures of Implementation of the Initiatives

The Variables: Types of Implementation

FAITH-BASED LIAISONS. Implementation of the initiatives can be measured in a number of ways. The first measure I used was whether a state had a faith-based liaison (FBL). This is a dichotomous variable representing whether a state had created a liaison position in a given year, and it is important because appointment of liaisons was the most common type of state implementation of the initiatives. In addition, by measuring this variable over time, I was able to assess how other time-varying covariates (such as gross state product and poverty rates) had affected state creation of liaison positions.

In addition to the quantitative data collected about FBLs, I conducted interviews with 30 of the 34 state liaisons that were in place at the time of my interviews. The interviews consisted of qualitative questions regarding their duties and motivations for taking the positions, as well as questions about the exact nature of the position and the types of activities in which they were involved. Interviews were taped and then transcribed, and the information from them is used to illuminate the patterns found in the quantitative data.

OFFICES OF FAITH-BASED AND COMMUNITY INITIATIVES. I also created a dichotomous variable representing whether a state had created an OFBCI in a given year. While similar in some ways to liaison positions, OFBCIs are important because they signify a step up in formalization of implementation. Therefore, while appointing a liaison is the most common form of implementation, the creation of an OFBCI illustrates a greater commitment to the initiatives on the part of a state.

LEGISLATIVE CHANGES. The third dependent variable used in this analysis was the total number of faith-based laws enacted by a state between 1996 and 2007. This reflects a different avenue to implementation: whereas FBLs and OFBCIs were generally administrative appointments, the number of laws reflects activity by state legislatures. Considering both paths gives a fuller understanding of the initiatives' effects on the state policy environment.

Data Collection Methods

Data on executive orders and legislative changes related to the faith-based initiatives were collected from LexisNexis, an Internet search engine used in legal research. Using search terms related to the initiatives (such as "faith-based" or "charitable choice"), at this early point in data collection I was able to identify the creation of FBL/OFBCIs in 14 states; of these, four positions were created by law, and ten were created by executive order. LexisNexis data included the date of appointment, how each FBL was appointed (law or executive order), and an official description of the position for each state.

Fewer than half of the liaison positions were created through these formal mechanisms. Most liaisons were administratively appointed, and LexisNexis contains no information about such positions. To determine which states had administratively appointed liaisons, I contacted the White House Office of Faith-Based and Community Initiatives (OFBCI), the Roundtable for Research on Religion and Social Welfare Policy, and the Center for Public Justice. Each of these organizations had been studying the initiatives and working with liaisons for some time; they were able to provide lists of state liaisons and of states without liaisons. From these lists and the LexisNexis data, I categorized each state as having a liaison position created by legislation, by the governor or a state agency head, or having no liaison. The list of state liaisons used for this research was in congruence with those of the White House and the Roundtable in late 2005.

I also used LexisNexis to collect data on all other legislative changes made at the state level; between 1996 and 2007, there were 271 laws passed in 41 states. LexisNexis data included date of passage and the content of each law. Most of these legislative changes either encouraged state organizations to contract with faith-based groups for specific purposes, added representatives from faith-based groups to state advisory boards, or specifically encouraged government agencies to reach out to faith-based organizations when contracting for services.

Independent Variables of Theoretical Interest

As discussed above, a number of factors may have influenced whether a particular state implemented the faith-based initiatives. The measures that follow were used to test whether such implementation, as expressed by states' creation of FBL positions and OFBCIs and degree of legislative change, has been a result of efforts to fight poverty—as its supporters claim—or of other factors.

Strength of Evangelical Movement in Politics

The first social-movement variable I used was a measure of the strength of the evangelical movement in a state, the index of the influence of the evangelical movement in the state Republican Party developed by Green and his colleagues (Conger and Green 2002; Green, Guth, and Wilcox 1998). Ranging from 1 (least influential) to 5 (most influential),[1] the scale incorporates several measures from interviews and other sources. The 1994 data were collected from *Campaigns and Elections Magazine* using two types of informants: state-level political insiders and evangelical movement activists; the study was repeated in similar fashion in 2000. From these data, they coded the strength of the evangelical movement into categories. While these data are not perfect, as Green and his colleagues acknowledge, they provide an important measure of evangelical movement strength. Since data were collected only in 1994 and 2000, in my analysis I used the last available year's score for each state.

From this scale, I created two dummy variables to test both high and medium levels of evangelical movement influence. In the first case, states with a high evangelical influence (a score of 5 on Green's scale) were coded as 1, and all other states as 0; this variable identifies where the evangelical movement is the most influential. I also used a second dummy variable, looking at midlevels of evangelical movement influence. It was coded as 1 for states that received a 3 or 4 on the Green scale of implementation; all other states were coded as 0. In his own assessment of the measure, Green concluded that the key differences lay not in the difference between scores of 3 and 4, but between having a great deal of influence, some influence, and none. Therefore, this recoding of the scale into two binary variables is analogous to Green's own assessment of the importance of the evangelical movement within a state. The Green variable is useful because it examines the legitimized political actors of the evangelical movement within a state.

I also tested a measure of white evangelical presence from Glenmary's (2000) research on state denominational membership; however, it was highly correlated with a strong conservative political environment and was not a significant predictor in any models. Therefore, it was not included in the final models. This indicates that it is not just the presence of possible religious supporters but also the activity of movement activists within state politics that is key to faith-based policy implementation.

Previous Policy Success of the Resurgent Evangelical Movement

The presence of laws prohibiting gay marriage can be taken as a measure of previous success of the conservative evangelical movement in influencing public policy. Using data collected by the National Gay and Lesbian Rights Taskforce (2006) on several categories of such laws, states were coded on a scale of 0 to 4. A score of 0 indicated that there were no such policies on a state's books; a score of 4 indicated especially restrictive and strong antigay marriage and family policies.

Problem-Driven Policy

Two measures were used to test whether implementation of the faith-based initiatives was driven by a need to solve the problem of poverty: state poverty rates and the fiscal burden of welfare programs upon a state. Poverty rates, measured as the percentage of population living below the federal poverty level, were taken from the U.S. Census Bureau (1996–2005). The strength of a state's welfare program was defined as the proportion of children eligible (by federal standards) that actually received funds from the state's Temporary Assistance to Needy Families (TANF) fund. Since passage of the 1996 welfare reform bill, states have been able to make their own policies regarding welfare coverage within the context of federal guidelines; this measure was therefore a good way to estimate whether states with a strong social safety net would create these policies, or whether they would be created only by states in need of greater services to the poor because state programs did not offer adequate coverage. Data for this variable also came from the U.S. Census Bureau (1996–2005) and from the Center for Children in Poverty; TANF data were available only for 1993, 1996, and 2002, so for intervening years the last available year's figures were used.[2]

Politics-Driven Policy

Political conservatism, favorable to free-market and religious activity, was represented by the percentage of the population that voted for the Republican presidential candidate in the previous election. Data for the 1996, 2000, and 2004 presidential elections were compiled from the U.S. Census Bureau (1996–2005); for nonelection years, data from the most recent presidential election were used.

Control Variables

In addition to these theoretically relevant variables, the policy literature suggests that the sociodemographic and economic characteristics of each state should be taken into account (Burstein 1998; Burstein and Linton 2002; Evans 1996; Grogan 1994; Haider-Markel 1998; Lin 2000; Nice 1994; Raeburn 2004; Soule 1997; Soule and Earl 2001; Soule and Olzak 2004; Soule and Zylan 1997; Strang and Soule 1998).

Sociodemographics

Since race may be an important factor in determining policy implementation (Nice 1994; Soule and Zylan 1997), the percentage of the population that was African American was considered in the models. Annual data for this variable were collected from U.S. Census Bureau (1996–2005).

Economics

States with fewer economic resources may be less likely to appoint FBLs, since such innovations would be seen as too costly (Nice 1994).[3] This factor was included as a control in the models, in the form of the per capita gross state product (U.S. Census Bureau, 1996–2005).

Time

I also examined change over time by including a dummy variable to test the effect of the 2004 presidential election on the appointment of liaisons; appointment of a liaison before 2005 was assigned a value of 0, and appointment in 2005 was assigned a value of 1. While many policies may progress linearly over time, for the faith-based initiatives there is reason to believe that a significant effect of time occurred after the 2004 presidential election. President Bush's 2004 reelection apparently did reduce the risks of policy adoption: twenty-four states had appointed liaisons in the eight years ending in 2004, and 10 states appointed FBLs in 2005 alone—an increase in the annual rate of nearly 50 percent. A summary of variables is included in Table 6.1.

Statistical Tests

I used two types of analysis on these data: event-history analysis and negative binomial regression.[4] By doing so, I was able to begin to understand the underlying reasons for a variety of faith-based practices, including the creation of FBL positions and overall implementation of the faith-based initiatives.

Event-History Analysis

To analyze the creation of FBL positions and OFBCIs, I used discrete time event–history analysis (Allison 1995) to analyze longitudinal data on the dichotomous dependent variable representing whether a state had appointed a liaison in a given year. Using event-history analysis allowed the assessment of the rate at which each state had appointed a liaison. It also allowed modeling of the time-varying covariates on the hazard rate of ratification by a given state in a given year. Data were arranged by state and year; once a state had created a liaison position, subsequent years were removed from the analysis, as the state was no longer at risk of appointing a liaison.

This method was used to study the rate of policy implementation for several reasons. First, implementation of a liaison could occur only at discrete periods in time (years). Second, except as noted above, state-level covariants were also measured in discrete (yearly) increments. Finally, there were a number of "ties" in the data since many states created liaisons in the same year, rendering the logit model for discrete time event–history analysis appropriate (Allison 1995). Analysis was done using the STATA 8 statistical software package.

Negative Binomial Regression

I used negative binomial regression to analyze the number of laws passed at the state level. Unlike event-history analysis, this does not look at the year in which a state implemented such policies, but rather at the total number of laws enacted from 1996 to 2007. I tested whether the negative binomial distribution was a significant improvement over the Poisson regression by performing a likelihood ratio test; the fit of the negative binomial model was significantly better than the Poisson model. Again, data were analyzed using STATA 8 statistical software.

Results

In Chapter 6, Table 6.2 presents the results of a set of models designed to test the above hypotheses. Models 1 to 5 examine state implementation of the initiatives by creation of FBL positions, whereas model 6 examines implementation by means of OFBCIs. In this section, I address models 1–4 in Table 6.2. The final versions of the models are discussed in Chapter 6.

Effects on Probability of Appointment of Faith-Based Liaisons

STRENGTH OF EVANGELICAL MOVEMENT IN POLITICS. Model 1 examined the effect of the strength of the evangelical movement in a state on the likelihood of the state's creating a liaison position. According to previous research on social movements (Soule 2004; Soule and Olzak 2004), states with greater social movement strength in state politics should be more likely to implement policies that favor that movement. Therefore, evangelical movement strength should favor implementation of an FBL position. Model 1 bore this out: states with a stronger evangelical movement presence in politics were more likely to appoint FBLs. Both variables (moderate evangelical movement presence and strong presence) were significant. In fact, when there was a strong evangelical movement presence in the state Republican Party, the odds a state would create an FBL were more than three and half times higher than when there was low movement presence.[5]

PREVIOUS SUCCESS OF MOVEMENT. Model 2 examined the direct effect of a state policy environment that had already been influenced by the conservative evangelical movement. This was significant in the expected direction: states in which the conservative evangelical movement had previously influenced policy were more likely to appoint a FBL. If a state had extremely conservative anti–gay-marriage policies in place, it increased the odds of the state appointing a liaison by a factor of two and a half. The nature of both policies examined suggests that it was not just any religious movement that was making inroads, but rather a certain brand of evangelical religion that was seeking, and achieving, a role in state politics.

PROBLEM-DRIVEN FACTORS. Model 3 tested whether indicators of a greater problem with poverty—a higher poverty rate or higher TANF coverage—increased the likelihood of a state's appointing a liaison. This did not find support in the model. Results for poverty rates were significant in none of the models, except in the nested models, when poverty was significant—but in a direction opposite to that predicted. In addition, the policy literature suggests that states with greater welfare needs should have a higher likelihood of appointing liaisons, the results suggested this: states with a greater welfare need were more likely to appoint liaisons. Together, these findings provide little support for the proposition that creating liaison positions was a response to problems of poverty, rather it is a response to a tattered safety net.

POLITICS-DRIVEN FACTORS. Model 4 examined the effect of political conservatism on implementation of the initiatives. Although states with a Republican majority in the previous presidential election were significantly more likely to appoint liaisons, this effect was small, and it dropped out of the two final models when the evangelical movement variables were included. So although there is some support for the argument made in the policy literature that states with more conservative voting populations are more likely to adopt policies that are religious in nature and allow greater free-market access, the final models suggest that this variable was not significant when taking the social movement strength into account.

SOCIAL MOVEMENTS OR POLITICS AND POVERTY? Finally, model 5 is the full model, incorporating all variables tested in the direct models. The variable representing the strongest evangelical movement influence on the Republican Party was significant; however, the medium-level evangelical movement influence was no longer significant. States in which the resurgent evangelical movement was the most influential—having either enacted law reflecting their religious ideals or becoming part of the state party— were most likely to create liaison positions. As in the direct-effect model, the presence of strong evangelical movement influence in state politics more than quadrupled the likelihood that a liaison would be appointed in that state. This indicates that it was not just evangelical presence in politics, but a strong, effective presence, through which players were able to enact policies that strongly favor their goals, that increased the likelihood that liaisons would be appointed.

I also included the three political and economic variables from the policy literature theory in the full model. When they were included, Republican voting rates were no longer significant. This model further supports the overall findings of the direct-effects models—namely, that a state's poverty problems were not significant predictors of implementation of faith-based initiatives, but having a previous policy climate friendly toward the resurgent evangelical movement was a significant predictor, as was a fiscal need to reach out to these groups because of limited welfare coverage.

Effects on Probability of Establishment of Offices or Passage of Legislation

These followed patterns similar to those described above. Details can be found in Chapter 6.

Appendix B: Faith-Based Liaison Interview Schedule

Section 1: State Administrative Enactment of Charitable Choice Practices

First, I'd like you to answer some questions about your job as an FBL and what your state is doing to implement the faith-based initiatives.

1. Could you tell me specifically what you do as an FBL? How have you tried to get religious or community groups involved in social services?
2. Were you hired in order to be the FBL, or were you already in state government before taking the assignment? (What was your occupation before you became an FBL?)
3. How did you learn about this position?
4. Who hired you for this position?
5. When did you take this assignment?
6. Is this your only job, or is it just one of many?
7. What are your other duties?
8. How much time does the FBL part of your job take?
9. Why did you decide to become an FBL?
10. What office are you located in (e.g., Department of Education, Health and Human Services, governor's office, etc.)?
11. Whom do you report to?
12. Do the faith-based initiatives have their own office? If so, where?
13. Do you have a budget for your duties? If so, what do you use it for?
14. Now I want to ask you about some specific items that other states have done, and I want to know if any of this is happening in your state. If you could please tell me yes or no and, if yes, what the date was that each was implemented.

A. OFBCI Yes / No / Date _____
B. Web site about faith-based initiatives Yes / No / Date _____
C. Set-aside special funds for the initiatives Yes / No / Date _____
D. A listserv for FBOs and CBOs Yes / No / Date _____
E. Technical assistance seminars aimed at FBOs and CBOs Yes / No / Date _____
F. Grant-writing programs aimed at religious leaders Yes / No / Date _____
G. Waiver of licensing requirements for FBOs Yes / No / Date _____
H. Recruitment of specific organizations to run programs (please list)? Yes / No / Date _____
I. An advisory board to focus on faith-based initiatives (if yes: Who is on the board?)? Yes / No / Date _____
J. Startup funds for FBOs or CBOs Yes / No / Date _____
K. Changes in the state constitution's language regarding church-state separation Yes / No / Date _____
L. Other _____

15. Have you experienced any opposition to these programs? If so, from whom and regarding what?

Section 2: FBL Ties to Other State FBLs/Organizations

I'd also like to ask you a few questions about your relationship with the federal OFBCI.

1. Who have you had contact with in the federal government in regard to faith-based initiatives? (Get names and the departments they are in.)
2. What was this contact regarding (i.e., conferences, technical assistance)?
3. How often do you have contact with these individuals?
4. What were the dates of this contact?
5. More specifically, how would you describe your relationship with the federal OFBCI?

    A. Have you been to any conferences they've sponsored? Where? Year?
    B. What kind of information did you get from them? What was it? Year?
    C. Have you had other kinds of contact that I haven't asked about explicitly?

6. Have you been to any other conferences not sponsored by the federal office? Where? When?

Now I'm going to ask you a few questions about your relationship with FBLs in other states. This is to help me understand what kind of relationship states have with one another and whether this has influenced faith-based initiatives in your state.

1. Please look at this list [of liaisons from other states]. Could you check which FBLs you know?
2. Of those you know, how many times have you had contact with them over the last year?

3. What was the context of this contact?
4. Have you worked with any of these individuals before?
5. Would you consider any of these to be your friends?

Section 3: Demographics

1. What is your religion?
2. What is your race?
3. Sex M / F (filled in without asking)
4. Age?

LIST OF STATE FAITH-BASED LIAISONS

STATE ABBREVIATION	NAMES(S)
AK	Lamar Jensen, Whitney Brewster, Stephanie Wheeler
AL	Terri Hasdorff
AR	Chris Pyle, Beth Garrison
AZ	Byron Garrett
CA	Open?
CO	Kevin Richards, Cameron Lynch
CT	Jim Brennan, Brian Matteo, Michael Murphy
DC	Dorris Howard, Pat Henry, Susan Newman, Deborah Murphy
FL	Mark Nelson, Liza McFadden
GA	Jennifer Sullivan
HI	Sam Aiona
ID	Blossom Johnson, Tammy Payne, Rico Barrera, Tom Farley, Shane Stenquist, Kathy Russell
IL	Derrius Colvin, Fred Nettles
IN	Emmerson Allen
KS	Linda Weaver, Jeremy Anderson
KY	Brian Crall
LA	Johnny Anderson
MD	John Heath
MI	Greg Roberts, Wanda Bostic
MA	Peter Flariety
MT	David Young, Hank Hudson
NC	Diana Wilson, Sonya Barnes
NE	Caroline Walles
NJ	Edward Laporte
OH	Krista Sisterhen
OK	Bradley Yarbrough
PA	Abass Kamara, Gilbert Gomez
SC	Gene Beckman, Harry Prim
TX	Janie Young, Beau Egert
UT	Bill Crim, Steve Klass
VA	Jane Brown
WY	Andy Aldrich

Appendix C: Raw Data Collected from Faith-Based Liaisons (2004–2005)

Unless otherwise noted, data in this table were collected during interviews between 2004 and 2005. When possible, I have noted significant changes in the data. However, since the faith-based initiative is a continuously changing and growing set of policies and practices, some of these data have changed since my qualitative data collection officially ended in 2005.

DATA COLLECTED	AL	AK	AZ[1]	AR
General Information				
State has FBL	x	x	x	x
State has OFBCI	x	x	—	—
Year FBL/OFBCI created	2003	2005	2003	2004
FBL position created by law	—	—	—	—
FBL created by executive order	x	x	—	—
FBL created by other means	—	—	x	x
Data Collected from Interviews & Surveys with FBLs				
State Information				
Conferences for FBOs	x	planned	x	x
Web site or e-mail listserv	x	x	x	x
Tech. assistance seminars for FBOs	x	planned	—	x
Grant-writing programs for FBOs	x	planned	—	x
Recruitment of groups for programs	—	x	x	—
Advisory board to focus on FBOs	x	x	—	x
Startup funds for FBOs/CBOs	—	planned ($60K)	—	—
Funding offered by state office	—	—	—	—
FBL Position				
Location of Liaison Position in Government Structure				
No position created	—	—	—	—
Position vacant or unfunded	—	—	—	—
FBL in the governor's office	x	—	x	x
FBL in state agency	—	HHS[2]	—	—
OFBCI under governor, but established in different way	—	—	—	—
OFBCI under a state agency	x	x	—	—
FBL funded by CCF funds	—	—	—	—
OFBCI primarily private funded, but connected to governor	—	—	—	—
Characteristics of FBL Position				
Status of position	P/T	P/T	P/T	P/T
Other employees in the OFBCI?	yes	no	no	no
State OFBCI budget	no[3]	salary	no	salary
Freq. of progress reports from FBL	—	—	—	—
FBL reports to	COS[4]	deputy secretary[5]	governor	governor's office
FBL Network				
# liaisons FBL reports knowing	10	2	5	3
Contact with White House OFBCI				
FBL connected to White House?	x	x	x	x
Freq. of contact with White House	bi-weekly	once	monthly	once
FBL attended White House confs	x	—	x	x
FBL rcvd. info. from White House	x	—	x	x
Federal gov't contacts about FBOs, other than White House OFBCI	HHS[2]	—	HHS,[2] DOL,[6] HUD[7]	HHS[2]
Level of Activity				
FBL budget to fund FBOs	—	—	—	—
Contract with intermediary orgs	—	—	—	—
Network with state agencies & FBOs	x	x	x	x
Hold state conferences	x	planned	x	x

DATA COLLECTED	CA	CO	CT[1]	DC
General Information				
State has FBL	x	x	x	x
State has OFBCI	—	—	x[8]	—
Year FBL/OFBCI created	1999	2001	2003	1999
FBL position created by law	—	—	—	—
FBL created by executive order	—	—	x	—
FBL created by other means	x	x	—	x
Data Collected from Interviews & Surveys with FBLs				
State Information				
Conferences for FBOs	—	x	x	x
Web site or e-mail listserv	—	x	x	x
Tech. assistance seminars for FBOs	—	x	x	x
Grant-writing programs for FBOs	—	—	x	x
Recruitment of groups for programs	—	—	x	—
Advisory board to focus on FBOs	—	—	x	—
Startup funds for FBOs/CBOs	—	x	x	x
Funding offered by state office	—	—	—	x
FBL Position				
Location of Liaison Position in Government Structure				
No position created	—	—	—	—
Position vacant or unfunded	x	—	x	—
FBL in the governor's office	—	—	x	x
FBL in state agency	—	HHS[2]	—	—
OFBCI under governor, but established in different way	—	—	—	—
OFBCI under a state agency	—	—	—	—
FBL funded by CCF funds	—	—	—	—
OFBCI primarily private funded, but connected to governor	—	—	—	—
Characteristics of FBL Position				
Status of position	—	P/T	P/T	P/T
Other employees in the OFBCI?	—	no		yes
State OFBCI budget	—	no[9]	$150K (2003)	salary+ $10K
Freq. of progress reports from FBL	—	—	—	—
FBL reports to:	—	HHS[2]	Advisory Council[10]	mayor
FBL Network				
# liaisons FBL reports knowing	—	2	3	0
Contact with White House OFBCI				
FBL connected to White House?	—	0	x	x
Freq. of contact with White House	—	none	regularly	monthly
FBL attended White House confs	—	x	x	x
FBL rcvd. info. from White House	—	0	x	x
Federal gov't contacts about FBOs, other than White House OFBCI	—	none	—	HHS,[2] DOJ,[11] HUD[7]
Level of Activity				
FBL budget to fund FBOs	—	—	—	RFP[12]
Contract with intermediary orgs	—	—	—	—
Network w/state agencies & FBOs	—	x	x	x
Hold state conferences	—	x	x	x

(continued)

DATA COLLECTED	DE	FL	GA	HI
General Information				
State has FBL	—	x	x	x
State has OFBCI	—	x	—	x
Year FBL/OFBCI created	—	2004	2004	2004
FBL position created by law	—	—	—	—
FBL created by executive order	—	x	—	—
FBL created by other means	—	—	x	x
Data Collected from Interviews & Surveys with FBLs				
State Information				
Conferences for FBOs	—	x	—	x
Web site or e-mail listserv	—	x	—	x
Tech. assistance seminars for FBOs	—	x	—	x
Grant-writing programs for FBOs	—	x	—	x
Recruitment of groups for programs	—	—	—	—
Advisory board to focus on FBOs	—	x	—	x
Startup funds for FBOs/CBOs	—	x	—	—
Funding offered by state office	—	x	—	—
FBL Position				
Location of Liaison Position in Government Structure				
No position created	x	—	—	—
Position vacant or unfunded	—	—	—	—
FBL in the governor's office	—	—	—	x
FBL in state agency	—	—	Family Services	—
OFBCI under governor, but established in different way	—	x	—	—
OFBCI under a state agency	—	—	—	—
FBL funded by CCF funds	—	—	—	—
OFBCI primarily private funded, but connected to governor	—	x	—	—
Characteristics of FBL Position				
Status of position	—	F/T	P/T	P/T
Other employees in the OFBCI?	—	yes		no
State OFBCI budget	—	salary, travel, materials	salary	no
Freq. of progress reports from FBL	—	monthly	—	—.
FBL reports to:	—	governor	division head	DOL[6]
FBL Network				
# liaisons FBL reports knowing	—	7	1	0
Contact with White House OFBCI				
FBL connected to White House?	—	x	—	x
Freq. of contact with White House	—	bi-weekly	—	maybe monthly
FBL attended White House confs	—	x	x	0
FBL rcvd. info. from White House	—	x	x	0
Federal gov't contacts about FBOs, other than White House OFBCI	—	HHS,[2] DOCF[13], DOE,[14] HUD[7]	—	HHS,[2] DOF,[13] HUD[7]
Level of Activity				
FBL budget to fund FBOs	—	—	—	—
Contract with intermediary orgs	—	—	—	—
Network w/state agencies & FBOs	—	x	x	x
Hold state conferences	—	x	—	x

DATA COLLECTED	IA	ID[15]	IL	IN
General Information				
State has FBL	x[8]	e-mail clearinghouse	—	x
State has OFBCI	—	—	—	x
Year FBL/OFBCI created		2004		2005
FBL position created by law	—	—	—	—
FBL created by executive order	—	—	—	x
FBL created by other means	—	x	—	—
Data Collected from Interviews & Surveys with FBLs				
State Information				
Conferences for FBOs	—	—	—	x
Web site or e-mail listserv	—	x	—	x
Tech. assistance seminars for FBOs	—	—	—	x
Grant-writing programs for FBOs	—	—	—	x
Recruitment of groups for programs	—	—	—	—
Advisory board to focus on FBOs	—	x	—	x
Startup funds for FBOs/CBOs	—	—	—	—
Funding offered by state office	—	—	—	—
FBL Position				
Location of Liaison Position in Government Structure				
No position created	—	—	—	—
Position vacant or unfunded	—	x	—	—
FBL in the governor's office	—	—	—	x
FBL in state agency	—	Children & Families	—	—
OFBCI under governor, but established in different way	—	—	—	—
OFBCI under a state agency	—	—	—	—
FBL funded by CCF funds	—	—	—	—
OFBCI primarily private funded, but connected to governor	—	—	—	—
Characteristics of FBL Position				
Status of position	—	P/T	—	F/T
Other employees in the OFBCI?				
State OFBCI budget	—	no	—	no[17]
Freq. of progress reports from FBL	—	—	—	—
FBL reports to:	—	advisory board	—	governor
FBL Network				
# liaisons FBL reports knowing	—	2 (3 states)	—	2
Contact with White House OFBCI				
FBL connected to White House?	—	x	—	x
Freq. of contact with White House	—	little; varies	—	few times
FBL attended White House confs	—	x	—	x
FBL rcvd. info. from White House	—	x	—	x
Federal gov't contacts about FBOs, other than White House OFBCI	—	HHS[2]	—	e-mail (HHS[2])
Level of Activity				
FBL budget to fund FBOs	—	—	—	—
Contract with intermediary orgs	—	—	—	—
Network w/state agencies & FBOs	—	x	—	x
Hold state conferences	—	—	—	x

(continued)

DATA COLLECTED	KS	KY	LA	MA
General Information				
State has FBL	x	x	x	—
State has OFBCI	—	x[8]	x	—
Year FBL/OFBCI created	2004	2005	2004	2005
FBL position created by law	—	—	—	—
FBL created by executive order	—	—		x
FBL created by other means	x	—	x	—
Data Collected from Interviews & Surveys with FBLs				
State Information				
Conferences for FBOs	—	—	—	x
Web site or e-mail listserv	x	—	x	—
Tech. assistance seminars for FBOs	—	—	—	—
Grant-writing programs for FBOs	—	—	—	—
Recruits specific groups for programs	—	—	—	—
Advisory board to focus on FBOs	—	—	—	—
Startup funds for FBOs/CBOs	—	—	—	—
Funding offered by state office	—	—	—	—
FBL Position				
Location of Liaison Position in Government Structure				
No position created	—	—	—	—
Position vacant or unfunded	—	—	—	—
FBL in the governor's office	x	—	x	—
FBL in state agency	—	—	—	—
OFBCI under governor, but established in different way	—	—	—	—
OFBCI under a state agency	—	—	—	—
FBL funded by CCF funds	—	—	—	—
OFBCI primarily private funded, but connected to governor	—	—	—	—
Characteristics of FBL Position				
Status of position	P/T	—	F/T	—
Other employees in the OFBCI?	no	—	—	—
State OFBCI budget	no[17]	—	—	—
Freq. of progress reports from FBL	—	—	—	—
FBL reports to:	no one	—	—	—
FBL Network				
# liaisons FBL reports knowing	0	—	—	—
Contact with White House OFBCI				
FBL connected to White House?	0	—	x	—
Freq. of contact with White House	0	—	—	—
FBL attended White House confs	0	—	—	—
FBL rcvd. info. from White House	0	—	—	—
Federal gov't contacts about FBOs, other than White House OFBCI	none	—	—	—
Level of Activity				
FBL budget to fund FBOs	—	—	—	—
Contract with intermediary orgs	—	—	—	—
Network w/state agencies & FBOs	—	—	—	—
Hold state conferences	—	—	—	x

DATA COLLECTED	MD[1]	MI	MN	MO
General Information				
State has FBL	x	x	x	x[8]
State has OFBCI	x	x	x	—
Year FBL/OFBCI created	2004	2004	2004	2007
FBL position created by law	—	—	—	x
FBL created by executive order	x	x	x	—
FBL created by other means	—	—	—	—
Data Collected from Interviews & Surveys with FBLs				
State Information				
Conferences for FBOs	x[18]	x	—	—
Web site or e-mail listserv	x	x	x	—
Tech. assistance seminars for FBOs	—	x	—	—
Grant-writing programs for FBOs	—	—	—	—
Recruits specific groups for programs	—	—	—	—
Advisory board to focus on FBOs	—	x	x	—
Startup funds for FBOs/CBOs	—	—	—	—
Funding offered by state office	—	—	—	—
FBL Position				
Location of Liaison Position in Government Structure				
No position created	—	—	—	x
Position vacant or unfunded	—	—	—	—
FBL in the governor's office	x	x	x	—
FBL in state agency	—	—	—	—
OFBCI under governor, but established in different way	—	—	—	—
OFBCI under a state agency	—	—	—	—
FBL funded by CCF funds	—	—	—	—
OFBCI primarily private funded, but connected to governor	—	—	—	—
Characteristics of FBL Position				
Status of position	F/T	F/T	F/T	—
Other employees in the OFBCI?	yes		no	—
State OFBCI budget	—	small salary, expenses	salary	—
Freq. of progress reports from FBL	—	—	—	—
FBL reports to:	governor	COS[4]	governor's office	—
FBL Network				
# liaisons FBL reports knowing	3	4	7	—
Contact with White House OFBCI				
FBL connected to White House?	x	x	x	—
Freq. of contact with White House	weekly	occasionally	once	—
FBL attended White House confs	3	x	0	—
FBL rcvd. info. from White House	x	x	0	—
Federal gov't contacts about FBOs, other than WHouse OFBCI	HHS,[2] DOL,[6] DOJ[11]	HHS,[2] DOL,[6] HUD,[7] DOJ,[11] DOE,[14] AG,[19] SBA[20]	—	—
Level of Activity				
FBL budget to fund FBOs	—	—	—	—
Contract with intermediary orgs	—	—	—	—
Network w/state agencies & FBOs	x	x	x	—
Hold state conferences	x	x	—	—

(continued)

DATA COLLECTED	MS	MT[21]	NC	ND
General Information				
State has FBL	x[8]	x	x	x
State has OFBCI	—	x	x	x
Year FBL/OFBCI created	—	2002	2005	2005
FBL position created by law	—	—	—	x
FBL created by executive order	—	—	—	—
FBL created by other means	—	x	x	—
Data Collected from Interviews & Surveys with FBLs				
State Information				
Conferences for FBOs	—	x	—	—
Web site or e-mail listserv	—	x	—	x
Tech. assistance seminars for FBOs	—	—	—	—
Grant-writing programs for FBOs	—	x	—	—
Recruits specific groups for programs	—	x	—	—
Advisory board to focus on FBOs	—	x	—	x
Startup funds for FBOs/CBOs	—	x	—	—
Funding offered by state office	—	x	—	—
FBL Position				
Location of Liaison Position in Government Structure				
No position created	x	—	—	x
Position vacant or unfunded	—	—	—	—
FBL in the governor's office	—	—	x	x
FBL in state agency	—	MSU[22]	—	—
OFBCI under governor, but established in different way	—	—	—	—
OFBCI under a state agency	—	—	—	—
FBL funded by CCF funds	—	x	—	—
OFBCI primarily private funded, but connected to governor	—	—	—	—
Characteristics of FBL Position				
Status of position	—	P/T	F/T	P/T
Other employees in the OFBCI?	—	yes	no	no
State OFBCI budget	—	CCF[23] funds	no	no
Freq. of progress reports from FBL	—	—	discretionary	discretionary
FBL reports to:	—	CCF & Adv. board	COS[4]	COS[4]
FBL Network				
# liaisons FBL reports knowing	—	2	0	4
Contact with White House OFBCI				
FBL connected to White House?	—	x	0	x
Freq. of contact with White House	—	quarterly	none	1 call; conf.
FBL attended White House confs	—	x	0	x
FBL rcvd. info. from White House	—	0	0	x
Federal gov't contacts about FBOs, other than White House OFBCI	—	HHS[2]	none	—
Level of Activity				
FBL budget to fund FBOs	—	X	—	—
Contract with intermediary orgs	—	—	—	—
Network w/state agencies & FBOs	—	x	x	agencies only
Hold state conferences	—	x	—	—

DATA COLLECTED	NE[21]	NJ	NH	NM[1]
General Information				
State has FBL	x	x	x[8]	x
State has OFBCI	—	x	—	x
Year FBL/OFBCI created	2003	1999	—	2005
FBL position created by law	—	—	—	—
FBL created by executive order	—	x	—	x
FBL created by other means	—	—	—	—
Data Collected from Interviews & Surveys with FBLs				
State Information				
Conferences for FBOs	x	x	—	x[24]
Web site or e-mail listserv	x	x	—	x
Tech. assistance seminars for FBOs	x	x	—	—
Grant-writing programs for FBOs	x	x	—	—
Recruits specific groups for programs	x	x	—	—
Advisory board to focus on FBOs	x	x	—	—
Startup funds for FBOs/CBOs	x	x	—	—
Funding offered by state office	x	x	—	—
FBL Position				
Location of Liaison Position in Government Structure				
No position created	—	—	x	—
Position vacant or unfunded	—	—	—	—
FBL in the governor's office	—	x	—	x
FBL in state agency	—	—	—	—
OFBCI under governor, but established in different way	—	—	—	—
OFBCI under a state agency	—	Lieut. Governor	—	—
FBL funded by CCF funds	x	—	—	—
OFBCI primarily private funded, but connected to governor	—	—	—	—
Characteristics of FBL Position				
Status of position	F/T	F/T	—	F/T
Other employees in the OFBCI?	yes	yes	—	—
State OFBCI budget	$1.1 m (annual)	$4 m (annual)	—	salary
Freq. of progress reports from FBL	—	—	—	—
FBL reports to:	CCF[23]	Sec. of State	—	governor
FBL Network				
# liaisons FBL reports knowing	0	6	—	2
Contact with White House OFBCI				
FBL connected to White House?	HHS[2]	x	—	x
Freq. of contact with White House	monthly	4–5 calls	—	semi-frequent
FBL attended White House confs	x	0	—	0
FBL rcvd. info. from White House	x	0	—	0
Federal gov't contacts about FBOs, other than White House OFBCI	—	—	—	e-mail, personal meetings w/HHS[2]
Level of Activity				
FBL budget to fund FBOs	—	X	—	—
Contract with intermediary orgs	—	—	—	—
Network w/state agencies & FBOs	x	x	—	x
Hold state conferences	x	x	—	x[24]

(continued)

DATA COLLECTED	NV	NY	OH	OK
General Information				
State has FBL	—	x	x	x
State has OFBCI	—	—	x	x
Year FBL/OFBCI created	—	2003	2003	2000
FBL position created by law	—	—	x	—
FBL created by executive order	—	—	—	—
FBL created by other means	—	x	—	x
Data Collected from Interviews & Surveys with FBLs				
State Information				
Conferences for FBOs	—	x	x	x
Web site or e-mail listserv	—	x	x	x
Tech. assistance seminars for FBOs	—	x	x	—
Grant-writing programs for FBOs	—	x	x	x
Recruits specific groups for programs	—	—	x	x
Advisory board to focus on FBOs	—	x	x	—
Startup funds for FBOs/CBOs	—	—	x	—
Funding offered by state office	—	—	x	—
FBL Position				
Location of Liaison Position in Government Structure				
No position created	—	—	—	—
Position vacant or unfunded	—	—	—	—
FBL in the governor's office	—	x	x	—
FBL in state agency	—	—	—	HHS[2]
OFBCI under governor, but established in different way	—	—	—	—
OFBCI under a state agency	—	—	—	HHS[2]
FBL funded by CCF funds	—	—	x	—
OFBCI primarily private funded, but connected to governor	—	—	—	—
Characteristics of FBL Position				
Status of position	—	P/T	F/T	F/T
Other employees in the OFBCI?	—	yes	yes	yes
State OFBCI budget	—	no	$750K	$130K+salary
Freq. of progress reports from FBL	—	—	—	—
FBL reports to:	—	Family & Comm.	governor	HHS[2] director
FBL Network				
# liaisons FBL reports knowing	—	1	14	17
Contact with White House OFBCI				
FBL connected to White House?	—	x	x	x
Freq. of contact with White House	—	semi-regular	monthly	monthly
FBL attended White House confs	—	x	x	x
FBL rcvd. info. from White House	—	x	x	x
Federal gov't contacts about FBOs, other than White House OFBCI	—	HHS,[2] HUD,[7] DOL[6]?	HHS[2]	HHS,[2] DOL,[6] DOJ,[11] DOE,[14] AG,[19] CCS[25]
Level of Activity				
FBL budget to fund FBOs	—	—	RFP[12]	—
Contract with intermediary orgs	—	—	—	x
Network w/state agencies & FBOs	—	x	x	x
Hold state conferences	—	x	x	x

DATA COLLECTED	OR	PA	RI	SC[27]
General Information				
State has FBL	—	—	—	x
State has OFBCI	—	—	—	—
Year FBL/OFBCI created	—	—	—	1999
FBL position created by law	—	—	—	—
FBL created by executive order	—	—	—	—
FBL created by other means	—	—	—	x
Data Collected from Interviews & Surveys with FBLs				
State Information				
Conferences for FBOs	—	—	—	—
Web site or e-mail listserv	—	—	—	x
Tech. assistance seminars for FBOs	—	—	—	—
Grant-writing programs for FBOs	—	—	—	—
Recruitment of groups for programs	—	—	—	—
Advisory board to focus on FBOs	—	—	—	—
Startup funds for FBOs/CBOs	—	—	—	x
Funding offered by state office	—	—	—	—
FBL Position				
Location of Liaison Position in Government Structure				
No position created	x	—	x	—
Position vacant or unfunded	—	—	—	x
FBL in the governor's office	—	—	—	—
FBL in state agency	—	—	—	—
OFBCI under governor, but established in different way	—	—	—	—
OFBCI under a state agency	—	—	—	—
FBL funded by CCF funds	—	—	—	—
OFBCI primarily private funded, but connected to governor	—	—	—	—
Characteristics of FBL Position				
Status of position	—	—	—	P/T
Other employees in the OFBCI?	—	—	—	no
State OFBCI budget	—	—	—	planned, but not yet
Freq. of progress reports from FBL	—	—	—	—
FBL reports to:	—	—	—	alcohol/drug admin
FBL Network				
# liaisons FBL reports knowing	—	—	—	0
Contact with White House OFBCI				
FBL connected to White House?	—	—	—	—
Freq. of contact with White House	—	—	—	—
FBL attended White House confs	—	—	—	0
FBL rcvd. info. from White House	—	—	—	0
Federal gov't contacts about FBOs, other than White House OFBCI	—	—	—	HHS[2]
Level of Activity				
FBL budget to fund FBOs	—	—	—	—
Contract with intermediary orgs	—	—	—	—
Network w/state agencies & FBOs	—	—	—	x
Hold state conferences	—	—	—	—

(*continued*)

DATA COLLECTED	SD	TN	TX	UT
General Information				
State has FBL	—	—	x	x
State has OFBCI	—	—	x	x[8]
Year FBL/OFBCI created	—	—	1999	in progress
FBL position created by law	—	—	—	—
FBL created by executive order	—	—	x	—
FBL created by other means	—	—	—	x
Data Collected from Interviews & Surveys with FBLs				
State Information				
Conferences for FBOs	—	—	—	x[26]
Web site or e-mail listserv	—	—	x	x
Tech. assistance seminars for FBOs	—	—	—	x
Grant-writing programs for FBOs	—	—	—	x
Recruitment of groups for programs	—	—	—	—
Advisory board to focus on FBOs	—	—	x	x
Startup funds for FBOs/CBOs	—	—	—	—
Funding offered by state office	—	—	—	—
FBL Position				
Location of Liaison Position in Government Structure				
No position created	—	x	—	—
Position vacant or unfunded	—	—	—	—
FBL in the governor's office	—	—	x	—
FBL in state agency	—	—	—	—
OFBCI under governor, but established in different way	—	—	x	—
OFBCI under a state agency	—	—	—	—
FBL funded by CCF funds	—	—	—	—
OFBCI primarily private funded, but connected to governor	—	—	x	—
Characteristics of FBL Position				
Status of position	—	—	F/T	P/T
Other employees in the OFBCI?	—	—	no	no
State OFBCI budget	—	—	salary	—
Freq. of progress reports from FBL	—	—	—	—
FBL reports to:	—	—	foundation CEO	—
FBL Network				
# liaisons FBL reports knowing	—	—	17	—
Contact with White House OFBCI				
FBL connected to White House?	—	—	x	—
Freq. of contact with White House	—	—	several times	—
FBL attended White House confs	—	—	—	—
FBL rcvd. info. from White House	—	—	—	—
Federal gov't contacts about FBOs, other than White House OFBCI	—	—	DOL,[6] HUD,[7] DOE,[14]USDA,[27] U.S. Freedom Corps	—
Level of Activity				
FBL budget to fund FBOs	—	—	—	—
Contract with intermediary orgs	—	—	—	—
Network w/state agencies & FBOs	—	—	x	—
Hold state conferences	—	—	—	in past

DATA COLLECTED	VA	VT	WA	WI
General Information				
State has FBL	x	—	x[8]	x[8]
State has OFBCI	x	—	—	x[28]
Year FBL/OFBCI created	2003	—	—	2006[28]
FBL position created by law	x	—	—	—
FBL created by executive order	—	—	—	—
FBL created by other means	—	—	—	—
Data Collected from Interviews & Surveys with FBLs				
State Information				
Conferences for FBOs	x	—	—	—
Web site or e-mail listserv	x	—	—	x
Tech. assistance seminars for FBOs	x	—	—	—
Grant-writing programs for FBOs	x	—	—	—
Recruitment of groups for programs	—	—	—	—
Advisory board to focus on FBOs	x	—	—	—
Startup funds for FBOs/CBOs	—	—	—	—
Funding offered by state office	—	—	—	—
FBL Position				
Location of Liaison Position in Government Structure				
No position created	—	x	x	—
Position vacant or unfunded	—	—	—	—
FBL in the governor's office	x	—	—	—
FBL in state agency	—	—	—	—
OFBCI under governor, but established in different way	—	—	—	—
OFBCI under a state agency	—	—	—	—
FBL funded by CCF funds	—	—	—	—
OFBCI primarily private funded, but connected to governor	—	—	—	—
Characteristics of FBL Position				
Status of position	P/T	—	—	—
Other employees in the OFBCI?	no	—	—	—
State OFBCI budget	no	—	—	—
Freq. of progress reports from FBL	—	—	—	—
FBL reports to:	Comm. of Social Serv	—	—	—
FBL Network				
# liaisons FBL reports knowing	11	—	—	—
Contact with White House OFBCI				
FBL connected to White House?	x	—	—	—
Freq. of contact with White House	quarterly	—	—	—
FBL attended White House confs	x	—	—	—
FBL rcvd. info. from White House	x	—	—	—
Federal gov't contacts about FBOs, other than White House OFBCI	HHS,[2] DOL,[6] DOJ[11]	—	—	—
Level of Activity				
FBL budget to fund FBOs	—	—	—	—
Contract with intermediary orgs	—	—	—	—
Network w/state agencies & FBOs	x	—	—	—
Hold state conferences	x	—	—	—

(*continued*)

DATA COLLECTED	WV	WY
General Information		
State has FBL	—	x
State has OFBCI	—	x
Year FBL/OFBCI created	—	2004
FBL position created by law	—	—
FBL created by executive order	—	—
FBL created by other means	—	x
Data Collected from Interviews & Surveys with FBLs		
State Information		
Conferences for FBOs	—	x
Web site or e-mail listserv	—	x
Tech. assistance seminars for FBOs	—	x
Grant-writing programs for FBOs	—	x
Recruitment of groups for programs	—	x
Advisory board to focus on FBOs	—	x
Startup funds for FBOs/CBOs	—	x[29]
Funding offered by state office	—	—
FBL Position		
Location of Liaison Position in Government Structure		
No position created	x	—
Position vacant or unfunded	—	—
FBL in the governor's office	—	—
FBL in state agency	—	Families & Children
OFBCI under governor, but established in different way	—	—
OFBCI under a state agency	—	—
FBL funded by CCF funds	—	—
OFBCI primarily private funded, but connected to governor	—	—
Characteristics of FBL Position		
Status of position	—	P/T
Other employees in the OFBCI?	—	no
State OFBCI budget	—	salary[30]
Freq. of progress reports from FBL	—	—
FBL reports to:	—	dir. Dept. of Family
FBL Network		
# liaisons FBL reports knowing	—	1
Contact with White House OFBCI		
FBL connected to White House?	—	—
Freq. of contact with White House	—	—
FBL attended White House confs	—	x
FBL rcvd. info. from White House	—	no
Federal gov't contacts about FBOs, other than White House OFBCI	—	ACF[31]
Level of Activity		
FBL budget to fund FBOs	—	—
Contract with intermediary orgs	—	x
Network w/state agencies & FBOs	—	x
Hold state conferences	—	—

NOTES

1. State is difficult to categorize: it has an unusual FBL structure, with many people in different offices taking responsibility.

2. Department of Health and Human Services.

3. The OFBCI does not have a budget, but has AmeriCorps, workforce development money.

4. Governor's Chief of Staff.

5. Deputy Secretary in the Governor's Office.

6. Department of Labor.

7. Department of Housing and Urban Development.

8. Office or liaison position created after I completed interviews in spring of 2005.

9. There is no state budget, but Compassion Capital Fund (CCF) and Temporary Aid to Needy Families (TANF) money is available for startups.

10. Advisory Council in the Department of Family Services.

11. Department of Justice.

12. Request for proposals.

13. Department of Children and Families.

14. Department of Education.

15. The liaison interviewed was not the same as the one listed on the White House OFBCI listing of state FBLs.

16. The OFBCI does not have a budget, but has access to AmeriCorps, staff, etc.

17. The OFBCI does not have a budget but has some staffing from workforce development.

18. Offers conferences in partnership with others.

19. Department of Agriculture.

20. Small Business Administration.

21. Liaison was funded through CCF before the office began; MT now has an FBL.

22. Montana State University.

23. CCF.

24. No conference had been offered at the time of the interview, but has been since.

25. Corporation for National and Community Service.

26. Utah had offered conferences, but no longer had an FBL at the time of my interview.

27. U.S. Department of Agriculture.

28. OFBCI created after my interview with FBL.

29. Funded by TANF, CCF, Faith Initiatives of Wyoming, and state partner funds.

30. Salary paid with TANF funds.

31. Administration for Children and Families.

Notes

PREFACE

1. Data on faith-based organizations (FBOs) are not currently gathered in a consistent, systematic way across all 50 states. First, the very definition of FBO is rather ambiguous; many surveys allow organizations to self-identify as faith-based, but outside entities may see them differently.
Second, independent surveys have yielded very different results. For example, the White House attempted to determine how many FBOs states had contracted with; on review, their tally of FBOs included some city governments. Third, many FBOs operate without anyone knowing they exist. In the end, exhaustive knowledge about the faith-based sector is simply not yet available. For purposes of this study, organizations were considered faith-based if they—or one of the people interviewed— considered them so.

CHAPTER I

1. Other conferences had been partially sponsored by the federal government, but were held at the state level and had been presented as nonpartisan roundtables on the faith-based initiatives, according to Kuo (2006a).

2. Flowers (2005), for example, disagrees with this interpretation. I take no stand on whether the interpretation is correct; rather I take as my starting point that the cultural and legal norm when the initiatives began in 1996 was (and had been for 40 or 50 years) one of separation rather than of cooperation.

3. Olasky coined the phrase "armies of compassion" in his 1996 article.

4. Over the last eight years, Supreme Court cases include *Hein v. Freedom from Religion Foundation*, a 2007 decision limiting taxpayer lawsuits on behalf of preserving a separationist interpretation of the First Amendment (Hughes 2008); *Elk Grove v. Newdow*, which ruled in 2004 that the parents of a schoolchild could not bring a lawsuit challenging the use of the Pledge of Allegiance and the statement "under God" because they did not have standing; *Zelman v. Harris-Simpson*, a 2002 decision in which the court found that voucher programs do not violate church-state constitutional requirements; and *Mitchell v. Helms*, in 2000, in which the Court found states could fund religious schools through instructional materials and equipment, even though these funds and materials might be used for religious purposes.

Policies that demonstrate a similar trend include pharmacists' conscience clauses, gay marriage and family policies, abortion restrictions, and school board policies allowing the teaching of intelligent design in science classes.

5. But see also Farris, Nathan, and Wright 2004. See Bartkowski and Regis 2003, Ragan and Wright 2005, and Wineburg 2001 for other descriptions of the initiative at the state level.

6. At the time of my data collection, 34 states had liaison positions; since then, 5 states have created positions. This work is based on the interviews I did with 30 of the original 34 liaisons.

7. It may in fact be that this otherworldly norm is an approach taken by some evangelicals during certain periods of American politics and that evangelicals and fundamentalists have moved in and out of the political realm throughout American history (Marsden 2006).

8. Also important to this is something that both Lindsay and I have found: that even in circumstances of collaborative support and cultural goods being produced, there are still barriers and difficulties to implementation. In fact, the attainment of some level of success and the need to reach out to others are the very things that create the barriers to idealized implementation. The history of the faith-based initiatives is an excellent example of how a social movement can attempt to create new policies and new political actors to further movement action and goals, and still be faced with political and bureaucratic inertia.

9. A more detailed description of methods can be found in appendix A, liaison survey questions can be found in appendix B, and appendix C contains a summary of the raw data.

10. At this writing, states with FBL position created by law are Iowa, Kentucky, and Missouri. States with FBL position created by executive order are Alabama, Alaska, Florida, Indiana, Massachusetts, Maryland, Michigan, Minnesota, New Jersey, New Mexico, and Texas.

11. "States" in this case includes the District of Columbia; a former liaison from Utah was also interviewed. When several staff members of a state OFBCI were interviewed, data used here are from the primary FBL. These interviews were completed in March 2005. Several additional states have created faith-based liaison positions and/or Offices of Faith-Based and Community Initiatives since then.

12. This aspect of the project bears repeating in the future, because recent conversations with liaisons and others have led me to believe that the level of connectivity has changed since 2004, when state FBLs had their first national

meeting. They have since had additional meetings, but I have not been allowed to attend.

CHAPTER 2

1. See also Cosgrove 2001 and Monsma 1996.

2. Stem cell research, gay marriage, and abortion are all issue areas that are known as "morality politics" and have become key issues within conservative political and religious circles (Leland 2005). A 2005 Pew Research study found that the greatest opposition to stem cell research came from conservative evangelicals and members of the Republican Party. "Opposition to stem cell research is greatest among white evangelical Protestants, 58 percent of whom believe that protecting potential life of embryos is more important. But mainline Protestants are strongly in favor of the research, with 69 percent believing that stem cell research's benefits outweigh the costs. And despite Vatican objections to embryonic stem cell research, a solid majority of Catholics (63 percent) support such research. Politically, the stem cell issue could prove beneficial for the Democratic Party. Fully two-thirds of Democrats (68 percent) favor stem cell research, but so too do 58 percent of independents. By contrast, Republicans are divided on the issue, with 45 percent favoring the research and 45 percent believing that it is more important to protect the potential life of embryos."

3. The departments with Agency Centers for Faith-Based and Community Initiatives are the Agency for International Development, Department of Agriculture, Department of Commerce, Department of Education, Department of Health and Human Services, Department of Homeland Security, Department of Housing and Urban Development, Department of Justice, Department of Labor, Small Business Administration, and Department of Veterans Affairs.

4. Although this brighter line existed, these groups did not have any problems providing social services without the Charitable Choice rules allowing religious hiring preferences. This lends additional support to the conclusion that these laws were really symbols of accommodation, showing the groups that those who supported the laws were friendly to the groups' missions.

5. The story of South Carolina is probably the most different, in that the liaison I spoke with had been doing a lot of work out of the office with substance abuse programs but had little contact with the governor or other state officials.

6. The funding of the Catholic hospital eventually made it to the Supreme Court in *Bradford vs. Roberts* and was held to be constitutionally sound (Buckley 2002).

CHAPTER 3

1. See http://www.whitehouse.gov/government/fbci/contact-states.html for a current list of state liaisons. This list changes periodically. For example, California, Illinois, and Pennsylvania had liaisons during the period in which I collected data, but they do not have any at the time of this writing.

2. Until recently the liaison in Oklahoma, Yarbrough was one of the first liaisons to fully grasp the constitutional issues related to the initiatives. He wrote

about the faith-based initiatives and their relationship to the Constitution, arguing that the initiatives were not a violation of the establishment clause, and that Oklahoma should aggressively implement these programs.

Yarbrough had been in the position longer than other liaisons, and most considered him one of the most helpful and informative liaisons. While he was able to create innovative programs, he had to rely on getting organizations to volunteer their efforts, rather than being able to fund their work through his office. One liaison described him as innovative but ultimately lacking in the authority to accomplish much at the state level.

3. The exception to this was North Dakota, in which the liaison was not able to do any networking with FBOs; his outreach was all to state agencies. But he had only been in the position for a couple of months and was also the governor's chief of staff. The position had been created through legislation, and its responsibilities were added to his numerous existing duties (Dec. 28, 2005).

4. In late 2008, 17 states with Web sites for information related to the faith-based initiatives were: Alabama (www.servealabama.gov), Alaska (www.hss.state.ak.us/fbci/), Arkansas (www.state.ar.us/dhs/adov), Connecticut (www.confrenceofchurches.org, designated as the state's OFBCI), Florida (http://www.volunteerfloridafoundation.org/about_faithbased.php), Illinois (http://www.dhs.state.il.us/page.aspx?item=30909), Indiana (www.IN.gov/ofbci/), Michigan (www.michigan/gov/outreach), Minnesota (www.faithandcommunity.state.mn.us), New Mexico (http://www.nmaging.state.nm.us/Faith_Based_Initiatives.html), North Dakota (http://governor.state.nd.us/misc/2006-faith-based.html), Ohio (http://governor.ohio.gov/Default.aspx?alias=governor.ohio.gov/fbci), Oklahoma (www.faithlinksok.org), Texas (www.onestarfoundation.org), Virginia (www.dss.virginia.gov/community/faith.html), Wisconsin (http://cfbp.wisconsin.gov/), and Wyoming (http://dfsweb.state.wy.us/faithBased.html). This list was compiled from the federal Web sites http://www.whitehouse.gov/government/fbci/contact-states.html and http://www.nyswtwrn.com/CCC/grants/Faith.pdf.

5. As noted earlier, the Utah position lost its funding, but the liaison continued in a volunteer capacity until 2007, when a new position was created.

CHAPTER 4

1. I am referring in this section to state appropriations. Colorado, Montana, Nebraska, and Ohio have also been able to provide money to FBOs or their state OFBCI through federal Compassion Capital Fund grants.

2. Although there have been several lawsuits against state government implementation that have been successful, the most important lawsuit against the federal government, *Hein v. Freedom from Religion Foundation*, which argued that the federal government could not use taxpayer dollars to fund religion through faith-based conferences, was settled in favor of the federal government. A majority of the Supreme Court justices found that the foundation did not have standing to bring the lawsuit. "The nation's highest court ruled that taxpayers may not mount legal challenges against the government over funding to religious organizations unless Congress has specifically authorized the programs that provide the money. Citizens may not sue over

purely discretionary actions of the President and his administration paid for out of general administrative funds, the court determined. That meant taxpayers had no right to sue the White House faith-based office over its conferences or other activities; lacking congressional support, the federal Faith-Based and Community Initiative has been advanced largely by executive orders issued by the President rather than legislative action" (Roundtable on Religion and Social Welfare Policy 2007).

CHAPTER 5

1. At the time of my interviews, only liaisons from Kansas, North Carolina, and Minnesota reported neither attending nor holding any conferences.

2. See, for example, Frazier 1974, Harris 1999, Lincoln 1974, 1999, Lincoln and Mamayia 1990, Paris 1991, and Walsh 2001. In addition, Jenkins and Eckert (1986), McAdam (1982), and Morris (1984) discuss the role of the church in the Civil Rights movement, and Calhoun-Brown (1996) and McClerking and McDaniel (2005) look at its role in voting rights and segregation issues.

3. Numerous new studies point to this changing, with the evangelical population being less likely to be Republican and more likely to believe that other issues, such as poverty and the environment, are also issues that they should be concerned about. For a discussion of this trend, see Nejfelt 2008.

4. For a discussion of conservative policies, such as those regarding gay marriage, in the black church, see Lawton 2004.

5. The election of the first African American president in 2008 was, of course, not a part of this pattern. However, it is too early to tell what the longer term effects of the election of Barack Obama may be.

6. It is possible that since Hurricane Katrina, the ability of the Republican Party to chip away at the Democrats' black voting base may be more limited. Nonetheless, religion is still playing a larger role in politics: there is now a greater willingness within the Democratic Party to welcome faith and the role of faith in public life. As a Democratic president, Barack Obama is supporting a version of the faith-based initiatives. It seems probable that both major parties will come to support faith-based policies relevant to black churches.

CHAPTER 6

1. While Catholics have become an important part of this alliance, the original group that created and implemented Charitable Choice and the faith-based initiatives consisted primarily of conservative evangelicals.

2. While I include poverty rates as a theoretically relevant variable here, it is also important as a control variable, because it could be that states with higher poverty rates would be more likely to provide services.

3. Data on the number of children eligible versus those actually covered were only available for 1993, 1996, and 2002. Therefore, for intervening years I used the last available year's figures in my data set.

CHAPTER 7

1. For example, groups such as the Southern Baptists and the mission shelter movement do not want to partner with government, and they see the initiatives as harmful to religious freedom because of the potential for government intrusion. And, as I noted earlier, many religious groups have a primary goal of serving the spiritual, rather than material, needs of society.

2. While some states do highlight the importance of community organizations, this has almost always come second to highlighting the importance of FBOs.

3. An exception is the case of *Hein v. Freedom from Religion Foundation*, which has left the question of religious hiring largely open. Questions about funding programs through vouchers is still largely unanswered, although most legal scholars believe that funding inherently religious programs through vouchers will pass constitutional tests.

APPENDIX A

1. In 2000 Green and Conger recoded the variable to a three-point scale, but showed, for each state, whether there had been any change from the original coding conducted in 1994. When there had been a change I coded that as a 1-point change on the original five-point scale. I have spoken with Green about this coding, and he concurred that it is an accurate representation of the movement strength.

2. The original faith-based measures implemented in 1996 focused almost exclusively on TANF. Therefore, assessing a state's willingness to allow people access to these programs was seen as a good way to measure this original intent in comparison to its faith-based policies.

3. While this hypothesis is the most theoretically sound assumption, it may also be true that states in fiscal crisis may see the faith-based initiatives and relying upon churches to provide social services as a cost-efficient alternative when limited resources are available. Therefore, they may be more likely to create faith-based practices.

4. Data were also analyzed using logistic regression. The same variables that were significant in the event-history analysis were significant in the logistic regression analysis; however, it was not possible to control for time or the interaction effect of time and TANF recipients. Therefore, only the event-history results are presented.

5. While it was not significant over time, liaisons were created by twice as many Republican (22) as Democratic (11) governors, adding further qualitative evidence to support this hypothesis.

References

Abbott, Andrew. 1988. *The System of Professions*. Chicago: University of Chicago Press.

Allard, Scott W. 2008. *Mismatches and Unmet Needs: The New Geography of Welfare Policy*. New Haven, CT: Yale University Press.

Allison, Paul. 1995. *Survival Analysis Using the SAS System: A Practical Guide*. Cary, NC: SAS Institute.

Andrews, Kenneth. 2001. "Social Movements and Policy Implementation: The Mississippi Civil Rights Movement and the War on Poverty, 1965 to 1971." *American Sociological Review* 66:71–95.

Aronson, Rancy. 2004. "The Jesus Factor." *Frontline*, PBS, April 29. Retrieved November 15, 2004 (http://www.pbs.org/wgbh/pages/frontline/shows/jesus/view/).

Ashcroft, John. 1999. "The Charitable Choice Expansion Act: A Blueprint for Unleashing the Cultural Remedy to Societal Ills." (Press Release, November 5). Retrieved December 2, 1999 (http://www.senate.gov/~ashcroft/charity-do.htm).

Bartkowski, John, and Helen Regis. 2003. *The Faith-Based Initiatives: Religion, Race, and Poverty in the Post-Welfare Era*. New York: New York University Press.

Belluck, Pam. 2006. "The Not-So United States." *New York Times*, April 23. Retrieved February 3, 2008 (http://www.nytimes.com/2006/04/23/weekinreview/23belluck.html?pagewanted=1&_r=1&fta=y).

Benford, Robert and David Snow. 2000. "Framing Processes and Social Movements: An Overview and Assessment." *Annual Review of Sociology* 26:611–639.

Berry, William D., Evan J. Ringquist, Richard C. Fording, and Russell L. Hanson. 1998. "Measuring Citizen and Government Ideology in the American States, 1960–93." *American Journal of Political Science* 42:327–348.

———. 2005. "Assessing Dynamic Measures of State Citizen Ideology: Revalidating Our Measure by Way of Replying to Brace, Arceneaux, Johnson and Ulbig." Department of Political Science, Florida State University, Tallahassee. Unpublished manuscript.

Bielefeld, Wolfgang, and Shelia Seuss-Kennedy. 2003. *Charitable Choice: First Results from Three States*. Indianapolis: Indiana University–Purdue University Indianapolis. Retrieved April 5, 2004 (http://ccr.urbancenter.iupui.edu/PDFs/Interim%20report/Interim%20report%20PDF.pdf).

Bischoff, Laura. 2007. "Inquiry, Audit Due for Faith-Based Expenditures: A Review Shows Questionable Outlays by the Contractor That Administered $22 Million." *Dayton (Ohio) Daily News*, March 10. Retrieved January 22, 2008 (http://www. daytondailynews.com/n/content/oh/story/news/local/2007/03/09/ ddn031007auditinside.html).

Black, Amy, Douglas L. Koopman, and David K. Ryden. 2006. *Of Little Faith: The Politics of George W. Bush's Faith-based Initiatives*. Washington, DC: Georgetown University Press.

Blee, Kathleen, and Verta Taylor. 2002. "Semi-Structured Interviewing in Social Movement Research." Pp. 92–117 in *Methods of Social Movement Research*, edited by Bert Klandermans and Suzanne Staggenborg. Minneapolis: University of Minnesota Press.

Boehlert, Eric, and Jamison Foser. 2005. "Kondracke Claimed *NY Times* Columnist Dowd 'Is Turning Out to be the Randall Terry of the Left.'" *County Fair* (media blog), March 20. Retrieved February 22, 2005 (http://mediamatters.org/items/ 200503300003).

Brysk, Alison. 1995. "'Hearts and Minds': Bringing Symbolic Politics Back In." *Polity* 27:559.

Buckley, Thomas. 2002. "Church, State and the Faith-Based Initiative." *America: The National Catholic Weekly*, November 11. Retrieved June 22, 2009 (https://www. americamagazine.org/content/article.cfm?article_id=2601).

Bullock, Charles S., III, and Charles Lamb. 1984. *Implementation of Civil Rights Policy*. Monterey, CA: Brooks/Cole.

Burke, Daniel. 2008. "Obama Says He Will Expand Bush's Faith-Based Program." *Pew Center Religion and Public Life*, July 1. Retrieved November 6, 2008 (http:// pewforum.org/news/display.php?NewsID=15983).

Burstein, Paul. 1998. "Interest Organizations, Political Parties, and the Study of Democratic Politics." Pp. 39–56 in *Social Movements and American Political Institutions*, edited by A. N. Costain and A. S. McFarland. New York: Rowman & Littlefield.

Burstein, Paul, and April Linton. 2002. "The Impact of Political Parties, Interest Groups, and Social Movement Organizations on Public Policy: Some Recent Evidence and Theoretical Concerns." *Social Forces* 81:381–408.

Bush, George W. 2001. "Executive Order 13199 of January 29, 2001: Establishment of White House Office of Faith-Based and Community Initiatives." 66 *Federal Register* 21 (January 31):8500. Retrieved March 9, 2003 (http://frwebgate.access.gpo.gov/ cgi-bin/getdoc.cgi?dbname=2001_register&docid=01-2852-filed.pdf).

———. 2004. "America's Compassion in Action: Remarks by the President at the First White House National Conference on Faith-Based and Community Initiatives."

Text of speech, press release, June 1, White House Office of the Press Secretary. Retrieved September 15, 2005 (http://www.whitehouse.gov/news/releases/2004/06/20040601-10.html).

———. 2006. "President Attends National Republican Congressional Committee Dinner." Press release, March 16, White House Office of the Press Secretary. Retrieved May 12, 2006 (http://www.whitehouse.gov/news/releases/2006/03/20060316-16.html).

———. 2008a. "President Bush Delivers State of the Union Address." Text of speech, press release, January 28, White House Office of the Press Secretary. Retrieved February 23, 2008 (http://www.whitehouse.gov/news/releases/2008/01/20080128-13.html).

———. 2008b. "Remarks during a Visit to the Jericho Program in Baltimore, Maryland." *Weekly Compilation of Presidential Documents* 44(4):126–128. Retrieved February 23, 2008 (http://fdsys.gpo.gov/fdsys/pkg/WCPD-2008-02-04/pdf/WCPD-2008-02-04-Pg126.pdf).

Calhoun-Brown, A. 1996. "African American Churches and Policy Mobilization." *Journal of Politics* 58:935–953.

Casanova, Jose. 1994. *Public Religions in the Modern World.* Chicago: University of Chicago Press.

Center for Public Justice. 2006. "A Guide to Charitable Choice–Appendix." Washington DC: Center for Public Justice. Retrieved January 8, 2008 (http://www.cpjustice.org/charitablechoice/guide/appendix).

———. 2008. "Indirect Government Funding." Washington DC: Center for Public Justice. Retrieved June 28, 2009 (http://www.cpjustice.org/node/1672).

Chaves, Mark. 1994. "Secularization as Declining Religious Authority." *Social Forces* 72:749–774.

———. 1999. "Religious Congregations and Welfare Reform: Who Will Take Advantage of the Faith-Based Initiatives?" *American Sociological Review* 64:836–846.

———. 2001. "Going on Faith: Six Myths about Faith-Based Initiatives." *Christian Century*, September 12–19, 20–23.

———. 2004. *Congregations in America.* Cambridge, MA: Harvard University Press.

Chaves, Mark, and William Tsitsos. 2001. "Congregations and Social Services: What They Do, How They Do It, and With Whom." *Nonprofit and Voluntary Sector Quarterly* 30:660–683.

Chaves, Mark, and Robert Wineburg. 2008. "Did the Faith-Based Initiative Change Congregations?" Duke University, Chapel Hill, NC. Unpublished manuscript.

Cnaan, Ram, Robert Wineburg, and Stephanie Boddie. 1999. *The Newer Deal: Social Work and Religion in Partnership.* New York: Columbia University Press.

Cobb, Roger, and Charles Elder. 1972. "Individual Orientations in the Study of Political Symbolism." *Social Science Quarterly* 4:305–332.

———. 1973. "The Political Uses of Symbolism." *American Politics Research* 1:305–338.

Colson, Charles, and Nancy Pearcy. 1999. *How Now Shall We Live?* Carol Stream, IL: Tyndale House.

Conger, Kimberly. 2008a. "A Matter of Context: Christian Right Influence in State Republican Parties." Iowa State University, Ames. Unpublished manuscript.

————. 2008b. "Moral Values Issues and Policy Party Organizations: Cycles of Conflict and Accommodation of the Christian Right in State-Level Republican Parties." Iowa State University, Ames. Unpublished manuscript.

Conger, Kimberly, and John Green. 2002. "Spreading Out and Digging In: Christian Conservatives and State Republican Parties." *Campaigns and Elections Magazine* (February): 58.

Cooperman, Alan, and Jim VandeHei. 2005. "Ex-Aide Questions Bush Vow to Back Faith-Based Efforts." *Washington Post*, February 15, A1. Retrieved February 19, 2005 (http://www.washingtonpost.com/wp-dyn/articles/A24561-2005Feb14.html).

Cosgrove, John. 2001. "Religious Congregations as Mediators of Devolution: A Study of Parish-Based Services." Pp. 331–350 in *Social Work in the Era of Devolution: Toward a Just Practice*, edited by Rosa Perez-Koenig and Barry Rock. New York: Fordham University Press.

Deutscher, Irwin. 1966. "Words and Deeds: Social Science and Social Policy." *Social Problems* 13:235–254.

Dilulio, John. 2007. *Godly Republic: A Centrist Blueprint for America's Faith-Based Future.* Berkeley: University of California Press.

Dionne, E. J. 2008. *Souled Out: Reclaiming Faith and Politics after the Religious Right.* Princeton, NJ: Princeton University Press.

Domke, David, and Kevin Coe. 2007. *The God Strategy: How Religion Became a Political Weapon in America.* New York: Oxford University Press.

Donohue, Bill. 2008. "Obama's Faith-Based Gambit Is a Fraud." Press release, July 2, Catholic League for Religious and Civil Rights, New York. Retrieved July 3, 2008 (http://www.catholicleague.org/release.php?id=1455).

Ebaugh, Helen R. 2003 "The Faith-Based Initiative in Texas: A Case Study." Report of the Roundtable on Religion and Social Welfare Policy. Albany, NY: Rockefeller Institute of Government, State University of New York. Retrieved January 18, 2005 (http://www.religionandsocialpolicy.org/docs/events/2003_annual_conference/case_study_2003_texas.pdf).

Edelman, Murray. 1964. *The Symbolic Use of Politics.* Urbana: University of Illinois Press.

————. 1971. *Politics as Symbolic Action.* Chicago, IL: Markham.

Edsall, Thomas. 2006. "Grants Flow to Bush Allies on Social Issues." *Washington Post*, March 21. Retrieved July 8, 2008 (http://www.washingtonpost.com/wp-dyn/content/article/2006/03/21/AR2006032101723_pf.html).

Ender, Philip. 2005. "Applied Categorical and Nonnormal Data Analysis: Negative Binomial Models." Los Angeles: UCLA Graduate School of Education and Information Studies. Retrieved October 3, 2006 (http://www.gseis.ucla.edu/courses/ed231c/notes1/nbreg1.html).

Evans, Diana. 1996. "Before the Roll Call: Interest Group Lobbying and Public Policy Outcomes in House Committees." *Political Research Quarterly* 49:287–304.

Fairhurst, Libby. 2006. "Little Evidence to Back Claim of Reduced Recidivism by Faith-Based Prison Programs." *State: The Faculty/Staff Bulletin of Florida State University* 41(9):5. Retrieved July 6, 2008 (http://unicomm.fsu.edu/state/Issues/2006/State11202006.pdf).

Farris, Anne. 2008. "Bush Promotes Faith-Based Initiatives in Final State of the Union Address." Report of the Roundtable on Religion and Social Welfare Policy. Albany,

NY: Rockefeller Institute of Government, State University of New York. Retrieved July 2, 2008 (http://www.religionandsocialpolicy.org/news/article.cfm?id=7651).

Farris, Anne, Richard Nathan, and David Wright. 2004. "The Expanding Administrative Presidency: George Bush and the Faith-based initiatives." Report of the Roundtable on Religion and Social Welfare Policy. Albany, NY: Rockefeller Institute of Government, State University of New York. Retrieved 8 October 2004 (http://www.religionandsocialpolicy.org/docs/policy/ FB_Administrative_Presidency_ Report_1008_04.pdf).

Fineman, Stephen. 1998. "Street-Level Bureaucrats and the Social Construction of Environmental Control." *Organization Studies* 19:953–974.

Fischer, Frank, Gerald Miller, and Mara S. Sidney. 2006. *Handbook of Public Policy Analysis: Theories, Politics, and Methods.* Boca Raton, FL: CRC Press.

Flowers, Ronald Bruce. 2005. *The Godless Court?* Louisville, KY: Westminster John Knox.

Formicola, Jo Renee, Mary C. Segers, and Paul Weber, eds. 2003. *Faith-Based Initiatives and the Bush Administration: The Good, the Bad, and the Ugly.* New York: Rowman & Littlefield.

Frazier, E. F. [1964] 1974. *The Black Church in America.* New York: Knopf.

Freedom from Religion Foundation. 2004. "Foundation Wins Second Lawsuit on Faith-Based Funding in Its Montana 'Parish Nursing' Case." Press release, October 27, Freedom from Religion Foundation, Madison, Wisconsin. Retrieved July 2, 2008 (http://www.ffrf.org/news/2004/MTdecision.php).

———. 2002. "Federal Court Halts Public Funding of Faith Works" Press release, January 2 Freedom from Religion Foundation, Madison, Wisconsin. Retrieved June 26, 2009 (http://www.ffrf.org/news/2002/fwvictory.html).

Gamson, William. 1975. *The Strategy of Social Protest.* Homewood, IL: Dorsey.

Giugini, Marco, Doug McAdam, and Charles Tilly. 1999. *How Social Movements Matter.* Minneapolis: University of Minnesota Press.

Glenmary Research Center. 2000. "Religious Congregations Membership Study 2000." Glenmary Home Missioners, Cincinnati, Ohio. Retrieved September 19, 2004 (http://www.glenmary.org/grc/grc_RCMS2000.htm).

Granholm, Jennifer. 2007. "Dear Friends." State of Michigan Governor's Office of Community and Faith-Based Initiatives Web site. Retrieved July 5, 2008 (http:// www.michigan.gov/outreach/0,1607,7-203-113610-,00.html).

Green, John. 2007. "American Congregations and Social Service Programs: Results of a Survey." *Roundtable for Research on Religion and Social Welfare Policy.* Retrieved June 3, 2008 (http://www.pewtrusts.org/uploadedFiles/wwwpewtrustsorg/Reports/ Religion_in_public_life/American%20Congregations%20Report1.pdf).

Green, John C., James L. Guth, and Clyde Wilcox. 1998. "Less Than Conquerors: The Christian Right in State Republican Parties." Pp. 117–135 in *Social Movements and American Political Institutions*, edited by A. N. Costain and A. S. McFarland. New York: Rowman & Littlefield.

Green, John, Mark Rozell, and Clyde Wilcox. 2003. *The Evangelical Movement in American Politics: Marching to the Millennium.* Washington, DC: Georgetown University Press.

Green, John, and Amy Sherman. 2002. *Fruitful Collaborations: A Survey of Government Funded Faith-Based Programs in Fifteen States.* Charlottesville, VA: Hudson Institute.

Retrieved September 4, 2002 (http://www.hudson.org/files/publications/fruitful_collab.pdf).

Grogan, Colleen. 1994. "Political and Economic Factors Influencing State Medicaid Policy." *Political Research Quarterly* 47:589–622.

Gross, Terry. 2006. "Defending Faith-Based Initiatives." Interview with H. James Towey, October 18, NPR. Transcript retrieved October 22, 2006 (http://www.npr.org/templates/story/story.php?storyId=6289877).

Gushee, David. 2008. *The Future of Faith in American Politics*. Waco, TX: Baylor University Press.

Hagerty, Barbara Bradley. 2008. "Religious Right Weighs Next Political Steps." *All Things Considered*, National Public Radio, November 13. Retrieved November 15, 2008 (http://www.npr.org/templates/story/story.php?storyId=96970061).

Haider-Markel, Donald P. 1998. "The Politics of Social Regulatory Policy: State and Federal Hate Crime Policy and Implementation Effort." *Political Research Quarterly* 51: 69–88.

Hall, Richard. 1987. *Organizations: Structures, Procedures, and Outcomes*. Englewood Cliffs, NJ: Prentice-Hall.

Hamburger, Tom, Nicole Riccardi and Peter Wallsten. 2005. "Bush Rewarded by Black Pastors' Faith." *Los Angeles Times*, January 18: Retrieved June 22, 2009 (http://articles.latimes.com/2005/jan/18/nation/na-faith18).

Harris, Frederick. 1999. *Something Within: Religion in African-American Political Activism*. New York: Oxford University Press.

———. 2001. "Black Churches and Civic Traditions: Outreach, Activism, and the Politics of Public Funding of Faith-Based Ministries." Chapter 7 in *Can Charitable Choice Work? Covering Religion's Impact on Urban Affairs and Social Services*, edited by Andrew Walsh. Hartford, CT: Trinity College and the Pew Program on Religion and the News Media.

Health and Human Services, U. S. Department of. 2004. "What Is Charitable Choice?" Washington DC: U.S. Department of Health and Human Services. Retrieved February 9, 2005 (http://www.hhs.gov/fbci/choice.html).

Henriques, Diana. 2006. "As Exemptions Grow, Religion Outweighs Regulation." *New York Times*, October 8. Retrieved October 8, 2006 (http://select.nytimes.com/gst/abstract.html?res=F3061EF939540C7B8CDDA90994DE404482).

Hudson, Deal. 2008. *Onward Christian Soldiers*. New York: Simon & Schuster.

Hughes, Claire. 2006. "Potential for Widespread Fallout in Ruling against Iowa Faith-Based Prison Program." Press release, December 5, Pew Charitable Trusts, Washington, DC. Retrieved March 10, 2007 (http://www.religionandsocialpolicy.org/news/article.cfm?id=4384).

———. 2007a. "Congregations Delivering Services without Government Funds." Press release, December 5, Roundtable on Religion and Social Welfare Policy. Albany, NY: Rockefeller Institute of Government, State University of New York. Retrieved January 8, 2008. (http://www.pewtrusts.org/news_room_detail.aspx?id=31928).

———. 2007b. *"Ohio Faith-Based Operation Subject of Investigation under New Governor." Report of the Roundtable on Religion and Social Welfare Policy*. Albany, NY: Rockefeller Institute of Government, State University of New York. Retrieved June 6, 2008 (http://www.religionandsocialpolicy.org/news/article.cfm?id=6206).

———. 2008. "One-Year-Old Supreme Court Decision Ripples through Church-State Lawsuits." *Report of the Roundtable on Religion and Social Welfare Policy.* Albany, NY: Rockefeller Institute of Government, State University of New York. Retrieved October 23, 2008 (http://www.religionandsocialpolicy.org/news/article.cfm?id=8463).

Hutchinson, Earl. 2006. *The Emerging Black GOP.* Los Angeles, CA: Middle Passage.

Jacobson, Jonathan, Shawn Marsh, and Pamela Winston. 2005. "State and Local Contracting for Social Services under Charitable Choice." Princeton, NJ: Mathematica Policy Research.

Jenkins, Craig, and Craig Eckert. 1986. "Channeling Black Insurgency: Elite Patronage and Professional Social Movement Organizations in the Development of the Black Movement." *American Sociological Review* 51:812–829.

Jenkins, Craig, and Charles Perrow. 1977. "Insurgency of the Powerless: Farm Worker Movements (1942–1972)." *American Sociological Review* 42:249–268.

Johnson, Byron. 2004 "Religious Programs and Recidivism among Former Inmates in Prison Fellowship Program: A Long-Term Follow-Up Study." *Justice Quarterly* 21:329–354.

Junti, Meri, and Clive Potter. 2002. "Interpreting and Reinterpreting Agri-Environmental Policy: Communication, Trust, and Knowledge in the Implementation Process." *Sociologia Ruralis* 42:215–232.

Kahn, Peggy. 2001. "'Governor Eagle Wants Ladies to Work': Single Mothers, Work-First Welfare Policy and Post-Secondary Education in Michigan." *Journal of Poverty* 5:17–38.

Kaler, Amy, and Susan C. Watkins. 2001. "Disobedient Distributors: Street-Level Bureaucrats and Would-Be Patrons in Community-Based Family Planning Programs in Rural Kenya." *Studies in Family Planning* 32:254–269.

Keiser, Lael R. 2001. "Street-Level Bureaucrats, Administrative Power, and the Manipulation of Federal Social Security Disability Programs." *State Politics and Policy Quarterly* 1:144–164.

Klandermans, Bert, and Suzanne Staggenborg. 2002. "Introduction." Pp. ix–xx in *Methods of Social Movement Research*, edited by Bert Klandermans and Suzanne Staggenborg. Minneapolis: University of Minnesota Press.

Klandermans, Bert, Suzanne Staggenborg, and Sidney Tarrow. 2002. "Blending Methods and Building Theories in Social Movement Research." Pp. 314–349 in *Methods of Social Movement Research*, edited by Bert Klandermans and Suzanne Staggenborg. Minneapolis: University of Minnesota Press.

Kniss, Fred, and Gene Burns. 2004. "Religious Movements." Pp. 694–715 in *The Blackwell Companion to Social Movements*, edited by D. A. Snow, S. A. Soule, and H. Kriesi. Oxford, UK: Blackwell.

Kuo, David. 2006a. "Please, Keep Faith." Beverly Hills, CA: Beliefnet. Retrieved October 17, 2006 (http://www.beliefnet.com/story/160/story_16092_1.html).

———. 2006b. *Tempting Faith: An Inside Story of Political Seduction.* New York: Free Press.

Kuo, David, and John Dilulio. 2008. "The Faith to Outlast Politics." *New York Times*, January 29. (http://www.nytimes.com/2008/01/29/opinion/29kuo.html?_r=1&scp=1&sq=kuo,%20david&st=cse).

Lawton, Kim. 2004. "Black Churches and Gay Marriage." *Religion and Ethics Newsweekly*, PBS, July 16. Transcript retrieved March 4, 2005 (http://www.pbs.org/wnet/religionandethics/week746/feature.html).

Leland, John. 2005. "One More 'Moral Value': Fighting Poverty." *New York Times*, January 30. Retrieved November 18, 2008 (http://www.nytimes.com/2005/01/30/politics/30poverty.html).

Lichterman, Paul. 2002. "Seeing Structure Happen: Theory Driven Participant Observation." Pp. 118–145 in *Methods of Social Movement Research*, edited by Bert Klandermans and Suzanne Staggenborg. Minneapolis: University of Minnesota Press.

———. 2005. *Elusive Togetherness: Church Groups Trying to Bridge Community Divisions.* Princeton, NJ: Princeton University Press.

Lin, Ann Chin. 2000. *Reform in the Making: The Implementation of Social Policy in Prison.* Princeton, NJ: Princeton University Press.

Lincoln, C. Eric. 1974. *The Black Experience in Religion.* Garden City, NY: Anchor.

———. 1999. *Race, Religion, and the Continuing American Dilemma.* New York: Hill & Wang.

Lincoln, C. Eric, and Lawrence Mamiya. 1990. *The Black Church in the African-American Experience.* Durham, NC: Duke University Press.

Lindsay, Michael. 2006. *Faith in the Halls of Power: How Evangelicals Joined the American Elite.* New York: Oxford University Press.

———. 2008. "Evangelicals in the Power Elite: Elite Cohesion Advancing a Movement." *American Sociological Review* 73:60–82.

Lipsky, Michael. 1971. "Street-Level Bureaucracy and the Analysis of Urban Reform." *Urban Affairs Quarterly* 6:391–409.

Lockard, Duane. 1968. *Toward Equal Opportunity: A Study of State and Local Antidiscrimination Laws.* Princeton, NJ: Princeton University Press.

Loconte, Joseph. 2002. "Keeping the Faith." *FirstThings* 123 (May):14–16. Retrieved September 24, 2002 (http://www.heritage.org/Press/Commentary/ed092402a.cfm).

———. 2004. "Faith, Hope and Politics." Washington, DC: Heritage Foundation. Retrieved February 19, 2004 (http://www.heritage.org/Press/Commentary/ed021904b.cfm).

Lowi, Theodore. 1964. "American Business, Public Policy, Case Studies and Political Theory." *World Politics* 16:677–715.

———. 1969. *The End of Liberalism: Ideology, Policy, and the Crisis of Public Authority.* New York: W.W. Norton.

Lupu, Ira, and Robert Tuttle. 2003. "The State of the Law." Report of the Roundtable on Religion and Social Welfare Policy. Albany, NY: Rockefeller Institute of Government, State University of New York. Retrieved December 9, 2004 (http://www.religionandsocialpolicy.org/docs/transcripts/12-1-003_state_of_the_law_transcript.pdf).

Marsden, George. [1982] 2006. *Fundamentalism and American Culture: The Shaping of Twentieth-Century Evangelicalism: 1870–1925.* New York: Oxford University Press.

Maupin, James R. 1993. "Control, Efficiency, and the Street-Level Bureaucrat." *Journal of Public Administration Research and Theory* 3:335–357.

McAdam, Doug. 1982. *Political Process and the Development of Black Insurgency, 1930–1970.* Chicago: University of Chicago Press.

McAdam, Doug, and Yang Su. 2002. "The War at Home: Anti-War Protests and Congressional Voting, 1965–73." *American Sociological Review* 67:696–721.

McCammon, Holly J., Karen E. Campbell, Ellen M. Granberg, and Christine Mowery. 2001. "How Movements Win: Gendered Opportunity Structures and U.S. Women's Suffrage Movements, 1866 to 1919." *American Sociological Review* 66:49–70.

McClerking, Harwood, and Eric McDaniel. 2005. "Belonging and Doing: Political Churches and Black Political Participation." *Political Psychology* 26:721–733.

McRoberts, Omar. 2006. "Social Welfare Policy and State 'Regulation' of Religion: Black Denominations in Three Policy Eras." Department of Sociology, University of Chicago. Unpublished manuscript.

McVeigh, Rory, Daniel Myers, and David Sikkink. 2004. "Corn, Klansmen, and Coolidge: Structure and Framing in Social Movements." *Social Forces* 83:653–690.

Mears, Daniel, Caterina G. Romam, Ashley Wolff, and Janeen Buck. 2006. "Faith-Based Efforts to Improve Prisoner Reentry: Assessing the Logic and Evidence." *Journal of Criminal Justice* 34:351–367.

Miceli, Melinda. 2005. "Morality Politics vs. Identity Politics: Framing Processes and Competition among Christian Right and Gay Social Movement Organizations." *Sociological Forum* 20:589–612.

Milward, Brinton, and Keith Provan. 2002. "Governing the Hollow State." *Journal of Public Administration Research and Theory* 10:359–380.

Monsma, Stephen V. 1996. *When Sacred and Secular Mix: Religious Nonprofit Organizations and Public Money.* Lanham, MD: Rowman & Littlefield.

———. 2004. *Putting Faith in Partnerships: Welfare-to-Work in Four Cities.* Ann Arbor: University of Michigan Press.

Monsma, Stephen, and Christopher Soper. 2006. *Faith, Hope, and Jobs: Welfare to Work in Los Angeles.* Washington, DC: Georgetown University Press.

Montiel, Lisa, and Mark Ragan. 2006. "Getting a Piece of the Pie: Federal Grants to Faith-Based Social Service Organizations." Report of the Roundtable on Religion and Social Welfare Policy. Albany, NY: Rockefeller Institute of Government, State University of New York. Retrieved September 24, 2005 (http://www. religionandsocialpolicy.org/docs/research/federal_grants_report_2-14-06.pdf).

Mooney, Alexandra. 2009. "Controversy Surrounds Obama's Faith Office." C NNPolitics.com, February 5. Retrieved June 23, 2009 (http://edition.cnn.com/ 2009/POLITICS/02/05/obama.faith.based/).

Mooney, Christopher, and Mei-Hsien Lee. 1995. "Legislating Morality in the American States: The Case of Pre-Roe Abortion Reform." *American Journal of Political Science* 39:599–627.

Morris, Aldon D. 1984. *The Origins of the Civil Rights Movement: Black Communities Organizing for Change.* New York: Free Press.

National Gay and Lesbian Rights Taskforce. 2006. "Anti-Gay Marriage Measures in the U.S." Washington, DC: National Gay and Lesbian Rights Taskforce. Retrieved February 21, 2006 (http://www.thetaskforce.org/downloads/marriagemap.pdf).

Nejfelt, Dan. 2008. "New Poll Demonstrates Evangelicals' Political Diversity." Washington, DC: *Faith in Public Life*, February 11. Retrieved July 6, 2008 (http:// blog.faithinpubliclife.org/2008/02/exit_polls_evangelicals_vote_f.html).

Nice, David. 1994. *Policy Innovation in State Government.* Ames: Iowa State Press.

Office of Community Services. 2008. "Compassion Capital Fund Fact Sheet." Washington, DC: Office of Community Services, U.S. Department of Health and

Human Services. Retrieved February 27, 2008 (http://www.acf.hhs.gov/programs/ccf/about_ccf/facts.html).

O'Keefe, Mark. 2002. "Federal, State Agencies Quietly Foster Faith-Based Initiatives." Listserv update. Retrieved June 28, 2008 (http://lists101.his.com/pipermail/smartmarriages/2002-March/001026.html).

Olasky, Marvin. 1996. *Renewing American Compassion: How Compassion for the Needy Can Turn Ordinary Citizens into Heroes.* New York: Free Press.

O'Neill, Michael. 1989. *The Third America: The Emergence of the Nonprofit Sector in the United States.* San Francisco, CA: Jossey-Bass.

Paris, Peter. 1991. *Black Religious Leaders: Conflict in Unity.* Louisville, KY: Westminster/John Knox.

Parsa, Misagh. 1989. *Social Origins of the Iranian Revolution.* New Brunswick, NJ: Rutgers.

Pattillo-McCoy, Patricia. 1998. "Church Culture as a Strategy of Action in the Black Community." *American Sociological Review* 63:767–784.

Pedriana, Nicholas. 2006. "From Protective to Equal Treatment: Legal Framing Processes and Transformation of the Women's Movement in the 1960s." *American Journal of Sociology* 111:1718–1761.

Pew Charitable Trusts. 2000. "Religion and Politics: The Ambivalent Majority." Survey report, September 20. Retrieved June 15, 2006 (http://people-press.org/report/32/religion-and-politics-the-ambivalent-majority).

———. 2001. "Faith-Based Funding Backed, but Church-State Doubts Abound." Survey report, April 10. Retrieved August 10, 2006 (http://people-press.org/report/15/faith-based-funding-backed-but-church-state-doubts-abound).

———. 2003. "Religion and Politics: Contention and Consensus." Survey report, July 24. Retrieved June 15, 2006. (http://people-press.org/report/189/religion-and-politics-contention-and-consensus).

———. 2005. "More See Benefits of Stem Cell Research: Opinions Divide along Religious Lines." Commentary, May 23. Retrieved June 20, 2006 (http://people-press.org/commentary/?analysisid=111).

———. 2008. "Gay Marriage Is Back on The Radar for Republicans, Evangelicals." Survey report, June 12. Retrieved June 17, 2008 (http://pewresearch.org/pubs/868/gay-marriage).

Piven, Frances Fox, and Richard Cloward. 1977. *Poor People's Movements.* New York: Vintage.

Prottas, Jeffrey M. 1978. "The Power of the Street-Level Bureaucrat in Public Service Bureaucracies." *Urban Affairs Quarterly* 13:285–312.

Raeburn, Nicole C. 2004. "Working It Out: The Emergence and Diffusion of the Workplace Movement for Lesbian, Gay, and Bisexual Rights." *Research in Social Movements, Conflicts, and Change* 25:187–230.

Ragan, Mark, Lisa Montiel, and David Wright. 2003. "Scanning the Policy Environment of Faith-Based Social Services in the United States: Results from a 50 State Study." Report of the Roundtable on Religion and Social Welfare Policy. Albany, NY: Rockefeller Institute of Government, State University of New York. Retrieved November 17, 2003 (http://www.religionandsocialpolicy.org/docs/ events/2003_annual_conference/11-17-2003_state_scan.pdf).

Ragan, Mark, and David Wright. 2005. "Scanning the Policy Environment of Faith-Based Social Services in the United States: What Has Changed Since 2002? Results from a 50 State Study." Report of the Roundtable on Religion and Social Welfare Policy. Albany, NY: Rockefeller Institute of Government, State University of New York. Retrieved September 24, 2005 (http://www.religionandsocialpolicy. org/docs/policy/State_Scan_2005_report.pdf).

Regnerus, Mark, David Sikkink, and Christian Smith. 1999. "Who Votes with the Christian Right? Contextual and Individual Patterns of Electoral Influence." *Social Forces* 77:1375–1401.

Rehnquist, William. 1985. *U.S. Supreme Court Dissenting Opinion, Wallace v. Jaffree*. Retrieved March 18, 2006 (http://caselaw.lp.findlaw.com/scripts/getcase.pl? court=US&vol=472&invol=38).

Ridzi, Frank. 2004. "Making TANF Work: Organizational Restructuring, Staff Buy-In, and Performance Monitoring in Local Implementation." *Journal of Sociology and Social Welfare* 31(2):27–48.

Riesbrodt, Martin. 1993. *Pious Passion: The Emergence of Modern Fundamentalism in the United States and Iran*. Berkeley: University of California Press.

Roundtable on Religion and Social Welfare Policy. 2007. "Taxpayers' Right to Sue over Church-State Violations." Albany, NY: Nelson A. Rockefeller Institute of Government, State University of New York. Retrieved November 2008 (http://www.socialpolicyandreligion.org/resources/HeinvFFRF.cfm).

Sager, Rebecca. 2005. "Why Faith-Based Liaisons Are Important." Paper presented at the national conference of the American Sociological Association, August 18, Philadelphia, PA.

Sager, Rebecca. 2007a. "The Cultural Construction of State Sponsored Religion: Race, Politics, and State Implementation of the Faith-Based Initiative." *Journal of Church and State* 49:467–486.

———. 2007b. "The Importance of Faith-Based Liaisons." *Sociology of Religion* 68:97–109.

Sager, Rebecca, and Laura Stephens. 2005. "Serving Up Sermons: Clients' Reactions to Religious Elements at Congregation-Run Feeding Establishments." *Non-Profit and Voluntary Sector Quarterly* 34:297–315.

Santoro, Wayne A., and Gail M. McGuire. 1997. "Social Movement Insiders: The Impact of Institutional Activists on Affirmative Action and Comparable Worth Policies." *Social Problems* 44:503–519.

Seuss-Kennedy, Shelia, and Wolfgang Bielefeld. 2006. *Charitable Choice at Work: Evaluating Faith-Based Job Programs in the States*. Washington, DC: Georgetown University Press.

Sherman, Amy. 1999. "How Do Congregations Serve the Community? How Should They?" Conference address, The Alban Institute's First Annual National Conference, October 21, Hudson Institute, Washington, DC. Retrieved September 21, 2002 (http://www.hudson.org/index.cfm? fuseaction=publication_details&id=1912).

Singer, Paul, and Brian Friel. 2007. "Leaps of Faith." *National Journal*, January 5. Retrieved January 6, 2007 (http://www.nationaljournal.com/about/njweekly/ stories/2007/0105nj1.htm).

Skocpol, Theda, and Edward Amenta. 1986. "States and Social Policies." *Annual Review of Sociology* 12:131–157.

Skretny, John. 1998. "State Capacity, Policy Feedbacks, and Affirmative Action for Blacks, Women, and Latinos." *Research in Political Sociology* 8:279–310.

Slater, Wayne. 2007. "Young Evangelical Voters Diverge from Parents." *Dallas Morning News*, October 15. Retrieved November 18, 2008 (http://www.dallasnews.com/sharedcontent/dws/dn/latestnews/stories/101507dntexyouths.3a7dbb3.html).

Smith, Christian. 2000. *Christian America? What Evangelicals Really Want.* Berkeley: University of California Press.

———. 2003. *The Secular Revolution: Power, Interests, and Conflict in the Secularization of American Public Life.* Berkeley: University of California Press.

Smith, Christian, Michael Emerson, Sally Gallagher, Paul Kennedy, and David Sikkink. 1998. *American Evangelicalism: Embattled and Thriving.* Chicago: University of Chicago Press.

Smith, Drew. 2005. "Black Clergy and the Governmental Sector during George W. Bush's Presidency." Pp. 197–199 in *Black Churches and Local Politics: Clergy Influence, Organizational Partnerships, and Civic Empowerment,* edited by Drew Smith and Fredrick Harris. Lanham, MD: Rowman & Littlefield.

Smith, Drew, and Fredrick Harris, eds. 2005. *Black Churches and Local Politics: Clergy Influence, Organizational Partnerships, and Civic Empowerment.* Lanham, MD: Rowman & Littlefield.

Soule, Sarah. 1997. "The Student Divestment Movement in the United States and Tactical Diffusion: The Shantytown Protest." *Social Forces* 75:855–883.

———. 2004. "Going to the Chapel? Same-Sex Marriage Bans in the United States, 1973–2000." *Social Problems* 51:453–477.

Soule, Sarah, and Jennifer Earl. 2001. "The Enactment of State-Level Hate Crime Law in the United States: Intra- and Interstate Factors." *Sociological Perspectives* 44:281–305.

Soule, Sarah, and Susan Olzak. 2004. "What Is the Role of Social Movements in Shaping Public Policy? The Case of the Equal Rights Amendment." *American Sociological Review* 69:473–497.

Soule, Sarah, and Yvonne Zylan. 1997. "Runaway Train? The Diffusion of State-Level Reform in ADC/AFDC Eligibility Requirements, 1950–1967." *American Journal of Sociology* 103:733–762.

State of Florida. 2007. FL 2007 ALS 72. Retrieved from LexisNexis.

State of Georgia. 2006. ALS 601-HB1292. Retrieved from LexisNexis.

State of Louisiana. 1999. RS 15:828.2. Retrieved from LexisNexis.

———. 2001. LSA-RS 46:1455. Retrieved from LexisNexis.

———. 2004. LSA-RS 49:210–2. Retrieved from LexisNexis.

State of Maryland. 2003. 2003 MD ALS 202. Retrieved from LexisNexis.

State of New Jersey. 2006. 2006 NJ ALS 47. Retrieved from LexisNexis.

State of Ohio. 2007. 2007 Ohio HB 699. Retrieved from LexisNexis.

State of Wyoming. 2004. "Children and Families Initiative." Enrolled Act HEA0028. Chapter No. 44 Session Laws of Wyoming 2004.

Stearns, Linda B., and Paul D. Almeida. 2004. "The Formation of State Actor-Social Movement Coalitions and Favorable Policy Outcomes." *Social Problems* 51:478–504.

Stern, Marc. 2001. "Charitable Choice the Law as it is and May Be." Pp. 157–177 in *Can Charitable Choice Work?* edited by Andrew Walsh. Hartford, CT: Pew Program on Religion and the Media.

Stone, Clarence. 2005. "Rethinking the Policy-Politics Connection." *Policy Studies* 26:241–260.

Stone, Deborah. 1988. *The Policy Paradox: The Art of Political Decision Making.* New York: Norton.

Strang, David, and Sarah Soule. 1998. "Diffusion in Organizations and Social Movements: From Hybrid Corn to Poison Pills." *Annual Review of Sociology* 24:265–290.

Suskind, David. 2003. "Why Are These Men Laughing?" *Esquire,* January 1. Retrieved January 1, 2003 (http://www.ronsuskind.com/newsite/articles/archives/000032.html).

Tarrow, Sidney. 1998. *Power in Movement.* New York: Cambridge University Press.

University of Missouri-Columbia. 2007. "Religion And Healthcare Should Mix, Study Says." *ScienceDaily* (October 24). Retrieved January 3, 2009 (http://www.sciencedaily.com/releases/2007/10/071023104134.htm).

U.S. Census Bureau. 1993–2006. *Statistical Abstracts.* Retrieved February 2005 (http://www.census.gov/prod/www/abs/statab.html).

Wald, Kenneth D., and Jeffrey C. Corey. 2002. "The Evangelical Movement and Public Policy: Social Movement Elites as Institutional Activists." *State Politics and Policy Quarterly* 2:99–125.

Wallis, Jim. 2008. *God's Politics: Why the Right Gets It Wrong and the Left Doesn't Get It.* New York: Harper Collins.

Walsh, Andrew. 2001. *Can Charitable Choice Work? Covering Religion's Impact on Urban Affairs and Social Services.* Hartford, CT: Trinity College and the Pew Program on Religion and the News Media.

Weatherley, Richard, and Michael Lipsky. 1977. "Street-Level Bureaucrats and Institutional Innovation: Implementing Special-Education Reform." *Harvard Educational Review* 47:171–197.

Weber, Max. 1922. *The Sociology of Religion.* Boston: Beacon Press.

Weissert, Carol S. 1994. "Beyond the Organization: The Influence of Community and Personal Values on Street-Level Bureaucrats' Responsiveness." *Journal of Public Administration Research and Theory* 4:225–254.

Williams, Rhys, and Jeffrey Blackburn. 1996. "Many Are Called, but Few Obey: Ideological Commitment and Activism in Operation Rescue." In *Disruptive Religion: The Force of Faith in Social Movement Activism,* edited by Christian Smith. New York: Routledge.

Wineburg, Robert. 2001. *A Limited Partnership: The Politics of Religion, Welfare, and Social Science.* New York: Columbia University Press.

———. 2007. *Faith-Based Inefficiency: The Follies of Bush's Initiatives.* Westport, CT: Greenwood.

Winston, Pamela, Ann Person, and Elizabeth Clary. 2008. "The Role of State Faith Community Liaisons in Charitable Choice Implementation." Retrieved January 10, 2009 (http://aspe.hhs.gov/hsp/08/RoleFCL/index.shtml).

Wood, Richard. 2002. *Faith in Action: Religion, Race, and Democratic Organizing in America.* Chicago: University of Chicago Press.

Wuthnow, Robert, C. Hackett, and B. Y. Hsu. 2004. "The Effectiveness and Trustworthiness of Faith-Based and Other Service Organizations: A Study of Recipients' Perceptions." *Journal for the Scientific Study of Religion* 43:1–17.

Wysong, Earl, Richard Aniskiewicz, and David Wright. 1994. "Truth and DARE: Tracking Drug Education to Graduation and as Symbolic Politics." *Social Problems* 41:448–472.

Zald, Mayer. 2000. "Ideologically Structured Action: An Enlarged Agenda for Social Movement Research." *Mobilization: An International Journal* 5:1–16.

Zeleny, Jeff and Brian Knowlton. 2009. "Obama Borrows a Bush Policy to Court Evangelical" *New York Times* February 4. Retrieved June 23, 2009 (http://www.nytimes.com/2008/07/01/world/americas/01iht-campaign.4.14141355.html).

Zylan, Yvonne, and Sarah Soule. 2000. "Ending Welfare as We Know it (Again): Welfare State Retrenchment, 1989–1995." *Social Forces* 79:623–652.

Index